Delimiting the Law

Law and Social Theory

Series editors:
PETER FITZPATRICK
Professor of Law and Social Theory, University of Kent
COLIN PERRIN
Law School and Department of Philosophy,
University of Kent at Canterbury

Law and the Senses
EDITED BY LIONEL BENTLY AND LEO FLYNN

The Wrongs of Tort
JOANNE CONAGHAN AND WADE MANSELL

Dangerous Supplements
EDITED BY PETER FITZPATRICK

Disabling Laws, Enabling Acts
Disability Rights in Britain and America
CAROLINE GOODING

The Critical Lawyers' Handbook
EDITED BY IAN GRIGG-SPALL AND PADDY IRELAND

Foucault and the Law
ALAN HUNT AND GARY WICKHAM

Family Law Matters
KATHERINE O'DONOVAN

False Images
Law's Construction of the Refugee
PATRICIA TUITT

Contract
A Critical Commentary
JOHN WIGHTMAN

DELIMITING THE LAW
'Postmodernism' and the Politics of Law

MARGARET DAVIES

Pluto Press
LONDON • CHICAGO, IL

First published 1996 by Pluto Press
345 Archway Road, London N6 5AA
and 1436 West Randolph
Chicago, Illinois 60607, USA

British Library Cataloguing in Publication Data
A Catalogue record for this book is available from the British Library

ISBN 0 7453 1100 8 hbk

Library of Congress Cataloging in Publication Data are available

Designed and Produced for Pluto Press by
Chase Production Services, Chipping Norton, OX7 5QR
Typeset from disk by Stanford DTP Services, Milton Keynes
Printed in the EC by T J Press, Padstow, England

Contents

Dedication   vi

Introduction: Legal Theory and Contemporary Philosophy   1

PART ONE

1   The Limits of Law   13
2   The Limits of Interpretation   39
3   'Before the Law'   64
Interlude: The Decision   91

PART TWO

4   Repetition   103
5   After the Law   123

Conclusion: The End of the Beginning   143

Endnotes   154
Bibliography   172
Index   178

For my parents, Helen and John

Introduction
Legal Theory and
Contemporary Philosophy

CRITICAL 'JUSTICE'

When I was in the final stages of my doctoral work on Derrida and legal theory at the University of Sussex, an edition of the *Cardozo Law Review* appeared which was to alter radically the shape of contemporary 'postmodern'-inspired legal theory.[1] The edition, of course, contained the text of Derrida's 'Force of Law: The "Mystical Foundations of Authority"',[2] as well as an influential commentary on Derrida by Drucilla Cornell entitled 'The Violence of the Masquerade: Law Dressed Up as Justice'.[3] Most of the articles were subsequently republished in a book entitled *Deconstruction and the Possibility of Justice*, and with these publications a new space was opened in English-language legal theory, marked especially by two more significant works by Cornell – *The Philosophy of the Limit* and *Beyond Accommodation* – and by a renewed interest in law as an object of philosophical and cultural study.[4]

Exactly how to characterise this new 'space' in legal thought is not entirely obvious. Clearly, as one would expect from any dialogue using Derrida as a springboard, it is not reducible to the traditional spaces of legal theory. Just as clearly, and just as predictably, it is not by any means a closed field, but influences many areas. In order to begin to delineate the relationship of this new direction in legal thought to the legal philosophical tradition, let me begin by taking a couple of the most obvious of the traditional spaces of legal thought, natural law and positivism. Natural law is centrally about the relationship between law and ethics or morality. Assuming the existence of universal standards inherent in nature, particularly human nature, the question becomes – how does positive law relate to what is 'natural' in humanity? On the other side, positivism has always existed to deny any *necessary* relationship between law and its infinite others. Law is simply positive law, and has only contingent connections to human morality or ethical standards. As Douzinas and Warrington suggest, what this in fact has entailed is a collapse of law and justice in legal thinking: although positivist thought envisages a separation between what is legal and what is, strictly speaking, just, it also manages to reduce the

1

discourse of justice to that of law.[5] Justice becomes nothing more than law. So, speaking very roughly, legal philosophy has two of its spaces defined by a concern for, on the one hand, ethical standards, and, on the other, theorising the nature of positive law as distinct from ethical standards.

One of the major contributions of the critical theories of law – Realism, Critical Legal Studies, feminism, race theory – has been to demystify the positivist mentality of neutrality in the law: law cannot be apolitical or amoral because it so clearly represents a dominant view. In such a context 'justice' roughly means an absence of unfair discrimination on the basis of sex, race, socioeconomic background, sexual orientation, nationality. Justice does not have a precise content, because we have not yet, not nearly, attained the social conditions which are the prerequisite for a just means of ordering society.

For the moment let me call these movements 'critical theories', and allow me also to distinguish them from the 'postmodern'-influenced legal space which has been called by Douzinas and Warrington the 'jurisprudence of alterity'.[6] The distinction is not absolute, since 'critical' theorists have often been influenced in some way by the 'postmodern', and vice versa. None the less, I think it is possible to make some rough distinction between those whose major concern is the politics of positive law, and those whose focus has been a more philosophically radical consideration of the foundation and nature of law as an institution, and on the philosophical dimensions and limits of legal theory. This second arm of the anti-positivist revolution in legal thought is at least partly metadiscursive: in other words, it is not only about the nature of positive law, it is also about the way that the discourses of law and legal theory shape our understanding of it. But it is perhaps most clearly defined by its concern with absolute otherness or alterity as the focal point for an ethical understanding of law and justice. To use the terminology of Derrida's 'Force of Law', the law is the element of the process which is calculable, while justice is incalculable. Justice cannot simply be enshrined in a rule – because it demands a relation to the other, not just an appropriation of it; justice is thoroughly particular.

Of course, there is otherness and otherness. There is the otherness which is appropriated and defined by the law, like that pertaining to being a 'battered woman', where your experience is given a name and pathologised as a 'syndrome'. This is the otherness of the object.[7] But for law's inability to recognise it, there *would also be* the otherness of *being* a 'battered woman' and of realising that your experience is not reflected in the law. Such an other cannot be reduced to an object: it must be either totally erased, which has been the traditional legal alternative, or respected as a subject. The one sort of otherness is that which is simply given a peripheral place in the accepted cultural and legal definitions, while the other other has no simple place, though it threatens from everywhere to destabilise the established order.

The debate about natural law and positivism has been more or less overtaken by these developments. In the first place, the focus on language and ideology has resulted in a recognition that whatever is 'natural' is so only because of its position in a particular discursive configuration. The opposition between 'nature' and 'culture' is itself a construction of Western cultural conditions. Second, the *post*modern condition is partly characterised by critical reflection about the desire for philosophical grounding, in contrast to the 'modern' assumption that grounding is necessary (and the consequential search for grounds). Natural law and positivism, as I will explain further in this book, are traditions of thought which seek a philosophically absolute understanding of law and assume in the process that such a thing is possible.

I have said that there are basically two focal points of contemporary critical approaches to legal theory and law, that is, a concentration on the overtly political dimensions of law (including substantive law) and the 'postmodern' emphasis on the abstract structure of law and legal institutions. I have however always thought that one of the most crucial functions of postmodern thought is its potential for understanding the political structure of law. It has this potential without necessarily being tied to particular political goals or strategies, a property which has led some commentators to argue that postmodern thought is anti-political, and can only hinder contemporary struggles. This view is no doubt reinforced by the fact that a number of conservative thinkers have found support for their own objectives in postmodernism. However, one of the features of the new 'jurisprudence of alterity' which I have briefly described is that it brings out the question of power in relation to an understanding of the abstract nature of law, and explicitly recognises the ethical demands of otherness.

Given this background, my aim in this book is twofold. First, I aim to move towards an elaborated understanding of the relationship between the political goals of what I have temporarily termed 'critical theories' of law – feminism, race theory, Critical Legal Studies – and the new 'jurisprudence of alterity'. I have said before that 'postmodern' insights are crucial because they help to change the way we think the world, and therefore provide one of the crucial prerequisites for a non-oppressive social order.[8] However, I think that the connection can be made in a much stronger, less arbitrary, way. For me, postmodernism is about understanding the cultural thought-patterns which are the foundation of oppression in its Western manifestations. Feminism is not simply a beneficiary of the spaces opened up by thinking differently. An understanding of the philosophical foundations of Western thought is an understanding of the philosophical foundations of patriarchy. Law holds a central place here, because of its role in ordering society formally and informally.

Second, I aim to develop arguments about the usefulness of 'postmodern' thought, and in particular 'deconstruction', for traditional legal theory in a more sustained fashion than has been attempted elsewhere. Basically, the question is – what happens when you look at modern positivist assumptions through the lens of contemporary anti-foundationalist thought? In particular, what happens to legal sovereignty, legal reasoning, the structure of rules and the idea of a separate realm of law? What sense can be made of law in such a context?

The two parts of the book basically mirror these two aims, although the first part, as well as concentrating on the first aim, also anticipates and constructs the conditions for the second aim, which is more specifically dealt with in the second part of the book. The next two sections of this preface outline several of the issues associated with these two aims and their interrelationship.

LEGAL PHILOSOPHICAL OPPRESSION

The ethical implications of deconstruction can be related to the larger political questions with which critical scholars in law have been concerned over the past fifteen or so years. One of the most entrenched and dangerous ideas about law is that it is neutral. Feminists and other critical thinkers have, in a sustained and systematic way, exposed first the discrimination inherent in the content of substantive law, and second, the biases of legal institutions and procedures. One of the things this book is about is the oppressiveness built into the *thought* of law. I think it is possible to say that ideas about law, and by extension the thought of regulation and regularity which orders the Western mind, are built upon the structure of purity and exclusion which sets up the dualisms and hierarchies of dominance. In other words, a particular understanding of law and of the subject's relationship to the law shapes the Western world: oppression is not separable from the way we think about the law, and fundamental social change involves not only a rethinking of the content of the laws, but also a rethinking of the nature of law itself.

It is therefore not possible to say that the questions of legal theory are separate from questions of politics. It is no longer possible for legal philosophy to hide behind the idea that it is about abstractions or pure entities having nothing to do with gender, race, or class. As soon as we get over the old image of law as being something pure and different from other modes of social regulation, we must conclude that gender, race and class *are* legally created.

As will become evident throughout the book, it is at least in part, for me, the analysis of law through the insights of postmodern thought which enables the exposure of the relationship between the various modes of dominance built into law. In particular the work of Derrida, despite its shortcomings for a feminist, demands that close attention be given to all of the limits which define our mental and physical existences.

Let me take for a moment a problem which has been closely examined by feminists influenced by postmodern thought. One of the things which Derrida makes clear in his work is that categories constructed by the exclusion of an other are never pure: the category contains within it the trace of the other, and cannot be coherent or closed. The category 'man' can never be a pure category of thought (or, for that matter, of physical existence): its boundaries must continually be policed in order that the semblance of self-containment can be maintained. The instability of gender categories has been the source of much debate among queer theorists, who are working at the frontier of conventional categories of sex and sexuality. I accept the argument that gender is constructed and unstable and therefore contestable, and believe that this line of thought is important to feminists who wish to challenge the basic framework within which gender takes place. However, it is also important to recognise that the political situation within which we find ourselves does not allow us simply to choose gender freely. Systems of oppression which divide people hierarchically along various axes are still prevalent: in the case of sex it will not do simply to replace the conventional political situation with multiple sex categories (like the lesbian in a man's body) which, in the end, still build upon the dualistic order. Nor will it do to pretend that sex categories do not exist. In other words, it is necessary to continue to deal with the consequences of continued violent regulation of the categories of male and female, while recognising that they are not politically or conceptually simple or pure categories.

I mention this because it opens on to the adjacent philosophical problem I am concerned with here: it is not possible to eradicate the force of law by arguing for its conceptual instability. The theoretical argument may well be the thin end of the wedge and/or a useful tool in the process of countering the power of law to reinforce oppression, but by itself it will not eliminate the problem. What I want to do in this book is to expose the weaknesses of legal theory and provide some foundation for a strengthened political critique.

THE DECONSTRUCTION OF LAW AND LEGAL THEORY

In *The Philosophy of the Limit*, Drucilla Cornell describes two versions of the meeting of 'postmodern' discourse and law. Much of my formal

argument in this work broadly speaking follows the trajectory of the
first version of this confrontation which is described as follows:

> the Law of Law is only 'present' in its absolute absence. The 'never
> has been' of an unrecoverable past is understood as the lack of
> origin 'presentable' *only* as absence. The Law of Law, in other words,
> is the figure of an initial fragmentation ...[9]

Many of my formal arguments can be understood more or less in this
light. I tend not to use the 'present/absent' terminology, preferring to
remain within the 'legal/non-legal' disjunction set up by positivism,
since this constitutes my primary logical and political target. Of course,
the complexities and nuances in each context, and in relation to the
various legal theorists I consider, involve very different aspects of this
'postmodern' legal philosophical narrative. For instance, the theoretical
structure of 'the Law of the Law' as an 'institutional source'[10] which
limits the legal system shares similarities with the structure of 'the Law
of the Law' as a statement about the *concept* of law, which is a limitation
on how theorists have approached law. In fact, as the limit of law and
of the theoretical object of conventional jurisprudence, these are at
once the very same thing, while being quite different.[11] Similarly,
taking 'the Law of the Law' to refer to the structure of the relationship
between a norm and the decision in a particular case, we find the larger
structure mirrored, but not perfectly reproduced. As I argue in Chapters
4 and 5, the law of the law of a case is a semantically lower repetition
of the 'law of the law' itself.

The reason for all of these structural repetitions (or rather, iterations)
has to do with the theoretical reflexivity of the legal philosophical
project. As a theorist of the law, one is confronted with endlessly
interrelated dimensions of the law question. In the first place, we are
caught up in a relentlessly irreducible tautology, because our object
'law' is presupposed in our end, 'the law of law', while our end is
presupposed in our object. Let me try to explain this, slowly and
cautiously. Starting from the object of legal theory – 'law', our end has
traditionally been to explain what it is conceptually, to find the 'law
of the law'. But how can we possibly theorise the 'law of the law'? We
need to know what law is *before* we can even begin the quest – but that
is precisely what we are looking for! To put this another, perhaps more
familiar, way, our end, the 'law of the law', is surely embedded in our
object 'the law'. How on earth can we describe a law of law, when that
law must be comprehended in the law we want to describe? A meta-
theoretical paradox if ever I saw one.

The problem is resolved, or perhaps avoided or foreclosed, by Anglo-
American legal philosophies, which have since Austin tended to begin
with a presupposition about their object, law 'properly so called',

distinguishing it from their theoretical end. Their objects are (usually positive) prescriptions ('do *x* or else') while their end is a set of descriptive regularities ('law is ...'). Thus theorists of *the* law have confined their enquiries to a particular sort of law, positive prescriptive institutionalised laws, and tried to discern a law (as ultimate description and limit) of that law, coming up with various answers like the command of the sovereign, the rule of recognition, or the basic norm, all of which serve as a bedrock for legal authority, and as a limit to *the* law. The law of *the* law must, however, still be presupposed in the object in order for it to be confined as such. Positive law cannot be known as an object without presupposing its limitedness and distinguishability from those laws which are not, properly speaking, law. Moreover, it is clear that in making the distinction between the described concept of law, and the law itself, the positivists have assumed a radical separation between is and ought, a separation which is by no means entirely defensible, as I argue in Chapter 2. As one of the laws of positivism, this is/ought disjunction has received remarkably little critical attention.

Now, a second, less formal, reason for the endless iterations of the problem of the law of the law is simply that, in the way I understand the project, law is everywhere – in our metaphysics, our social environment, our ways of perceiving the world, the structure of our psyche, language, the 'descriptive' regularities of science (for instance) and so on. Thus the attempt to articulate a law of the law must be either a highly selective and artificially closed endeavour, like that of the positivists, or will become sensitive to the some of the ways in which our environment is structured by unceasing repetitions.

Third, to complicate matters, what if law is not that simple anyway? What if we discover at the place where we expect to find *the* law, or the essence of law, only paradox, ambiguity, contradiction, mystery and perhaps finally force – as Derrida has characterised the 'founding violence' of law? Then surely the theoretical complexity which we have already discovered even in our nice structure of laws as limits, reflections, and repetitions, will be hopelessly multiplied. Obviously this is an enquiry with neither a beginning nor an end.

Cornell's last sentence in the above quotation ends by amplifying 'an initial fragmentation' as 'the loss of the Good', which is where I depart from this first 'postmodern' story about law and join the second. The first version leaves behind any understanding of 'the Good' with its deconstruction of law: the Good is taken to be good only insofar as it is enshrined in the law, and so the deconstructive project deconstructs not only the law, but also its notion of the Good, leaving us with no particular ethical direction. In contrast, the second version of the 'postmodern' confrontation with law is described by Cornell as follows:

In Levinas' conception of the Good and, as I also argued, in Derrida's critical intervention into Levinas, the Good remains as the disruption of ontology that continually reopens the way beyond what 'is'. As the call to responsibility for the Other, the Law of the Law is irreducible to negative theology, or to the allegory of an 'initial' fragmentation that can only be indicated as absence.[12]

Law is on the one hand appropriation, reduction, objectification, force – everything antithetical to the notion of an 'ethical relation' with the other. Yet curiously, it is a thorough analysis of the law of this law which allows us to see the 'beyond', to see through it and at least imagine the other. In this book the Good is not reduced to its conventional legal, social, or political content, or to any content at all for that matter. It remains a projection beyond law, a 'beyond' which is opened up continually by an understanding and critique of the law of the law in all of its dimensions, and not just as a conceptual origin. Moreover, the ethical relation is posed specifically as involving a certain degree of self-reflection and the active subordination of the self to the other. If legal actors such as judges are to respond ethically to the others who are traditionally disregarded or appropriated by law, it can only be by adopting a reflective attitude to the history and ideology of legal exclusory practices.

THE BEGINNING OF THE END

Having explained the philosophical background, the aims and the hopes of this book, it now falls to mention a few less seriously theoretical, but equally important, matters.

First, the structure of the book needs some explanation. The main part of the text is divided into two sections. They are separated by a brief 'Interlude'. The first section contains three chapters, the main task of which is to delineate legal thought, taking first a broad view of the entire subject, secondly the question of language, and thirdly the conceptual and institutional conditions which have been said to exist 'before' the law. In these chapters I address explicitly some of the questions of politics which I have mentioned in this Introduction, and relate them to the jurisprudentially prevalent ideas about law. The 'Interlude' is, I have to admit, a set of reflections which has never quite fitted in any of the other chapters. This is not surprising, since it concerns the place of decisions and decision making in relation to the law, acts which themselves are never completely of the law, though never outside it either. The second part of the text builds on the first part, though not as a superstructure builds on an infrastructure. My aim in the second part is systematically to undo the theory of law: to see, as I have said, what happens to it when certain crucial aspects of the thought of Derrida are put alongside some of the foundations of positivist legal thought. In a sense, the first part of the book is an attempt to erect the ideational monolith of law, while the second part is an attempt to examine the bricks and mortar which hold it together. It does not work perfectly like that, of course, since my training in Derrida does not allow me simply to describe a philosophical system without at the same time at least sticking markers in its weak spots. In other words, much of the first part is also dedicated to highlighting the weaknesses of conventional ideas about law, even though I have left the more rigorous examination of the logical gaps in the law to the second part.

Secondly, a number of people have contributed to the text in a variety of ways, and I would like to take a moment to thank some of them. Although the work I have undertaken here began formally in 1988 when I began postgraduate study at the University of Sussex, two people at the University of Adelaide, where I studied undergraduate law and arts, influenced my ideas at an early stage – Rosemary Moore and Michael Detmold. If it had not been for their early enthusiasm I doubt that I would ever have taken this path. My studies in the United Kingdom were generously supported by the British Council. At Sussex, Geoffrey Bennington was my supervisor and gave me a great deal of support and intellectual inspiration for several years. I returned to Adelaide in 1991, and have continuously been encouraged by the scholarship and friendship of Judith Gardam, Mary Heath and Ngaire Naffine. I must also thank the editors of the Law and Social Theory series, Colin Perrin and Peter Fitzpatrick, who have been very thorough in their comments, not to mention patient. I would also like to thank all of the people at Pluto Press who have been involved in the publication of the book, in particular Anne Beech and Robert Webb, who have been extremely helpful throughout. In the final stages of writing Elizabeth Rawlings has been both very understanding and wonderful company. Most importantly, throughout this whole time, my parents have supported and followed my work, and I hope that we will continue to learn together for many years.

Part One

Part One

1
The Limits of Law

INTRODUCTION: THE BEGINNING OF THE END

The play of limits and transgression seems to be regulated by a
simple obstinacy: transgression incessantly crosses and recrosses a
line which closes up behind it in a wave of extremely short duration,
and thus is made to return once more right to the horizon of the
uncrossable.

Michel Foucault, 'Preface to Transgression'

A limit is an end to thought, an end to action and an end to how we
define ourselves.

As Foucault pointed out in his frequently quoted description of the
alternative system of classification or 'taxonomy' of Borges' Chinese
encyclopaedia,[1] the extraordinary thing is not so much that a different
taxonomy exists. This we can appreciate intellectually quite easily. The
extraordinary thing is that, in encountering the Chinese encyclopaedia,
we are forced to confront the limitation of our own thought. Trying
to *think* a taxonomy of animals which includes classifications like
'sucking pigs', 'embalmed', 'stray dogs', innumerable', 'drawn with a
very fine camelhair brush', and 'included in the present classification'
is quite impossible. We cannot think anything we like. Our thought
is limited by some natural or cultural norms of thinking, or, as Foucault
says, by 'all the familiar landmarks of my thought – *our* thought'. (And,
to be pedantic, dichotomising the possibilities like this, into either
'natural' or 'cultural' norms of thought, is itself an illustration of a
limitation, landmark, or law of modern thought. Why didn't I envisage
that our norms of thought have been laid down by a god or given to
me by my personal fairy?)

Thus, a limit is an end to thought – something is there preventing
us from thinking *that*. And, very often, there is something (our need
to go on, perhaps, or our belief in the non-arbitrary character of our
understandings) preventing us from even seeing that we are prevented
from thinking *that*. We are blind to the limitations of thought.

A limit is also, therefore, in a very obvious way, an end to action.
First, because theory and practice can never be separate – our interactions
with the world are shaped by the way we see it, just as the way we see

13

the world is shaped by our interactions. On a daily basis, we are confronted with the impossibility of *doing that*, whatever *that* is – getting a tattoo, for instance, is outside the comprehension of many people. Second, of course, limitations to action are not only due to the structures of our own thought. Things which we cannot do are determined by social limitations, including that institutionalised aspect of social regulation which we normally refer to as the 'law'. Like our thoughts, our actions are limited by some natural or cultural norms, including our norms of thought. In this case, within the standard thought framework of natural or cultural, it is possible to state reasonably clearly that some of our limitations of actions belong to a pre-subjective physical state of affairs. I am personally incapable of flying, though I continue to hope that the problem is that I simply haven't yet discovered how, or lack the imagination, or do not have certain access to the reality of my dreams. And some of our limitations are cultural. Declaring our non-mainstream sexuality to the world can result in violent social punishments.

A limit is also therefore, an end to our persons. We are defined, and define ourselves, in the world by our thoughts and our actions. We cannot *be* anybody or anything. Being women in a society which has certain definitions and expectations of women means, obviously, that in *being* we have to negotiate these definitions, some of which are internalised, some of which we struggle against and some of which we may accept reflectively as part of the human condition.

A limit is (on another hand) the beginning of thought, the beginning of action and the beginning of ourselves. Without the taxonomy which says that *that* is impossible to think, we would not be able to think *this*. The limit gives us a place to begin, a place to put our thoughts, a place to proceed and a place to make conclusions. The limit also, in some instances, empowers us to act and to be. There is a whole educational institution out there (and in here, for that matter) which is empowering me to write this book, and to be this person sitting at her computer (who is also incidentally thinking about aspects of her life 'outside' the ivory tower). However, I should also observe something which will be obvious to many, which is that the empowering side of a limit is not in itself necessarily a good thing: the existence of a limit which is *more* than a beginning for some – being also a head start or a downright predetermined victory – is only one aspect of an oppressive society. Being white and Anglo-Saxon in a society which excludes and marginalises those who come from other racial and cultural groups – being inside the category of people valued by a racist society – is an empowerment of a very concrete political sort in the current context, but can we claim that our white condition is better than that which might exist for us in a non-racist society?

To summarise (an activity which I fear will be frequently necessary in this book): a limit is an end and a beginning. The limit is the end or limitation of analysis beyond which it seems always impossible to reach, and is therefore also a failure and weakness in thought. Yet limits are formative and bind thought into a unitary form – they are the paths which we follow to determine our existences.

A crucial question which arises is – can we have law without oppression? If law just is this way of ordering the world into protected insides and devalued outsides, in all of their intersecting complexities, isn't oppression of some sort inevitable? The boundaries may shift and the protected categories may alter, but won't there always be an inside and an outside? The answer to this problem may lie in the metaphor of the path, which seems to present a concept of law as a personal journey, rather than something outside ourselves which binds us, and into which we attempt to fit ourselves (or take the consequences).[2] A singular path, of course, though it is something to follow, and gives us somewhere to go, may be just as limiting as an uncrossable frontier. Or a solution may lie in developing a concept of law which, although maintaining order, does not rely primarily on the difference between sameness and otherness, and works actively to subvert antagonism between the subject and the object. These are questions which remain to be explored.

The Western limit seems more like a circle than a path. In defining an area of things which are the same and an area of things which are the same in being different, it divides the world for its purposes into two, a division which in itself leads to no *different* place, just more of the same: two categories, two stereotypes, two streams of being (inside and outside). This feature of Western thought – our dichotomising habit – has been thoroughly canvassed and critiqued in contemporary theory.[3] We read repeatedly how Western thought works by dividing any particular terrain into two, one privileged and valued, and the *other* of necessity deviant and devalued. However, although this is now an old point, it cannot be emphasised too strongly, for not only are such dichotomies the instrument of arbitrary modes of thought which limit our imaginations and our theoretical possibilities, they are also the fundamental structure of oppressions in Western culture and in all of its imperialist modes.

Law is a limit which works in many dimensions. In fact (to stick my neck out) I would say that any limit is a law, because, tautologically, that is what a law is – something which defines an inside and an outside, gives us the possibilities and impossibilities of phenomena, and, in our culture, mediates oppression by defining and legitimating the categories of sameness and deviancy. Punishment flows from being outside, whether we are talking about a criminal law, or the social laws which regulate existence generally. Thus 'law' here is not just that aspect of social organisation which is institutionalised into a legal system. Laws are all of the circles and paths which contribute to and protect our understanding of the world, our interactions with it and the relationships which define our persons.

A limit, to my mind, invites transgressions. The recognition that it is impossible to think *that*, and therefore impossible to do that, or be like that, is sometimes (at least when the impossible option seems preferable to the existent one) an inspiration to make the attempt. Thinking outside what Monique Wittig has called the 'category of sex',[4] that is, the social significance of being female or male, is a challenge to existing presuppositions about sex and sexuality and therefore a necessary element of emancipatory thought, but it remains in absolute terms impossible. We cannot, as Wittig says, think outside the category of sex. The limits which are sexual stereotyping in many ways define our social perceptions, and it is not possible simply to step outside and ignore sex as a category. However, the aim of emancipating our thought from this prison makes it necessary to think and act outside, to refuse to be contained. The limit is therefore like a brick wall inviting us to think beyond it, but which at present cannot simply be smashed. The paradox of such laws is this struggle of necessity and impossibility: that it is at any given moment both necessary and impossible to transgress the limits which have been laid down. I should point out that a 'transgression' or 'subversion' does not involve the annihilation of law or of the certainty of our meanings (any more than a deconstruction is a destruction). Foucault has put it like this:

> The limit and transgression depend on each other for whatever density of being they possess: a limit could not exist if it were absolutely uncrossable and reciprocally, transgression would be pointless if it merely crossed a limit composed of illusions and shadows ...
>
>   Transgression contains nothing negative, but affirms limited being – affirms the limitedness into which it leaps as it opens this zone to existence for the first time.[5]

Foucault says that a transgression contains 'nothing negative', yet it is clear none the less, that in crossing a limit which sets itself up as uncrossable, a transgression does contain an element of negativity. A transgression is a challenge which demonstrates the permeability of our frontiers, and may in the process weaken or otherwise alter their rigidity. It does not destroy them. However the major point, that the transgression 'opens [a] zone to existence for the first time', is what I see as the central liberating potential of the attempt to think the other of that which is within the domain of our everyday representations.

The transgressability of limits and our responsibility to undertake this task in the context of legal thought is the major political/theoretical focus of this book. My aim is to consider the limits of legal thought – both the limits which are the *content* of legal thought (laws as limits), and the limits which define jurisprudence and 'law' as a distinct terrain of thought. In other words, apart from law as a philosophical concept, the book is about the 'laws' of jurisprudence – jurisprudence as an institution. It is crucial to recognise that law is multi-dimensional, that is, that the 'laws' which make up our world as thinking and acting beings operate on a variety of levels, which cannot ultimately be separated out into distinct objects of analysis. It is not possible, for instance, to factor out the laws which structure the understanding or the laws of logic, in order to achieve a 'pure' analysis of legal institutions. It is not possible to discount 'discourse' and the laws of language in our quest for an understanding of the conventions of philosophical processes.

The fact that each potential object of legal analysis is permeated with every other suggests that what is in fact necessary is an appreciation of the ways that the different layers of laws interact, and a resistance to the closure which legal analysis inevitably solicits. Thus, the laws which define jurisprudence as the philosophy of law, must be regarded not simply as the frontier of jurisprudential analysis, but also as integral to the study of substantive law. The limitations which jurisprudence has placed on its subject matter are inevitably reflected in what we regard as 'law', and what is inside the realm of things which are legitimately studied at law school and considered by a court in determining a case. I will come back to this question of the frontier of jurisprudence in the next section.

It should therefore be borne in mind throughout that a norm, or a law, is never something simply 'within' a closed system: a law is never simply a rule of a game, never a prescription which is entire in itself and which just belongs inside a certain structure of norms. The political significance of this fundamental insight relates to the point already made about dualistic thought: the refusal to accept the closed terrains of conventional legal thought is an anti-conservative step which hopefully, in the right contexts, can open the domain of law to presently unthinkable possibilities. One such possibility, for instance, is the acceptance of multiplicity in social organisation rather than the simple division of social categories into same and different.

THE LIMITS (AND CENTRES) OF LEGAL PHILOSOPHY

What does a game look like that is everywhere bound by rules? whose rules never let a doubt creep in, but stop up the cracks where it might?
Ludwig Wittgenstein, *Philosophical Investigations*, § 84.

It was John Austin – the patriarch of contemporary legal thought – who set the modern limit to jurisprudential investigation by insisting upon a distinction between the science of jurisprudence and the science of legislation, or between the study of law as it is, and speculation about what it ought to be.[6] According to Austin, the 'province' of jurisprudence is determined by laws 'properly so called', which he defined as the positive commands of a sovereign. Laws laid down by the correct legal mechanism qualified as being within the domain of jurisprudence, while any other sort of law or norm, for instance laws of morality, language, etiquette or religion, did not qualify. The limit of jurisprudence was thus itself very clearly laid down by a philosophical legislator.

The proper terrain of jurisprudence was therefore claimed as legally institutionalised laws. Laws 'properly so called' were, in this way, the property of jurisprudence, being the proper content of the new science. Jurisprudence owns law, as English literature owns George Eliot. And the property, that is the legitimacy (being their essential characteristic), of the laws conceptualised within this limit, was that they had been set in place by a sovereign – a supreme owner of the entire legal system. In thus setting a limit to jurisprudence Austin at once staked a claim for legal science which was protected from the realms of ethics, legislation, sociology, political science and other contiguous disciplines. The determination of the province of jurisprudence was, in the manner I have already outlined, both an end and a beginning – a limit which in the one movement established a new science and put an end to various non-legal questionings.

The property metaphor, which is Austin's, is no accident, though nor are its implications easy to unfold. (In fact, another theme of this book is this idea of law as property, and it will take some time to examine its dimensions.) Like law, property is a mechanism of exclusion: as Kevin Gray has argued, the hallmark of a property right in the common law tradition is not so much the positive ability which one has to alienate or use an object of property, but the existence of excludability.[7] A property (right) is a limit which excludes others from the use and enjoyment of an object. The object's relationship to its owner, and to other people and potential owners, is defined by this zone of inclusion and exclusion. Douzinas and Warrington have very accurately described the self-appropriation of jurisprudence in the following terms:

> Jurisprudence sets itself the task of determining what is proper to law and of keeping outside law's empire the non-legal, the extraneous, law's other. It has spent unlimited effort and energy demarcating the boundaries that enclose law within its sovereign terrain, giving it its internal purity, and its external power and right to hold court over the other realms ... Jurisprudence's task is to impose upon law

the law of purity and of order, of clear boundaries and of well-policed checkpoints.[8]

In legal philosophy, law 'properly so called' is the exclusive terrain of the legal philosophers: though political theorists, sociologists and the like may have certain aspects of law, and various sorts of conventions as their theoretical objects, the essential legal question – the *validity* of law – belongs to the legal theorist. At the same time, questions of morality and politics are excluded from the domain of legal theory, as belonging properly to other areas of thought. The discipline thereby established has very clear frontiers in which can be observed the connection between legitimacy and property: the essential question of legitimacy is the question which is the property of legal philosophy – it both belongs to legal philosophy and is the universal characteristic (or property) of legal thought. At the same time the legitimacy of the terrain of legal theory is defined by the exclusory zone which determines that some things – laws 'properly so called' – are within its domain, while other things – basically everything else – are not.

Hans Kelsen had a similar view of the limits of jurisprudence. The 'pure' theory of law was, he claimed, a science of law, not a politics – it was concerned with what law is, not with what it ought to be.[9] Its purity was assured by an exclusion of everything *other* to law from its area of knowledge:

> That all this is described as a 'pure' theory of law means that it is concerned solely with that part of knowledge which deals with law, excluding from such knowledge everything which does not strictly belong to the subject-matter law. That is, it endeavours to free the science of law from all foreign elements. That is its fundamental methodological principle.[10]

Thus, the body of knowledge which is legal science is formed by a positive exclusion from consideration of everything which is other or 'foreign' to law. That the character of law itself may have been formed through this exclusion does not seem to have played a major role in the early theory of Kelsen, although he did recognise that the 'science of law' constitutes its theoretical objects.[11] (Though the assumption remains that drawing a rigid boundary around law ensures the purity of the science thereby established.) As Kelsen himself argues elsewhere, 'the norm functions as a scheme of interpretation':[12] imposing a norm on law in order to delimit an area which is legal theory in a way determines the nature of the content to be studied. The norm which provides that some 'laws' are within the domain of legal theory and others (social norms, for instance, or norms of language) are not, determines positively the nature of the law under consideration. The exclusion gives an identity to the theoretical object. However, positivism does not carry its understanding of posited laws as far as the conventions of personality, observation, or understanding. Such matters would obviously interfere with the purity of the jurisprudential enterprise. The 'pure', 'scientific' description of the laws of a legal system, requires that social and linguistic constructs remain unquestioned and are therefore naturalised.[13]

One limit of legal philosophy then, is this proprietary one set by Austin and reinforced by Kelsen. Although a positivist limit – because it proclaims and reinforces the distinction between legal thought and other sorts of enquiry – it has more or less determined the domain of all legal theory beyond positivism. The objects of legal thought generally – from critical legal studies and feminist legal theory to natural law theory and realism – remain Austin's 'proper laws' and their surrounding contexts, which also form the basis of legal education. The primary focus is still proper law, not 'improper laws' such as the one which says that men cannot wear dresses.

In this way traditional legal thinking is what Maria Lugones calls 'an exercise in purity'[14] – that is, an exercise which asserts control and dominance over heterogeneity by separating certain elements of existence from others, fragmenting the world in order to hierarchise it. Yet as Lugones explains, separation is not just this 'exercise in purity', the separation of the white from the yolk, or of (for instance) rationality from emotion, or law from society. Separation is also what happens when different elements refuse to become one, as the proponents of purity would like: the curdling of a mixture is a resistance to the imposition of unity, and an affirmation of multiplicity as opposed to fragmentation. To affirm a curdled separation rather than a pure one, is to resist the law of purity, or the purity of laws. For instance, Lugones suggests that we can see lesbian separatism not as a simplistic rejection of patriarchal law and the formation of an alternative 'pure' lifestyle, but as a curdled response to the demand for purity.[15] Separation from dominance must involve a recognition that the demand for purity is produced by the culture of dominance: the way to resist this is by affirming impurity and multiplicity – the curdled state of our selves and of our political and social existences.

Theoretically, what is perhaps required, as a form of resistance to the oppressive purity of legal thought, is an approach which refuses to be bound by the analytically pure categories of law and legal theory. As I will argue these categories are, in any case, the fictional constructs which mask normative multiplicity. Therefore, to quote Lugones: 'The reader needs to see ambiguity, see that the split-separated are also simultaneously the curdled-separated. Otherwise one is only seeing the success of oppression, seeing with the lover of purity's eyes.'[16] The response to legal theory's insistence on purity is not only to deal with the rationalistic, positivist arguments on their own terms, but to look beyond at the fragmented other of legal thought, and to articulate the interconnectedness of laws in every manifestation.

Apart from the external boundary of the province of jurisprudence, the area is defined by several other limits. The most obvious of these in the twentieth century has been the distinction drawn between natural law theory and positivism. The terrain of jurisprudence since Austin has been basically, though not entirely, demarcated by the opposition between theories which look at law originating in the nature of the world, and law originating in human association. The theories of natural law and positivism do not necessarily conflict, even on what has been considered to be the basic question of jurisprudence – what makes law valid? – because the 'laws' under consideration exist in different dimensions (if they exist at all). It is only when a positivist claims that natural law does not exist, or when a natural law theorist claims that a law made within a positive legal system is invalid if it is against natural law, that a conflict arises.[17] Otherwise, the difference is primarily one of focus.

In fact, the natural and the positive, in jurisprudence as in other areas, are inextricable, and only held apart by a theoretical terrain that insists on distinguishing them. On the positivist side, the integrity of description, the *is*, is protected from collapse by a natural law of textual and factual interpretation – words have a natural significance, objects fall naturally into classes of things. Notwithstanding his recognition of the constructedness of 'nature' and the 'real', Kelsen insisted on a strict distinction between the descriptive character of theory and the prescriptive character of law-making institutions. His 'descriptive ought'[18] does not name the necessarily prescriptive element of description (any description has the power of determining, constructing, or influencing meanings and actions): the 'descriptive ought' refers to the act of describing purely that which is inherently prescriptive. In order to be able to claim that what is going on is merely description, not prescription or evaluation of any sort, the positivists have had to resort to a rather naive scientific and linguistic naturalism. On the natural law side, as I will explain in a moment, Finnis needs to revert to some rather fuzzy notions of 'soundness' and 'authenticity' to justify his views about the universality of practical reason. Such obviously evaluative words stand out as the terminology of those who have the power to say that their own world view is the 'sound' or 'authentic' one, and which therefore is the view with the greatest claim to universality.

In fact, given the philosophical context of modern natural law and positivist theories, it may be that they have more in common than is generally supposed. The white male homogeneity of their proponents is certainly one major aspect of this commonality, but there are several others (which I would regard as related to the powerful social position of most of the writers involved). For instance, both approaches, at least in the modern context, tend to speak of law as something external to the individual, something which can be positively identified, and either followed or not followed. A law takes the form of a prescription which can be stated, and which is separate from our individual identities. Liberal legal theory has assumed absolutely the existence of a pre-legal subject who makes rational choices, rather than a subject who is constructed through the processes of law. Furthermore, both natural law and positivism are centred on the attempt to find the origin and general concept of law and legal authority. The approach has not been to follow threads or look for analogies throughout the texture of life, but rather to achieve a general theoretical description of legal authority. Joseph Raz puts it like this:

> A comprehensive investigation may result in what could be called a theory of legal system. Such a theory is general in that it claims to be true of all legal systems. If it is successful it elucidates the concept of a legal system, and forms part of general analytic jurisprudence.[19]

It is the general concept of law which rules jurisprudence, or as John Finnis has indicated, the central case: the theorist is concerned to discern the typical or focal case of law, in relation to which there may be any number of diversions or marginal cases. Jurisprudence is typically about describing the law of law – what is it about law which makes it law? – and therefore of finding the *essence* or core concept of law. This project is common to natural law and positivist approaches.[20]

Thus, in order to be a serious legal philosopher one must contemplate serious cases, not fantasies. The analytical limit of jurisprudence is not only the definition of its property, but the related demand that the properties or central characteristics of law be articulated. This is the perception of many legal thinkers who base their arguments upon what generally occurs, upon serious, central cases which are explained by a principle, norm, concept, or theory. Finnis, writing in an Aristotelian mood, explains:

> ... one's descriptive explanation of the central cases should be as conceptually rich and complex as is required to answer all appropriate questions about those central cases. And then one's account of the other instances can trace the network of similarities and differences, the analogies and disanalogies ... between them and the central cases. in this way, one uncovers the 'principle or rationale' on which the general term ... is extended from the central to the more or less borderline cases, from its focal to its secondary meanings.[21]

Law and its limits can therefore be solidly described in all of their integrity, centrality and unity 'without ignoring or banishing to another discipline the undeveloped, primitive, corrupt, deviant or other "qualified sense" or "extended sense" instances of the subject matter'.[22] In this way, the power of law defined and limited by its centre is such that it radiates its significance even to the edges of its domain, illuminating with the archetype of its own self the 'undeveloped, primitive, corrupt, [and] deviant', and generously adopting such marginal cases into the heart and warmth of normality. To be marginal or deviant nevertheless means to be subjected merci(less/full)y to the normal and acceptable paradigms. A similar move is made by H.L.A. Hart, who argued that the paradigm case of law exists where primitive or pre-legal systems are supplemented by a type of rule – the 'rule of recognition' – which binds everything into a whole and provides a mechanism for the identification and alteration of law.[23]

Yet, as Finnis argues (and clearly reveals through his language), the process of determining that something is a 'central' case is an evaluative one, requiring the theorist to make judgements about the nature of her (or, in Finnis' language, 'his') object. The marginal cases are primitive, undeveloped, deviant and corrupt. Central cases are strong and valued in their centrality. Surely this is the language of theoretical imperialism.

The method Finnis advocates as a way of avoiding the potential arbitrariness of individual evaluations is that of paying due attention to the requirements of practical reasonableness. According to Finnis, the universal or complete viewpoint can only be attained by a theorist who has a 'wide knowledge of the data, and penetrating understanding of other men's practical viewpoints and concerns'.[24] In combination with 'sound judgement about all aspects of genuine human flourishing and authentic practical reasonableness'[25] a theorist is, according to Finnis, able to develop an understanding of law which is 'potentially complete' and 'universal'.[26] What Finnis has not taken into account is that the 'sound' judgement and 'authentic' practical reason do not themselves exist in a neutral theoretical space, any more than the central cases of law do, but are constituted through the world view of the theorist. The common element between those who agree on what is 'sound' and 'authentic' may not be a universal practical reason, but rather the power of those who have been able to define the theoretical territory: the only question worth asking about this distinction between the centre and the margin is – just *who is it* who gets to say what is 'central', and where does *he* get his authority from?

Such a question seems to me to open up the whole terrain of academic institutional mystifications and the associated hierarchy of knowledges to a profound questioning. Does he get at least part of his authority to say what is central from his position as an Oxford professor whose word is valued because of this status? Do others listen respectfully and respond in kind essentially because they/we are also part of that institutional system? What is it that accords weight to benign views of current forms of legal organisation as something which, though not flawless, exist to secure human goods? What is it that privileges this view over that of the feminist or anarchist who sees in law a system which maintains the privilege of those with power to define reality and to benefit materially from those definitions? Why is the one view 'balanced' and the others 'political', if not outrightly hysterical? Is it an over-reaction to be so *angry* about this? And, who am I to talk, who also benefits enormously from this system of academic privilege?

My purpose in raising this matter (the voice of reason re-asserts itself) is simply to indicate the way in which what has been posited as the study of jurisprudence together with the laws or conventions of that terrain of 'knowledge' have an institutional history, and are inextricably linked with the laws and conventions of that institution. The 'institution' in question here is roughly legal and philosophical academia in a common law context, and is as limited and as hierarchical as the legal systems it theorises.

THE LIMITS OF THE LEGAL SYSTEM

As I have indicated, Austin determined the province of jurisprudence early in the nineteenth century. The territorial limits of Austin's province was the concept of laws 'properly so called'. Jurisprudence as an area of theory is limited by this concept, yet as I have suggested, this limitation is always a political boundary in that it excludes a realm of social, cultural and linguistic questioning in attempting to purify its concerns: in essence jurisprudence excludes reflection on its own constructedness through academic norms, and thus like many other academic discourses shrouds itself in a veil of naturalness.

The terrain of law, like the terrain of jurisprudence, has become naturalised by the enforcing of a limit to the concept of law through the notion of a 'legal system' which achieves theoretical and practical closure in its ultimate validating principle. 'Law' is only that which is within the limits of the legal system. The Western convention that men should not hold hands with each other in public, even when they are feeling affectionate, is not, according to positivist-inspired dogma, a law, because it does not attract enforcement by the institutions of the 'legal system'. This is to say that the legal system is conceptually limited in positivist thought by some frontier (or frontiers) unifying what *is* law. Everything that is law shares some mark or characteristic with everything else that is law, and this *property* of law is the defining boundary of the legal system. Whether or not something is within the system can be discerned by the presence of such a mark or characteristic.

Moreover, and very importantly for positivist thought, whether or not a set of rules is a legal system can be determined 'objectively' by the presence of such a unifying rule. It is true that in many cases the frontier is fuzzy: clearly positivists recognise some degree of uncertainty about the *precise* content of law, but the idea is that its general dimensions and characteristics are certain.

H.L.A. Hart, for instance, as is well known, postulates a system of primary and secondary rules which, unified under a comprehensive 'rule of recognition', are the necessary identifying features of a legal system. In order to demonstrate the necessity of this hierarchical system of rules to any 'developed' legal system, Hart begins by considering the nature of 'law' in 'primitive' communities, that is, societies without 'legislature, courts or officials of any kind', but only a 'general attitude of the group towards its own standard modes of behaviour'.[27] Such communities, according to Hart, have only primary rules of obligation which lay down basic standards of behaviour. Lacking the synthesising power of a rule of recognition this type of society has no centrally vested authority which can serve as the defining characteristic of law and is therefore no more than pre-legal: such an arrangement will only be viable for small groups of people:

> In any other conditions such a simple form of social control must prove defective and *will require supplementation* in different ways. In the first place, the rules by which the group lives will not form a system, but will simply be a set of separate standards, *without any identifying or common mark*, except of course that they are the rules which a particular group of human beings accepts.[28]

The first 'defect' of organisation of a society by primary rules alone is that the rules do not form a system, since they have no 'common mark', except (curiously) that they are accepted by a particular group of people. The mark which for Hart converts the pre-legal into the legal, the unsystematic into the systematic, and the primitive into the developed, and which is the remedy or supplement for the uncertainty of the frontiers of law, is the rule of recognition. This rule is that which is essentially the law of law, since it is the criterion for recognising a particular rule as legitimate within a legal system. For a set of rules to qualify as a legal system, there must be some authoritative or proper way of determining its content, and this function is fulfilled by the rule (or rules[29]) of recognition.

The rule of recognition therefore performs a dual function for Hart. From the internal point of view, the question 'what makes norm X law?' can be answered by reference to the rule of recognition. A norm is part of the law if it is recognised as such under the rule of recognition. From the external point of view, the existence of the rule of recognition is the criterion by which a set of norms can be scientifically identified as a legal system in a developed state. The rule of recognition therefore provides not only an internal criterion of identity and mark of legitimacy but also an external, 'objective' definition of law. Of the rule, Hart insists 'its existence is a matter of fact'.[30]

However, the empirical expression of the rule of recognition is deliberately left vague by Hart: exactly what the rule (or rules) of recognition are in a given legal system may not always be clear, although they may take the form of acceptance of some authoritative text, of judicial decisions, legislative or monarchical enactments, or customs as the basic source of legitimacy. Whatever the content of the rule, it clearly takes the form of acceptance or recognition by some relevant persons that certain norms count as law:

> For the most part the rule of recognition is not stated, but its existence is shown in the way in which particular rules are identified, either by courts or other officials or private persons or their advisers.[31]

As a largely unsupported empirically based description of the way that recognition of law occurs, Hart's position is unobjectionable: those who are given a certain privilege within the system of law have the power to say what the law is. Law is largely self-defining in practice because those who have power within the system have also the authority to recognise the law, that is, to say what constitutes law. In practice, law is an incestuous and homosocial boys' game, a conversation among reasonable men about the nature and dimensions of legal regulation.

As a theoretical statement attempting to prove that 'developed' law is closed and systematic (and therefore as a quasi-scientific apology for the legal status quo), Hart's analysis falls quite flat in ways which will be discussed at some length at various stages of this book. For a start, Hart simply excludes from the category of the legal everything which does not fit into a predetermined picture of law which just happens to correspond to that accepted by Western democratic states. The political nature of the exclusion is obvious: the central case of developed law is defined through the exclusion of the undeveloped and the primitive, and the theoretical basis for the exclusion is never made clear. What *is* clear is that Hart is simply disguising as a description of a universal concept of law something which simply empirically reflects a certain type of law. If you start with the assumption that the central case of law looks like British law seen through the eyes of a reasonable man, it is hardly surprising that the theoretical reduction of the central case reflects the characteristics of British law from this perspective, and not of Aboriginal law, or Islamic law, or the law of the Hopi Indians.

Nor is it surprising that the ensuing theoretical debate is largely conducted by those who have the background and the inclination to engage in it: it is hardly surprising, for instance, that there are few feminist critiques of Hart since the terms of the debate have been set in this way.

Secondly, Hart's thesis is plainly circular: the officials recognise the rule which recognises them as officials.[32] The rule of recognition owes its existence to the fact that certain officials recognise it, while the existence of officials within a legal system can only be due to their constitution *as* officials by the system. This type of logical aporia is in my view not peculiar to Hart, but indicative of both the impossibility and the oppressiveness of the positivist project.

It can only be theoretical force, or what Derrida tends to term violence, which is holding this conceptual system together. Hart's system involves actively neglecting those moments where political exclusions and definitions determine the shape of the explanation of law's legitimacy. In my view this type of theoretical force which defines legality in a particular exclusory and hierarchical fashion is obviously related to the coercion which holds existing legal systems together. The necessary contradictions of attempting to legitimate authority without reference to a supernatural order are being repressed here in the name of achieving an 'objective' explanation of law: such repressions also operate in practice in order to present some understanding of the legal which is distinct from the political.

In an analogous movement of limiting law to itself and thus in principled if not detailed support of Hart's totalisations of legal relations, Joseph Raz writes: 'By the thesis of the "limits of law" I mean the position that there *is a test* which distinguishes what is law from what is not' (emphasis in original).[33] Recognising that Hart's criterion for the identification of a legal system fails as a necessary condition for the self-determination of a legal order (there is no reason to suppose that different officials can't 'recognise' the system in accordance with different rules[34]) Raz nevertheless proposes a *test*, that is, a criterion by which the essential existence of a legal system can objectively be identified: 'If the thesis of the limits of law is right, there must be a criterion of identity which sets necessary and sufficient conditions, satisfaction of which is a mark that a standard is part of a legal system.'[35] Like Hart, Raz is committed to establishing the unity and self-identity of law, though not necessarily its internal coherence, by theorising a limit within which law always finds itself: he thus proposes an exclusive 'criterion of membership' for the legal club which denies entry to any prospective member not recognised by the law's 'primary organs'.[36]

The conceptual limit of the legal system is perhaps most interestingly theorised by Hans Kelsen. Kelsen's ideas are less empirically convincing that those of Hart (or even Austin), but more theoretically tight, though since Kelsen's methodology is more precise than Hart's, the gaps in the system are also more evident. In his early work Kelsen marks both the temporal and the conceptual origin of a legal system with the presupposition of a 'basic norm' – a legally unconditioned reason occasioned by the replacement of one legal system with another.[37] The basic norm is the first reason of a legal system and the only validating principle of its Historically First Constitution:[38] through that constitution, or a chain of constitutions which it has authorised, the basic norm is the unifying principle of the total system – it is 'the bond between all the different norms of which an order consists'.[39] Each norm in the system is justified by a higher and prior norm, and these relations of validity taken as a whole therefore constitute a hierarchy of norms generally authorised by the basic norm: in its role as the historically first reason of the system the basic norm is also the last reason discoverable in the chain of validity, marking as it does the invalidity of the prior system. The right of the present system of norms originates in the destruction of an other, earlier system of norms.

In Kelsen's later work, notably in *The General Theory of Norms*, the basic norm is theorised no longer as a hypothesis or presupposition, but as a fiction, which gives objectivity to an otherwise subjective set of norms. What Kelsen appears to mean by this is that the basic norm is a frame within which a norm which would otherwise have no basic reason for validity becomes objectively valid. A norm stating that the speed limit on a particular road is 60 kilometres per hour is only the subjective pronouncement of a legislature: what makes it objectively valid is its situation within the frame or limit which is provided by the basic norm. It is objective because the basic norm is a limit beyond which it is not possible to ask further questions about validity. The frame is a fiction because it has not itself been laid down, and no reason for its own validity exists. Nor does it have an empirical expression, but is, as Kelsen says, 'a merely thought norm'.[40] The fiction of a limit supplies the objectivity which is lacking in a norm. What is so interesting about this is that Kelsen recognises in his later work the contradictions inherent in the closed concept of law, and has not tried to resolve them.

Kelsen's structure is similar to Hart's in some ways because the basic norm performs the dual function of providing the basic reason for validity of a law, and of being the observable mark or criterion of identity of a legal system. The basic norm is at once the law of every law, being the ultimate condition for every law's existence, and the limit of legality which binds the system into a totality excluding the non-legal. In Kelsen's early work, the basic norm also delimited the legal order temporally, and demarcated a boundary which was under a previous legal regime strictly illegitimate, but which was definitive of legality under a new regime. The temporal aspect of Hart's rule of recognition is quite different, because it is described as developing out of a pre-legal system which gradually coheres and centralises authority until a point is reached when true legal systematicity (limitedness, identity) is attained.

The basic norm is at various stages of its history a hypothesis, a presupposition, an act of political force and a fiction. In every case the basic norm as the law of law represents a failure in the idea of the 'purity' of law and legal science, because it imports into the terrain of the legal something which is strictly speaking neither legal nor non-legal, while being at the same time the very essence of legality and its antithesis. Hart's attempt to limit law by reference to a rule of recognition is, as I have indicated, circular because its existence rests on recognition by the very subjects which it constitutes and governs. The choices with which positivism is faced are underlined by this overview of Hart and Kelsen: the concept of law in a positivist regime (and, I would suggest, its practical expression) is circular, contradictory, maintained by violence, exclusory, and/or (though I would put the emphasis on the 'and') inherently oppressive.

In no way, however, do these difficulties with positivism imply that a theory of natural law is preferable: both varieties of thought suffer from the aporia of any attempt to ground law absolutely. A theory of natural law rests on the belief that there are principles transcending human contingencies which are or at least ought to be encapsulated in positive law.[41] Yet, since 'nature' refuses to reveal its commands to us clearly and unambiguously; since the existence and identity of any God is (to say the least) controversial; and since even assuming a clear identity of any of the gods available her word seems never to be entirely transparent – acceptance of such a claim invariably relies upon the conferral of authority upon some human institution or individual to clarify the content of natural law. Personally I trust neither the Catholic Church nor the Natural Law Party (and not even John Finnis) to undertake this task, which is, in any case a thoroughly political one. In other words, until some revelation convinces me otherwise (and I do not question the revelations experienced by others, I simply find it hard to make any use of them) the idea of natural law remains reliant on human contingencies, and cannot therefore fulfil its own goal of ascertaining non-human foundations for law. These claims will be considered at greater length in later chapters of this work.

THE LIMITS OF LAWS

The discipline of legal theory and the positivist conception of law as limited and systematic are, in the way I have indicated, mutually supportive. Legal theory defines itself as such by taking as its central (and sometimes only) object laws 'properly so called', while lending support to the notion that institutional, limited, law *is* proper law, and that other sorts of norms are qualitatively different. Legal theory constitutes the object (proper law) which constitutes it as a discipline.[42] Interrogating these frontiers of jurisprudential enquiry, and exposing their political and institutional dimensions is crucial if legal thought is to move beyond its current positivist phase. The law of law, that is, what it is that gives law its identity, needs fundamental reformulation if the political dimensions of law are ever to change.

However, the notion of limitedness is not only definitive of the ideas of jurisprudence and of a legal system: it is inherent in the very concept of *a* law. Laws impose limitations and definitions of certain sorts on human action. Laws appear as limits or configurations of limits which give definition to acts. As a limit, a rule would represent the most impermeable frontier, while principles and standards would be less rigorous boundaries. On the one hand, the idea of the limitedness of laws is a useful, perhaps necessary, condition of existence: we need standards, principles, norms, rules and categories in order to be able to understand the world, make judgements and get on with life, and it is hard to see how laws can be conceived of as anything other than systems of limits which enable us to do these things.[43]

On the other hand, a limit excludes possibilities for alternative visions, and gives a certain privilege to those whose world views cohere with the dominant one. This is underlined by the way that the limitedness of laws has been theorised by positivist writers which often entrenches, even naturalises, particular ideas and systems, making them highly resistant to change. It also participates in the policing and enforcement of the boundary between law and non-law, and in particular excludes any serious challenge to the notion that law is singular and objectively applicable. The idea that *before* the law can even be established and interpreted an epistemological framework with all of its politically demarcated boundaries must exist has never been interrogated seriously by positivist writers. The limitedness of laws precludes such questioning from the beginning. In my view it is therefore necessary to look closely at the idea of a law and in particular at the types of boundaries which laws are said to establish and administer, in order to show how the limits of laws are of necessity permeable, how their essences are logically constructions and repressions of difference, and how separations between different types of norms are politically enforced and therefore open to being resisted and reconstructed where desirable.

With this in mind, the following is a brief sketch of some of the ways that the concept of *a* law is limited in legal philosophy: some preliminary difficulties with these notions are raised, though, again, the major part of the analysis takes place in later chapters.

The Norm as a Frame

As is evident in the work of all of the major positivist thinkers in the tradition of common law jurisprudence (including Kelsen), the idea of the highest reason of law provides both a mark and a limit of legality. This mark is the frontier between the legal and the non-legal. Similarly, the conventional understanding of a legal rule, principle, or standard is that it is a boundary which defines the limits of appropriate behaviour in the form of a prohibition or a conferral of powers. A norm sets up an inside and an outside, defining acceptable and unacceptable conduct, and bestowing the stamp of legality or illegality on every possible human action.

Many actions are in themselves not addressed by the law of the legal system, for instance whether I wear shorts or a frock to work, and are therefore by default stamped 'legal' whatever I decide. What is of no interest at all to positivist theorists is that such a decision is also determined in many ways by non-legal norms, such as those which set different dress codes for women and men, and those according to which dress is a relevant factor in determining standards of professionalism. The *legal* norm carries the criterion or identifying mark of a basic norm, rule of recognition, or sovereign command, while the other is not properly law, just a social standard. In both cases, however, the existence of the norm is the foundation for certain types of judgement – a judgment given by a legal judge in a wig and a robe, or a judgement by society and individual members of it.

This, I take it, is what Kelsen meant when he said that 'the norm functions as a scheme of interpretation'.[44] A norm lays down a criterion for categorisation and understanding: in itself an act has no particular legal significance, but the existence of a norm provides a frame through which to view it. Thus, to use Kelsen's example, in itself an act of killing has no particular legal significance, but the existence of a set of norms defining types of legal and illegal homicide provides a framework for categorising and judging such an act.

The understanding of the norm as a general limit within which certain particulars fall gives rise to a view of laws as essentially the major premise in a deduction. The general proposition 'if p then q' is a limit providing a criterion for judgement in cases of 'p'. The general norm of the law of negligence would be something like: 'if P owes a duty of care to D, has breached that duty, and caused damage which is not too remote, then P is liable to pay damages to D, providing that no defences can be established'. This norm is the major premise, and in order for a decision to be made against any plaintiff, it must be established that s/he owed a duty of care, breached it, and caused sufficiently proximate damage in a situation where no defences applied. In order to ascertain this, of course, a whole set of sub-norms, which determine whether or not a duty was owed, breached, and so on, must be considered, each of which also has a deductive operation: for instance, if P acted as a reasonable person in her position would have acted, then she did not breach her duty. The general norm sets a limit, within which particular cases either do or do not fall.

In *Legal Reasoning and Legal Theory*, Neil MacCormick argues first, that deductive reasoning in law is possible, and secondly, that all legal rules can be formulated as the major premise in a syllogism: deduction is therefore the archetype of legal reasoning. In order to illustrate the first point, MacCormick analyses a case where the rule clearly pre-existed, meaning that it was possible to reduce it to a set of propositions following a more complicated version of 'if p then q; p; therefore q'.[45] Where a rule 'if p then q' exists, and the content of 'p' is clear, the process of judgement simply takes the form of establishing whether in fact a case of 'p' has occurred. In 'rule' cases it is possible to come to a conclusion about the applicability of the law simply by determining whether or not the facts fit within the stated universal.

MacCormick himself notes two 'limits', that is, failures, to the applicability of deductive justification in legal thought. First, he notes that there will be a problem if the legal proposition is ambiguous, if its interpretation is not clear in a particular fact situation. In order to solve the problem of interpretation it is necessary to go beyond purely deductive reasoning in order to determine which interpretation is the legally appropriate one. Having done this, deduction once more takes over. 'Resolving the ambiguity in effect involves choosing between rival versions of the rule ... once that choice is made, a simple deductive justification follows.'[46] Of course, the basis upon which one version of the rule is seen to be legally preferred is an operation which must also be justified: this is what MacCormick refers to as the problem of interpretation.

The second 'limit' of deductive justification is one which MacCormick terms (quaintly, after a Scots form of pleading) the 'problem of relevancy'. Such a problem arises where there is no identifiable legal norm against which a case can be measured or, as MacCormick says, we 'run out of rules without running out of the need for legal decisions'.[47] In order to decide such a case, according to MacCormick, some universal must be endorsed which, as in other cases, takes the form 'if p then q'. MacCormick insists that formal justice requires the setting of some universal standard in order to decide a particular case.

MacCormick's argument is therefore an attempt to illustrate the pervasiveness of deduction by showing that even at the limits of deductive justification the universal form of argumentation reasserts itself, albeit after some process of interpretation or of gap-filling has taken place. MacCormick proceeds to elucidate the principles of interpretation and gap-filling which, he believes, judges ought to adhere to, and – in the majority of cases – in fact do adhere to. These involve not only the making of reasonable 'consequentialist' arguments which, as his term suggests, involve consideration of the consequences of adopting a particular rule, but also attempting to preserve the rationality, coherence, and internal logic of the legal system as a whole. Judicial development of the law must be extrapolation of the law: it must start with the central and clear cases in order to determine reasonable principles to apply where deductive justification is not possible:

> The point ... is to show that the decision contended for is thoroughly consistent with the body of existing legal rules and is a rational extrapolation from them, in the sense that the immediate policies and purposes which existing similar rules are conceived as being aimed at would be *pro tanto* controverted and subjected to irrational exceptions if the instant case were not decided analogously with them.[48]

First then, we have logic, of a sort, and when that fails, analogy, rational extrapolation, cohesiveness and the logic of the system and of common sense.

MacCormick's argument is an eminently reasonable one: it represents in fact, the voice of benevolent legal reason itself. Although clearly a positivist, MacCormick never denies (indeed vehemently asserts) that law is value-laden. Not only is law not value free, it is laden specifically with the values of those who have control over its various functions.[49] Yet MacCormick's argument is still essentially an apology for existing positive law, especially in so far as he reinforces the systemic and institutionalised aspects of law and legal reasoning which make it so resistant to radical revision. In MacCormick's work, emphasis is laid very squarely on the rational, the reasonable and the universalisable: neither the political structure and content of what conventionally counts as reasonableness nor the institutional construct of legal theory is ever seriously put into question.

To the syllogism itself ('if p then q; p; therefore q'), I am inclined to say 'so what?' Such a rule case is purely abstract and tautologous: stated as a logical proposition it is boringly obvious. The interesting questions relate to the practical matter of how such a formal argument has any application in law.

Several matters need to be noted here, which indicate the *non-logical* conditions of using formal logical arguments in law. First, as MacCormick himself notes, even if a syllogism is established, it is not possible to say that a particular decision follows logically. The decision of the judge is an *act*, not itself a logical conclusion made mechanically, and therefore involves the making of a choice. The judge exercises her will in deciding a case. She is not an automaton. At the very least a decision whether or not to apply the law must be made. In order to make the argument that a judge ought to decide in accordance with the conclusion of a syllogism, a further assumption must be made, which is that it is the duty of a judge to 'decide the case in accordance with the legal rights and liabilities of the parties'.[50] Compliance by judges rests firmly on acceptance of current legal institutions as on the whole fair and appropriate, which is, as MacCormick rightly points out 'an overtly political judgement'.[51] However, the political nature of such a position is frequently overlooked because of the grip which rationality and objectivity has on the legal imagination. The status quo can present itself as more or less rational, objective, and unobjectionable by erasing, or minimising the importance of, its political basis. In fact, this is precisely the sort of move made by MacCormick: although he recognises the political basis for accepting legal institutions as fair, he tends to minimise the theoretical importance of this by emphasising the common reason, rationality and good sense of legal subjects.

Secondly (and this is a point not dealt with fully by MacCormick), even assuming the transparency of the rule, that is, that its meaning is clear and precise, and that a judge ought to decide in accordance with it, a universal can never itself determine in advance what falls within its limits. The proposition 'if p then q' leaves quite open the practical question of whether a particular set of facts counts as a case of 'p'. This may seem to raise purely factual questions: can it be established that this is a case of 'p'? However, in the first place, there is never any such thing as a 'purely factual' question. The establishment of 'facts' as being of a particular type relies entirely on the ordering of the understanding, which is also in my view a political and culturally contingent matter. Moreover, the task of stating that a case falls within a particular rule involves a non-logical move, that of judgement. The point is hardly new, but it is very important. Kant wrote:

> If understanding in general is to be viewed as the faculty of rules, judgement will be the faculty of subsuming under rules; that is, of distinguishing whether something does or does not stand under a given rule ... General logic contains, and can contain, no rules for judgement.[52]

The point made by Kant is that logic is only an abstraction from content and that even though one rule may be clarified by means of another, subsumption under a rule will require the non-logical operation of judgement. There must be some 'third thing' which is neither concept nor object,[53] but which enables some decision to take place. By abstracting the content of legal decisions to a deductive form which makes decisions appear to be the result of logical extrapolation, MacCormick both maximises the hold which legal limitations have on the process of law, and minimises the agency and political responsibility of legal officials. The positivist thesis of the limits of law is, moreover, reinforced by the insistence on a peculiarly legal style of reasoning – one based on the limitations of law already established within the system.

All this may sound like so much abstract anti-positivist argument with little relevance to the concrete issues of law. However, the implications of failing to give central attention to the political structures underlying categorisation are huge. In determining that a particular case is a case of 'p', all sorts of differences are often either defined as irrelevant or simply ignored. To say, for instance, that for the purposes of defining provocation as a defence to assault or murder, the differences between a situation of domestic violence and a brawl in a pub are irrelevant, and therefore the same rules must apply, is an insultingly ignorant act of definitional violence against women perpetrated by the legal system, which has frequently resulted in actual physical violence in the form of incarceration or other punishment. It is the 'like' of analogy which enables the law to represent both cases as cases of some 'p', and therefore to treat them in the same way. What positivism as an approach to law does is to police such analogies, entrenching them, and disguising their arbitrary and political nature.

The positivist way of conceptualising a rule as the formative element of a legal system is as a boundary which encapsulates within its field the set of its possible instantiations, both past and future. The notion of the boundary sets up a reasonably determinate and static inside and outside. There will be determinate central cases where the law and the facts correspond unequivocally, making the decision justifiable deductively. There will be not-so-clear penumbral cases where problems of indeterminacy regarding either the facts or the law will have to be settled before the process of deduction can proceed. And there will be 'hard' cases where no rule will suffice to determine the outcome, meaning that the case will be solved by a very large component of judicial discretion (or delegated legislation) and by general legal principles. For the most part, the identity of law will be guaranteed by its correspondence with certain determinate normative limits. The 'exercise in purity' which characterises the discipline of jurisprudence is therefore also a hallmark of the legal approach to laws: the underlying project is always to establish the purity of core legal identities.

Individuation

The limit defined by the formula 'if p then q' is what Michael Detmold, arguing against the positivist thesis, calls the 'limit of rules'.[54] According to Detmold, demonstration of the existence of such a limit in no way proves the separation of law from non-law. It merely shows that 'inside' law there is a limit between what is inside the rule and what is outside it: showing that a legal rule has limits merely demonstrates its own self-containment and not that of an entire system.

But Joseph Raz, following Jeremy Bentham, highlights another limit which, he argues, connects the study of individual laws to the study of a legal system. In normal legal usage a 'rule', 'principle', 'doctrine' or 'norm' is not the same thing as the law on a particular topic or applicable to a particular case. Nor is a single posited legal instrument such as a statute – except in a loose sense – identical with a law. One 'law' could enshrine a number of rules, precedents, or doctrines. One statute might contain or contribute to several laws. With this in mind, Jeremy Bentham asks 'What is a law? What are the parts of a law? The subject of these questions, it is to be observed, is the *logical*, the *ideal*, the *intellectual* whole, not the *physical* one; the *law* and not the *statute*.'[55]

Raz argues that it is absolutely essential, if the limits of the entire system are to have any precise definition, for legal philosophy to have a way of delimiting each law as a single conceptual object, complete in itself and interconnecting with, though not transgressing the boundaries of, other similarly discrete legal units.[56] The identification of law on this level is what Raz calls the 'individuation' of laws. In order for law to make sense as a system, the elements of the system, individual laws, must be determinate and identifiable. In order for the universal concept of *the* law to make sense, it is necessary to have a picture of *a* law, and of how all of the instances of *a* law fit together to make *the* law. Yet it remains the case that *a* law, depending on one's criteria of individuation, could be manifested at innumerable levels of specificity. Presumably the limits of *a* law could be positioned exactly where the limit of law is, meaning that there would be only *one* law, and that it would be *the* law. Raz would reject such a possibility for simple pragmatic reasons. No single law should be too large, unmanageable, or internally conflicting:[57] law is limited on several levels at once and it is this which gives law its systematic character, *the* law representing the totality of lots of individuated instances of *a* law.

In this context it is useful to recall the answer to Wittgenstein's question 'what are the simple constituent parts of which reality is composed?' How is it, he asks, possible philosophically to distinguish conceptual units or logical atoms?

> ... isn't a chessboard, for instance, obviously, and absolutely, composite? – You are probably thinking of the composition out of thirty-two white and thirty-two black squares. But could we not also say, for instance, that it was composed of the colours black and white and the schema of squares? And if there are quite different ways of looking at it, do you still want to say that the chessboard is absolutely 'composite'? – Asking 'Is this object composite?' outside a particular language-game is like what a boy once did, who had to say whether

the verbs in certain sentences were in the active or passive voice, and who racked his brains over the question whether the verb 'to sleep' meant something active or passive. ...

To the philosophical question: 'Is the visual image of this tree composite, and what are its component parts' the correct answer is: 'That depends on what you understand by "composite"'. (And that is of course not an answer but a rejection of the question.)[58]

The analytical task of dividing the world up into parts which fit nicely together into wholes can thus only be understood within particular language games, where the meaning of the simple or the composite parts are absolutely clear. Such clarity is by no means assured, particularly in the case of something like law, where frequently there is disagreement about specific legal requirements, let alone abstract questions about the conceptual dimensions of a law. Even assuming clarity about what is simple (*a* law) and what is composite (*the* law), decisions about the placing of these limits can only be effected arbitrarily within the law language game, and cannot be justified absolutely.

DELIMITING THE LAW

The iniquitous thing about current understandings of law is not so much the claim to universality: although it is clear that any universal is a reduction of difference to singularity, it is the reduction, neglect or ignorance of *significant political* differences which is a problem, not the process of universalisation in itself. Indeed, making sense of the world is reliant on the drawing of general boundaries, but these do not have to be closed, fixed, or otherwise impermeable. Rather, the iniquitous thing about law at the present time is the myths of its purity, closure, and fixity: the blind insistence that 'proper' law is separate from the other sorts of norms which order society. In particular, real law and its abstract subjects are separated from the norms and relationships which construct the person as a knowing and existing social subject who has a sex, a race and a class. This separation protects law and legal theory from fundamental critique, because any analysis which does not have as its first point of departure law's story about itself is by definition not centrally about law, but about something else.

As far as I am concerned, the question for legal theory is not 'what is law?' in the abstract, as though we can discern a correct universal understanding of law which will hold for all time and for all types of social organisation. To assume this possibility would be to assume a natural law of the understanding, as though there is some correct way of seeing the world, and some certain method of distinguishing the universal from our experiences within a particular class, sex, race, culture (and so on). Moreover, the relationship between politics and knowledge – that what is widely recognised as knowledge is determined by those who have the power to define the world, and is therefore part of the structure of oppression – has been too clearly established for 'what is law?' to be asked in isolation. It is part of the ethical responsibility of theory to take these matters seriously (not to assimilate the stories of those defined as other, but to believe and act upon them), since failure to do so merely repeats and conserves traditional structures.

However, I do believe it is necessary to take seriously the question 'what concept of law pervades Western legal discourse?', a question which certainly involves looking at others' answers to 'what is law?' One issue around which this book is focused is the concept of law which lawyers, legal academics, legal theorists and others are working with – what is its political and theoretical background, and what are its implications in the world today? The overtly political dimension of this enquiry arises when we start to think about how the concept of law can be reformulated in order to respond to political and social conditions: in itself, critique is essential, but it is also necessary to use critique to attempt to transgress, and look beyond established understandings, in order to further our political goals.

2
The Limits of Interpretation

INTRODUCTION: THE LEGAL GAP

The use of the word 'rule' and the use of the word 'same' are interwoven. (As are the use of 'proposition' and the use of 'true'.)[1]

According to the traditional view held by both natural and positive law theorists, there are basically two possible positions in relation to the ideal of a norm – same and other, materially identical or different, inside or outside. The norm is a homogenising limit circumscribing a category of the same, determining what is identical and what is different, demarcating a present interior of like cases opposed to an exterior of cases which fail to fit the norm's paradigm and which possibly will not be measurable by any legal standard. At the borders, human finitude, perversity, or fallibility present some difficult, or deviant, or not-quite-normal, cases. But when such unpredictable cases arise, the law, in all of its omnipotent self-sufficiency, adopts the delinquent case into its fold, homogenising its peculiarities, reducing its differences and its idiosyncrasies, and reconsolidating the total control of the law. The case which is 'hard' because it is unprecedented, unexpected by a prior norm, undecided by existing law, obviously is not, according to legal thought and practice, undecidable. The law, through the intervention of a judge, solves the problem of the undecided simply by deciding or appropriating it, which means comprehending it, placing it inside or outside the boundary established by a norm. No case can be undecidable, because to be undecidable would mean – as far as the practical reason of the law is concerned – to be immobilised, suspended between practical alternatives, incapable of acting, or lost in the unthinkable space where there are no norms, nothing to go on.

Even the action of throwing a case out of court because its issues cannot be solved by law or are not within the jurisdiction of the court, an apparent case of legal undecidability, in effect establishes a boundary of exclusion reinforcing the interiority of law. Kelsen made such an argument in support of his assertion that there are no 'genuine' gaps in the law.[2] Either the case can be decided according to the law or it cannot be. However, such an argument shows rather that there are no gaps in the decidability of the law. A decision must be reached. We could argue that the law must therefore be composed *only* of gaps, otherwise a decision would be unnecessary.

The difficulty here is that the positivist thinking which pervades our view of law at this time sees law as a static structure out there and different from us: an abstract system of rules, doctrines, principles and so on, which have an existence independent of the process of their creation, construction, and application. Thus, the fact that decisions can always be made – in my view an indicator that law is a never-ending process of referrals to the past and deferrals to the future – gets interpreted as a sign of law's completeness. And the fact that it is a *judge* who makes the decision with all of (usually) his social and legal conditioning is repressed by the ideology of law. Despite continued criticism by some academics and legal professionals, the naive thought that judges simply apply the law has an enormous popular hold. Even the thought that *on the whole* judges apply the law and from time to time create it, opposes application and creation in a way which assumes that there is a system of norms which transcend human interactions, and neglects the dynamic of repetition which maintains legal assumptions and institutions.

The relationship of decisions to the law will be examined in detail in Chapters 4 and 5. For the moment it will suffice to say that every 'application' is in some sense also a re-creation of the law. And no 'creation' can exist in a vacuum, as though no law preceded it. In particular the thought that judges are non-political instruments or technicians of law casts law as the neutral arbiter and organiser of social relations, instead of the force which defines the limits of acceptable hierarchy and privilege. Accepting the status quo is as political a position as rejecting or questioning it: the difference, as many others have noted, is simply that conventional or predominant thinking has the power to define itself as true, as objective, and most importantly, as grounded or justified. Often there is some institutional context giving substance to the claims of justification: claims of scientific truth are backed by the weight of scientific convention, just as claims of legal truth are backed by the institutional weight, authority and force of legal traditions.

These myths of legal transcendence – essentially the thought that law and people are radically separate – are the forces which maintain legal order and authority in the current system. Whether it is the brute force of white patriarchal Western imperialism, or (what is often arguably much the same thing) the force of our ruling legal metaphors and conceptual structures, the force of law as we presently think of it always resides in its ultimate power to determine, define and exclude. For institutionalised law, as opposed to the norms which define our identities in their cultural context, this power has crystallised in the positivist era as the transcendence, neutrality and institutionalised character of the legal order. In other words, one of the foundations for legally-sanctioned oppression – which I see as the inability of law to appreciate (as opposed to appropriate) difference – is the positivist myth of the separation of law from its subjects.

The point which I wish to emphasise from Chapter 1 then, is that in positivism the structure of the rule, and the structure of the entire legal system, share certain crucial features. In particular, both the rule and the system are predicated on a fairly rigid inside/outside distinction – something is either legal or non-legal, it is either contained by a rule or it is not. The rule and the system combine to produce a set of definitions and determinations for our social existences which are, however, distinct from our selves. This mode of thought tends to essentialise and purify, and to appropriate instances where incommensurability may otherwise arise.

Lyotard calls instances where there is incommensurability between litigants a 'differend'.[3] A differend arises if the parties are not speaking the same language – either literally or in effect – or if there is no rule which can be applied to them in common. For instance, where an aboriginal person comes into conflict with white norms, or in a rape case where the woman's reality is different from the man's,[4] it is clear that there is no way of applying a single measure which will resolve the question to the satisfaction of all. Traditionally, as we know, the law has taken the side of the socially strongest in such disputes, often to the point where there is never even any recognisable conflict – the experience of the woman or the cultural context of the aboriginal person simply have not existed. In a sense, the law always artificially sets up a differend between itself and both parties to a dispute, because it requires them to submit to its set of norms and to speak its language.

The move towards mediation as a way of settling disputes is an interesting attempt to bring the law closer to the parties, and thus to minimise the difference between them and the norms by which they will be measured. It has also been shown, however, that where the artificial construct of the law offers some distance and protection from the other party by setting up a rule of judgment which, however unsatisfactory, belongs to neither party, mediation can actually exacerbate the differences by minimising this distance and allowing the dominant differend to be the one existing between the parties rather than that set up by the law.[5] In its clumsy way, the law is now in some small details practising reversal of the situation by empowering those who have traditionally been in the weaker position to speak, and trying to give credit to their narratives before the usual process of appropriation takes place. Such attempts remain partial and are invariably resubsumed by the master narrative.

All this is to indicate that, although those who make and administer the law are aware of the problem of the differend, or of incommensurability between the norms of the parties, the law as it presently stands is incapable of dealing with heterogeneity. Moreover, although in a sense everyone is alienated from the formal processes of law, the practice of the law has been to accord vast privileges to those who come closest to representing its own standard. This means that in setting up two differends, between itself and each of the respective parties, the person who is closest to the legal standard has a headstart in being recognised, heard, and believed. Far from being the case that there are no 'genuine' gaps in the law therefore, I would argue that what the law does in its dealings with legal persons is to set up a system of gaps, and that it is the inability of the law to recognise and deal with these gaps in all of their complexity which entrenches the legal and social privilege of certain groups. This is not to say that the solution is to find a way to close the gaps: in fact the law's conventional strategy is to close gaps by pretending that they do not exist, that is, by pretending that its version of the world is that which is or should be shared by everyone, or by finding a rule which seems appropriate to some and fits with the existing system but which, in its nature as a rule, excludes others. Current theory is in fact continually discovering the extent of these gaps, and this is an important part of the process of finding a way of dealing with them equitably.

The differend is clearly not simply a case of institutionalised laws being pitted against people who do not understand or accept them. As I indicated in Chapter 1, it is not possible ultimately to distinguish institutionalised laws from the other norms which shape our society: the attempt to do so is in reality a political and theoretical act of force which preserves the inequitable divisions enshrined in law. Thus, in thinking about law in this context it is important to bear in mind that I am speaking here not only of institutionalised law, but of the whole spectrum of norms – compulsory heterosexuality, the norms relating to sex and gender, cultural requirements, religious standards, moral ideals and so on. Although in many instances it is not possible to say that there is a *single* standard or set of requirements in social norms, and that much variation exists even within one group of people, it is still the case that certain standards are fairly common.

What I am interested in examining in this chapter is the way in which language and legal interpretation are part of this system of legal gaps. Institutionalised law is a 'discourse' – a system of linguistic and non-linguistic modes of categorisation, evaluation and transmission of meanings. In this context I am adopting the explanation of 'discourse' offered by Laclau and Mouffe:

> ... turning to the term discourse itself, we use it to emphasize the fact that every social configuration is *meaningful*. If I kick a spherical object in the street or if I kick a ball in a football match, the physical

fact is the same but its meaning is different. The object is a football only to the extent that it establishes a system of relations with other objects, and these relations are not given by the mere referential materiality of the objects, but are, rather, socially constructed. This systematic set of relations is what we call discourse.[6]

Legal discourse is that set of signifying practices contained in the institutionalised law and its surrounding context, including language and cultural norms, which interact to give certain acts a legal significance. It is important to note that legal discourse is not just the formal rules of the game of law, but includes all of the contextual systems which contribute to the significances established by law. I will come back to this point later in the chapter. To interact with the law is to play the legal language-game (since the law recognises no other) – the differend we are speaking of here (and elsewhere) is played out as at once a set of normative and discursive differences. In fact, differences in the 'languages' spoken by different groups of people *are* normative differences, simply because one 'language' and the world associated with it is generally valued above all others. In other words, as I will explain, language is normative, and law is a system of signification – signification and prescription are two fundamental functions of law and language, which combine to produce at the present time a legal discourse which is imperialistic and exclusionary.

My first task then, is to outline traditional jurisprudential assumptions about language, and to indicate the ways in which they have been overtaken by contemporary linguistic philosophy. The second section summarises what I see to be the common structure of law and language and develops the argument that they are ultimately indistinguishable. Finally, I will take a brief look at some of the modern jurisprudential work which takes interpretation as a central focus.

I should also say at this point that what I am doing here is continuing the building process which I began in Chapter 1 and which will be continued in Chapter 3. My aim is to present a picture of the interrelationship of the various dimensions of law, and the foundations of law (or the law of law) in order the more effectively to deconstruct it in Chapters 4 and 5. What I have to say here is partly descriptive of the position of language in the picture. I have also, where appropriate, made observations about the political and philosophical implications which arise generally. Chapters 4 and 5 continue the analysis in a more sustained and systematic fashion.

THE WORLD IN LANGUAGE

One classical ideal of literature is that it be as far as possible 'mimetic' or 'realistic' – such an understanding of the goal of literature assumes that the relationship between literature and the world which it represents is clear, direct and more or less unobstructed. A good writer would be one who has the insight to perceive and understand the world, and the linguistic facility to express it. The thought that language is expressive or representational presupposes that it expresses or represents something other than itself, some extra-linguistic 'reality'. The traditional notion of language is then that it re-presents some thing, bringing it into the present, making it present in its actual absence. In 'Différance' Derrida describes the 'classically determined structure of the sign' as follows:

> The sign is usually said to be put in the place of the thing itself, the present thing, 'thing' here standing equally for meaning or referent. The sign represents the present in its absence. It takes the place of the present ... The sign, in this sense, is deferred presence.[7]

Thus, an ideal or perfect language would be what literary theorists call transparent or clear, in that as the medium standing between the represented object and the mind of the reader, it would efface itself and its material existence.[8] What happens in the mind of the person who is at the receiving end of the communication should be as close as possible to what occurred in the mind of the sender of the message, and language is traditionally thought of as being nothing more than the medium of communication.

Wittgenstein summarised the ordinary assumption like this: 'These concepts: proposition, language, thought, world, stand in line one behind the other, each equivalent to each.'[9] In the tradition of language philosophy which Wittgenstein questions, language is to thought what thought is to reality, that is, the medium or container. First, there is reality, or the world, or objective truth, which becomes imprinted on the mind or is somehow intuited by the processes of the understanding. Then, thought is expressed in language as a set of propositions, and because language is imperfect and does not correspond exactly to thought or to the world, things are invariably lost or distorted on the way. The truth condition for a proposition is its correspondence to an actual state of affairs, a position usually attributed to the Wittgenstein of the *Tractatus Logico-Philosophicus*, described by Saul Kripke as follows:

> To each sentence there corresponds a (possible) fact. If such a fact obtains, the sentence is true; if not, false. For atomic sentences the relation between a sentence and the fact it alleges is one of simple correspondence or isomorphism.[10]

Simply, any statement of a constative type (which alleges a fact) is true if there is a condition in the real world which corresponds to the assertion made in the sentence.

Put at its simplest, the question here is, does meaning move from world to thought to language to proposition, or do language and other signifying processes have a central role in constructing the shape of the world? Do the world and thought have meaning independent of signification?

Legal thinkers have relied on the correspondence model of language in various ways, but have not taken it to its extremes. Where descriptions of facts are concerned, lawyers still tend to be highly resistant to the suggestion that facts are constructed by language: it is assumed that a reasonable, objective and neutral description can be obtained and that this description is not in itself a construction of the facts, but the truth, because it corresponds to a reasonable and objective perception of the facts which corresponds to the facts themselves. In some ways it is extraordinary that this idea still prevails, since the parties to a dispute invariably cast the 'facts' in a way which is most favourable to their argument: different descriptions of the facts are generally available, and it might be thought therefore that the idea could, with a little imagination, arise that different perceptions of the facts, and therefore different realities, actually exist. However, conflicting stories are apparently all part of the adversary system which supposes that the 'facts' as determined by the arbiter of facts, especially if this is the judge, and he is male, are – barring the odd mistake or bias – true and singular. Advocates and their clients may attempt to cast the facts in a particular light by their use of language. Judges, however, do not tell stories, but the truth. (What juries do is up to them, since they are not accountable for their determinations.)

On the level of the description of facts, then, the correspondence theory of language still has an enormous hold on practical legal thinking. The facts simply *are* a particular way, and the judge is the person in the best position to discern them. Critiques developed in particular by feminists and race theorists of the presumed objectivity of facts and of judges have so far had little impact on this assumption. Even the common and fairly obvious observation that facts are always in any case constructed by the law – law and facts are not separate, because what counts as a fact is made so by the law – has not substantially diminished our unfaltering belief in facts as absolute truths. The effect of this is that legal officers claim to be speaking the truth about the world through the law, whereas what frequently happens is that a differend between the experiences of the parties to an action and the legal construction of those experiences is established. This differend is entrenched by the correspondence theory of truth since only one truth – not a multiplicity – is recognised. Where other 'perspectives' are recognised, they are assumed to be subject to the view from nowhere supposedly held by the judge. No recognition that legal discourse itself is a perspective is built into the system.

So much for correspondence theory and its applicability to 'facts'. The situation in relation to 'law' is somewhat more complicated, partly because there are two sorts of correspondences to consider – that between language as an expressive medium and law, and that between law as a system of ordering the world and an assumed external reality. In what sense can legal language be said to 'correspond' to some ideal form of the law which is qualitatively different from legal discourse (where such a thing is thought to exist)? In what sense does the 'law' refer to something outside the legal order? Given that most twentieth century lawyers and legal thinkers find justification for their propositions of law in authoritative texts of varying sorts, there would seem to be little room for distinguishing 'law' from the texts in which it is contained. It would seem obvious that law is only legal discourse, that is, all of the linguistic and non-linguistic systems of signification which order our thoughts, actions and social existences. However, law has often been assumed to have some purely ideal existence beyond or behind texts, meaning that legal interpretation is assumed to be a process of discovering the correct single meaning of a text. This beyond or behind the text, the pure *thought* of law, is also sometimes assumed to latch on to a natural reality.

The latter point raises the problematic of natural law. Is there some external and eternal referent which the positive legal order does or ought to reflect? Take a proposition like the famous one of Lord Atkin in *Donoghue* v. *Stevenson*: 'You must take reasonable care to avoid acts or omissions which you can reasonably foresee would be likely to injure your neighbour.'[11] It is fairly clear that for a proposition like this it is going to be very difficult to find a factual truth condition outside legal texts. There is no 'fact' inherent in the nature of things which makes this true or false. It is, as a legal proposition, justified or not, or true within a particular authoritative set of norms, but it has no external reference in the world.

It is reasoning like this which is said to invalidate much natural law theory: as many of the positivists have written, norms are not susceptible to being grounded in facts about the world. Just because it will (naturally) hurt if I punch someone, does not mean that I should not do it.[12] It is not possible to derive an 'ought' from an 'is'. So, when the Natural Law Party conflates the laws or regularities of nature (how plants grow, how many times our hearts beat, the movement of the planets) with the laws or prescriptions of human existence ('what children need … is the love and warmth of mother at home'[13]) they are making an illicit jump from is to ought. In other words, the proposition of law cannot refer outside the law itself to some natural state of affairs: there is no correspondence to something 'real' as there would be if I said that there is a fly buzzing outside my window.

The assumed external referent of natural law has, however, at least in the modern tradition, not been 'is' statements about facts obtaining in the natural world, but rather other 'ought' statements, which can supposedly be derived from moral reasoning, or which are given to us by some deity. Is there some external referent for 'you must take reasonable care to avoid acts or omissions which you can reasonably foresee would be likely to injure your neighbour'? Lord Atkin himself referred his statement back to Christian ideals: he did not claim to derive the one from the other, but did note some equivalence. More to the point, John Finnis claims to be able to discern, in his reasonable way, what the natural 'goods' are, and how human coexistence can be ordered to attain them.[14] In this context there is assumed to be some law which exists independently of human creations, and a proposition of law is good in so far as it encapsulates that natural law. It would even be possible to say that such a proposition of law could be 'true' – that is, it is true that you should not injure your neighbour – since there is claimed to be an external, eternal and objective referent (a natural law) for such a proposition. The obvious problem here is that there is no established way of verifying the existence of such natural norms in the same way as there is general agreement about how to verify statements about objects. Positivist critique of this sort of position is not directly in conflict with natural law thought, and amounts either to a disagreement about the actual existence of a universally valid set of norms, or to a disagreement about the jurisprudential project – that we are aiming to describe what law is, not what it ought to be.

Classical common law theory also had a version of correspondence theory which related the truth of legal statements to some external referent. The objective referent here, however, was not something which inheres in nature, but rather the 'law' idealised and abstracted from legal tradition, custom and wisdom. The function of the judge in the classical common law period was not simply to read legal texts, but to declare the law. Legal knowledge was based not only on knowledge of the texts, but on an understanding of the deep structure, the artificial wisdom, of law which had arisen through custom and immemorial usage. Peter Goodrich summarises the classical common lawyer's approach to the relationship of law and texts as follows:

> In Coke's words, even where it is a matter of reading the law, it is a question of reading not simply the words of the text but also the tradition that accompanies them: the text is a mere representation of an external memory; it is a vestige in the classical sense of *vestigium*, an imprint, a footprint, a mark or trace of something, of some body, of some practice that passed on time out of mind or

countless years ago. Where it is a question of reading, then it is not
the words but the truth that is to be adhered to: *in lectione non verba
sed veritas est amanda.*[15]

Thus, as Blackstone famously said, judges are the 'living oracles' of the
law: '... judicial decisions are the principal and most authoritative
evidence' of the law, and are preserved as 'records' of it.[16] The true law,
in other words, exists in some space outside its material manifestations,
and legal propositions can be measured as statements of truth if they
correspond to this extra-textual law.

It was just such an understanding of the difference between the
language of law and the law itself which gave rise to the distinction
between the spirit and the letter of the law:

> ... it is not the words of the law, but the internal sense of it that makes
> the law, and our law (like all others) consists of two parts, viz. of
> body and soul, the letter of the law is the body of the law, and the
> sense and reason of the law is the soul of the law, *quia ratio legis est
> anima legis* [because the reason of the law is the soul of the law]. And
> the law may be resembled to a nut, which has a shell and a kernel
> within, the letter of the law represents the shell, and the sense of it
> the kernel, and as you will be no better for the nut if you make use
> only of the shell, so you will receive no benefit by the law, if you
> rely only upon the letter, and as the fruit and profit of the nut lies
> in the kernel, and not in the shell, so the fruit and profit of the law
> consists in the sense more than in the letter.[17]

The letter of the law according to Plowden is merely the outermost limit
of the expression of law which shrouds and protects its innermost sense
or content. The letter of the law is the communicating medium which
must be seen through, peeled away, cracked open, or pierced by our
legal insight. However the division letter/spirit does not map precisely
on to the distinction between language and meaning, or between the
sensible and the intelligible. It rather names something within the
intelligible, within meaning, which would duplicate some such
distinction. When we speak of the 'letter of the law' we do not refer
to the printed marks or to the phonic substance of any 'legal'
pronouncement, but rather to that interpretation of these tangible things
which we believe to be most proximate to them. The letter of the law
is the reading which is supposedly most formal, most tangible, most
precisely defined and closest to the physical aspect of legal expression.

Thus, the correspondence in question is not simply between the
language of the law and the law itself, but rather between the language
of the law and the letter of the law: the existence of a 'literal'
interpretation presupposes a meaning which directly corresponds to

the medium of expression, while the 'spirit' of the law would represent some deeper reality or underlying truth of the law. While the correspondence between the language of the law and its letter would be a fairly close one, that between the language/letter and the spirit of the law would exist on a different level altogether. The letter of the law names the correspondence between a legal articulation and its immediate, obvious, meaning. The spirit of the law cannot be tied down to any particular articulation, but is rather the life or movement of the whole of the law. As the meaning of the law it may be contained in legal texts, but it is not reducible to them – it rather exceeds them. Plowden's prescription to lawyers is that they pay heed to the deeper aspects of law's existence, its life and soul, and not merely to the superficial shell or body which contains it.[18] It therefore seems to be implied that there is *no* clear correspondence between the language of the law and the true law, though there is correspondence between the language of the law and its letter.

Just this sort of correspondence has been traced by Peter Goodrich through classical writings about the language of law. Goodrich describes in rich detail the forms and significances of early common law writing practices. Far from the movement towards plain language which is currently fashionable, the early writers were deliberately obscure in a seemingly paradoxical effort to represent their objects exactly. In fact, their understanding was that the construction of an artificial notation, a highly symbolic, technical and sacred means of recording legal transactions, could document the legal memory – not as scriptures or codifications of general principles, but rather as an endless catalogue of details, where each note faithfully re-presents a particular legal object:

> The linguistic note is a sign or mark that is attendant upon and stands in for an object. The legal note similarly represents and guarantees a specific transaction. Both senses of note involve a propriety relation in which the note is the mere mark or token of a real object, action or speech. In that respect it is the obvious duty of the custodians of the note, the notaries, to keep faith with the referent, to recollect the sender, of whose intention the note is never more than the symbol. Fidelity to meaning or to the conservation of authoritative prior meanings marks the legal writing systems examined in this chapter as systems of restriction: the note contracts; it reduces, it limits, it binds. It might also be said that in claiming to represent real properties it becomes a form of property, a unit in a system of exchange, a token of good faith, of propriety or of honour and of traditional virtues.[19]

The ideal of legal notation was as a language of proper names, each name referring singly and unproblematically to its object, though this was not because of the clarity or transparency of the language used, but rather its technical and artificial nature.

Finally, some of the Realists and Critical Legal Scholars have in this century made the argument that law should (and therefore can) reflect the 'real'. Much of their critique of law revolves around its technical and abstract nature – that it does not latch on to the real lives of real people and does not describe facts. For instance, Felix Cohen wrote that 'any word that cannot pay up in the currency of fact, upon demand, is to be declared bankrupt, and we are to have no further dealings with it'.[20] Cohen does not unfortunately identify for his readers the 'facts' which correspond to 'currency' and 'bankruptcy'. Similarly some of the early CLS writers assumed that their critique of existing law as ideological would expose a better, more true, reality, rather than just a different one,[21] and begin to provide the basis for a law which reflects social reality.

What all of these approaches to the relationship between meaning and its medium assume (whether we are talking about the world and the law, or about law and language) is that there is something external and original which can ground the law or its linguistic expression. The law reflects, represents, or is authorised by, some prior order. Language directly encapsulates legal meanings. Although these ideas about the relationship between language, law, and the 'real' reappear in various forms in contemporary thinking about law, a strict distinction between language and law is not universally maintained because of the recognition that law is itself an interpretive art, and that legal outcomes are shaped by the language of the law. Lawyers more than most people are aware of the way that one form of words can mean totally opposite things. Sometimes this sort of difficulty is cast as an indeterminacy in the law (the language is unclear, therefore the law is), and sometimes it is cast as an indeterminacy in language only[22] (the law is clear and we need to determine the 'correct' interpretation of the words). In the former case, law is recognised as unavoidably language-based, and in the latter case, it is thought of as something ideal outside a language which strives imperfectly to express it. In this way law is often idealised as something abstract and non-material – for instance in the idea of a *ratio decidendi,* or in the highest legitimating principles described by the positivists – which pre-exists and authorises legal language.

Moreover, while admitting a measured indeterminacy in the expression of norms, legal philosophy has largely failed to question its own language. Features of the language of jurisprudence, such as the mechanical imagery of positivism, the organic metaphors used by early common law writers,[23] or the eminent reasonableness and detachment of the language of John Finnis or H.L.A. Hart, provide obvious focal points for the demystification of legal philosophy's claims to be simply observing, describing, analysing, or reasoning about law. I do not wish to suggest that jurisprudence is somehow at fault for utilising a suggestive metaphorical terminology – the point is rather that the claim of scientificity can only be supported if there is a language of description which can represent its theoretical objects and their relationships in the absolute reality of their being. It is the significance of this assumption which traditionally-oriented legal philosophers have failed to grasp. The basic construction of a 'science' of law or of jurisprudence suggests the possibility of an analysis free from ideological, metaphorical, or linguistic contamination, a reality of law outside its determinations in the language of theory.

In contrast, an appreciation of legal discourse would challenge this series of correspondences by indicating the ways in which 'facts' or the 'real' or an idealised abstract 'law' are not prior to or separate from (and cannot be distilled out of) the discursive conventions of law and language. The natural world is a discursive construct, as is the legal world. Part of the difficulty here is that we are accustomed to speaking as though language and law are qualitatively different things which exist in different spaces as medium and meaning, or material and ideal. What I will look at in the next section is the ways in which language and law are the same thing, and exist in the same space.

'A RULE STANDS THERE LIKE A SIGN-POST'[24]

> The difference between *is* and *ought* cannot be explained further. We are immediately aware of this difference. Nobody can deny that the statement: 'something is' – that is, the statement by which an existent fact is described – is fundamentally different from the statement: 'something ought to be' – which is the statement by which a norm is described. Nobody can assert that from the statement that something is, follows a statement that something ought to be, or vice versa.[25]

Common sense – by which I mean a certain set of the norms which shape our understanding of the relationships between things – has traditionally distinguished description from prescription. Signs and norms exist separately, and come together when the norm is in need of expression. Signs encapsulate or express norms. Such a view is based on a realist approach to language, that is, the view that language is there to express or describe, not create, a pre-existing reality. I wish to begin by showing that this distinction cannot be analytically sustained, that norms and signs operate in a similar way, and cannot be practically or theoretically distinguished. In essence my argument is that what we call 'law' and what we think of as the language of law do not exist in different theoretical spaces. In pursuing this argument, I am aware that I am stuck in the language of description and prescription – a position which in itself demonstrates that the descriptive order is prescriptive of what I am saying, and that prescription sets up a system of significant differences which shape description.

In the conventional understanding of law which I have outlined, the norm (principle, doctrine, rule, etc.) represents an ideal and abstract entity which binds particulars together within a limit or frame which defines the inside and the outside of the rule. Kelsen, as I have already mentioned, said that the norm 'functions as a scheme of interpretation',[26] and in this insight is contained one of the crucial points of intersection between norms and signs. The norm categorises facts and actions, and gives them significance (and consequence) within a particular order. This is essentially the function of a sign – to set up a system of similarities and differences which allow us to understand the world. Thus the descriptive aspect of norms – that which says that certain sorts of human transactions are contracts, that others are defamation, and yet others are unlawful homicides – operates in the same way as signs which categorise some things as sheep, others as male, and yet others as writing. The norm imposes meaning on otherwise unregulated acts:

> The qualification of a certain act as the execution of the death penalty rather than as a murder – a qualification that cannot be perceived by the senses – results from a thinking process: from the confrontation of this act with the criminal code and the code of criminal procedure.[27]

The 'meaning' of an act, which is also its legal identity or character, is not derived from the act itself, but from normative categorisation of cases. Thus a norm is never purely prescriptive, because as well as specifying the consequences of a particular set of facts, it actually constructs the facts so that they make sense. The legal system is a signifying system writ large – it orders the world into categories, determines the way we interpret things, and attaches consequences to certain sorts of interactions. Law constructs its objects like a language.

This is somewhat at odds with a naturalistic view of language, which has traditionally assumed that language simply describes or encapsulates the world – that the categories enshrined in language are natural categories, motivated by the world. One of the major advances of the structuralist revolution in thinking about language was that it totally discredited the assumption that language reflects a pre-existing world. It was recognised instead that language constructs and shapes the world. What is interesting about Kelsen was that he applied his positivist views thoroughly to institutional law, while adhering to a view of theory which says that description is different from prescription, and that the position of the theorist in no way influences 'scientific' outcomes:

It is ... true that, according to Kant's epistemology, the science of law as cognition of the law, like any cognition, has a constitutive character – it 'creates' its object insofar as it comprehends the object as a meaningful whole. Just as the chaos of sensual preceptions becomes a cosmos, that is, 'nature' as a unified system, through the cognition of natural science, so the multitude of general and individual legal norms, created by the legal organs, becomes a unitary system, a legal 'order' through the science of law. But this 'creation' has a purely epistemological character. It is fundamentally different from the creation of objects by human labour or the creation of law by the legal authority.[28]

According to Kelsen, law is a signifying system and constructs its objects, legal theory is constitutive in that it creates order from a mass of otherwise unordered norms, but the task of description is different from prescription, because it is 'fundamentally different', and 'purely epistemological'. Kelsen explains that statements of law are not true or false, but rather valid or invalid, because they do not refer to an external object but rather receive authority from a higher norm. Theoretical or 'scientific' statements are true or false because they refer to an object, the legal system. What Kelsen neglects to explain is the difference between a law receiving its validity from a higher norm, and a statement about the law being justified by the framing theory which is there to make sense of the law I would argue that both are questions of justification or legitimation of a statement within a framing order. Where truth is only a question of justification – truth is legally established – then there can be no absolute difference between theory and law, description and prescription, norm and sign, ought and is.

As a signifying system, law is of course also reliant upon other signs – those of language and cultural meanings – to do its own work of construction. Language and cultural meanings are not only mediums for the expression of a rule, they participate in the process of definition and construction. For instance, equal opportunity legislation often says something like 'discrimination on the grounds of sex is unlawful'. Such a law responds to and relies upon a discursive and political context which divides people into two sexes, and attaches a great deal of significance to this division. If there were no 'sex' pre-existing such a law, it would have no meaning. If we ever reach a point where sex has no significance, at least in those areas the legislation is designed to address, it will become irrelevant. The signifying function of the law then, can never be separated from the signs of the linguistic and cultural orders, and the pretence of the law that it is in some way above or different to social constructions often entrenches, instead of rectifying, social inequities. For instance, a man who rapes a non-aboriginal stranger is more likely to be convicted than one who rapes an acquaintance or an aboriginal woman:[29] even though formally the law makes no distinction between these cases, society does, and it is legal *discourse*, not what is generally known as 'the law' (separate, transcendent) which determines the outcome.

One function of norms then, is to act as signs or limits which categorise the world. Norms are obviously also prescriptive in that certain consequences – judgements, evaluations, punishments – generally flow from their categorisations. In this sense signs are norms, because not only do they have a descriptive aspect, they also determine the shape of the world we inhabit. Language and cultural systems of meaning prescribe our thought and consequently our actions, and – as in any legal system – there are certain consequences which flow from failing to think or act in the prescribed manner. This prescriptive character of signification is often repressed or underestimated, largely because inbuilt into it is the idea that the system of categorisation which we use to understand the world is in some way natural – that it flows from the nature of things. The 'legal' dimension of one set of signs, those pertaining to sex, has been brilliantly expressed by Monique Wittig:

> For the category of sex is a totalitarian one, which to prove true has its inquisitions, its courts, its tribunals, its body of laws, its terrors, its tortures, its mutilations, its executions, its police. It shapes the mind as well as the body since it controls all mental production. It grips our minds in such a way that we cannot think outside of it.[30]

Sex is a category which shapes the way we think, and in so doing, determines the way we act. There is no clear distinction between 'is' and 'ought' here, because *being* and *doing* are not separate. As Judith Butler says, the category of sex is not only descriptive, but *normative* and is a 'regulatory practice' in that 'it produces the bodies it governs'.[31] The law of sex says that I am female. It makes my anatomy socially significant, and therefore requires me to act in a particular way or take the consequences. It also, in an interesting reversal which really reinforces the point, says that if I do not act in that particular way, I am not 'really' or 'truly' female. The identity and the normal (according to the norms) consequences of the identity are not distinguishable. As Andrea Dworkin argues, law has a dual function – to delineate the world, and to coerce it:

> There is an ecology of male dominance: a complex, delicate, deliberate interaction between it – our rain forest, our desert, our sea – and us, the fragile organisms breathing in and out inside it because of necessity, not choice. On one level, laws are diagrams of that ecology. They show the whole pattern of relations between us, the organisms,

and it, the environment. On another level, the more important one, laws are causal, not illustrative. They make us do certain things in certain ways. They keep some people on top and some people on the bottom. They punish those who do not comply. They force compliance in those who do not want to be punished. They produce fear. They create order. In this, their active meaning, laws are instrumental in organizing human energy, creativity, and potential into patterns of actual behaviour, including sexual behaviour. The purpose of laws on intercourse in a world of male dominance is to promote the power of men over women and to keep women sexually subjugated (accessible) to men.[32]

The creation of order is both an order of the understanding and a social order. Order is created through the double signifying/legislating movement of discursive systems.

All of this is to say that one of the distinctions which has been dear to jurisprudence, that between the is and the ought, in particular between the descriptive and the prescriptive orders of theory, is yet another way of masking the political character of our descriptions of the world. As I have explained, positivists have aimed to describe the legal system as it is, not as it ought to be. When Austin, Hart and Kelsen, following Hume,[33] insisted on a rigid separation of is and ought, they built into their theoretical approaches claims of personal disinterest, objectivity and scientificity, at the same time as they were capitalising on their ability to tap into the predominating rhetoric of scientific reasonableness to support their arguments. Yet, as I argued in the last chapter, the thesis of the limits of law is itself a political construct, as is the jurisprudential approach which takes an institutionally limited concept of law as its object. The act of theoretical force/denial is particularly evident in the case of Kelsen who recognised that legal institutional constructions are political, recognised the constructive nature of theory, and yet managed to argue that the descriptions (creations) of theory are 'fundamentally different' from the prescriptions (creations) of the legal order. Law's orders are different from jurisprudential order, even though both are created. Excluding politics as an explicit part of theory is as political an approach as including it, especially when it is only too obvious that the object under description reflects a particular political standpoint. It has been crucial to positivism to adhere to a naturalistic view of language (the view that language reflects the world, and does not construct it) because to do anything else would have totally undermined faith in both the objectivity of legal theory, and the neutrality of the law itself. It is as important to positivism that 'facts' be objectively discernible rather than constructed, as it is that there be identifiable procedures for discovering what is law and what is not law.

THE LIMITS OF INTERPRETATION

To interpret a text is to limit it – to say that it means one thing and not another. To defend a theory of interpretation is to prescribe in advance what limits (or lack of them) should be adhered to in interpretation. For instance, a theory of interpretation which says that the 'meaning' of the Constitution is to be found in the framers' intentions limits the constitutional meanings which can be found to whatever constructions can be made of the actions and utterances of a bunch of dead white men. A theory which says that the 'meaning' of the Constitution is to be found in the life of the text in the community places very different limits on the acceptable 'meanings' to be discerned. A theory of interpretation which says that there is no single meaning in a text or in the conventions which contextualise it, and that meaning is multi-layered and never total, begins to break down some of the limitations of saying that a single complete meaning can be attained, and opens the way for quite different interpretations of the one text to coexist. None the less, the limitations of our imaginations, of our conventional understanding of the world, and of our need to communicate, means that certain limits will always remain – they are just changing. Frequently, interpretive limits are not made explicitly as theoretical statements but are simply assumed by the interpreter: assumptions about gender are frequently of this order, and it is the task of feminist interpretation to unpack them – to put the gender question at the centre of interpretation instead of at the edges is one way of moving the boundaries.

The question of interpretation is then, generally framed as an examination of the nature and extent of the limitations which constrain readings of a text. In essence this is a question about the existence of rules, conventions, boundaries, or essential meanings which are supposedly external to the individual reader, and which limit the potential constructions of the object of interpretation. Theories of interpretation in this way target the relationship between the will and constraints 'external' to the will. Theorists who wish in some way to assert the objectivity or neutrality of their view of interpretation are invariably under pressure to minimise the role of the subject-position in interpretation. Those who wish to argue the political or 'subjective' nature of interpretation are at pains to present the constraints as less determinate, and therefore to maximise the role of the individual in making an interpretation. At their extremes these two positions are represented in theory respectively by formalism and Critical Legal Studies. A judge who can say that (usually) his interpretation of the law, and therefore his decision, is constrained by pre-existing limits is claiming generally to be making a non-political decision. Where interpretation is less constrained, questions of 'policy' are often considered, but even here, judges tend to present their arguments as 'public' not personal policy in order to give them the stamp of objective reasoning.

What is frequently overlooked is that not only do 'politics' come into play when it is a question of an individual making a choice, but that politics and objectivity are systemic. What is overlooked then, is that the limits of interpretation – like the limits of law – are themselves political since they are set up and informed by a specific system of power, and that it is not possible to avoid positioning oneself in relation to these limitations. Although it may be true to say that my reading of a text is in fact limited by linguistic and other social conventions, and that I have little choice about my interpretation if I want it to make sense to others, those conventions themselves can never be distinct from their political implications. There is no position which is not in some way political, even though the view from above has often claimed to be neutral. 'Objectivity', as the term is frequently used, suggests a view from outside, a disinterested view – the view which, as we know, the powerful have traditionally been able to claim for themselves in relegating every marginalised group of people to the realm of the interested, the subjective and the political. Objectivity, as Catharine MacKinnon has said 'is a figleaf for misogyny'[34] or, more generally, for the imperialism of the white Western heterosexual male.

In the male-monopolised tradition of jurisprudence, some such non-political constraints on interpretation are often posited. In the rest of this chapter I want to look briefly at two views of interpretation which – although recognising the political input in the processes of interpretation – still attempt to reserve some non-political dimension in relation to any interpretive judgement.

Frames

It is said that Kelsen does not have a theory of interpretation in the sense of providing some guide for determining how interpretations ought to be carried out.[35] He would have seen such an intervention in the process of making a judgment as quite beyond the bounds of legal theory, which, as I have indicated, he insisted was purely descriptive, not prescriptive. As a theorist Kelsen was determined to keep his theory 'pure' by rigidly policing the boundaries between it and what he saw as any sociological, moral, or political interference. I have already indicated the ways in which his general presuppositions about the 'purity' of the distinction between prescription and description are at odds with the recognition that legal theory constitutes its objects. At this point I want to elaborate on this problem in relation to his views on interpretation.

As I mentioned above, Kelsen said that norms provide a scheme for ordering and categorising experience. The law relating to homicide is a scheme for determining what counts as a lawful homicide and what counts as the various types of unlawful homicide. However, the law is only a *scheme*, it is not a total description, and cannot determine its results. Obviously there are many different ways in which, for instance, a manslaughter could occur, and the norm does not envisage every potential situation.[36] Even an individual norm, such as the declaration by a judge that a defendant must serve a certain prison sentence, cannot provide every detail of how the norm is to be carried out. The precise content of a norm is always therefore somewhat indeterminate: that is the nature of a norm.

Kelsen compared the norm to a frame which does not entirely determine its content: law is indeterminate in the sense that it does not address every possible outcome. Moreover, a higher norm provides a framing norm for lower norms. The task of interpretation, according to Kelsen, is simply the task of discovering the frame – its position and character – and not of determining the precise content of the frame. Of course, interpreting the frame will involve determining its *possible* content. For instance, a constitutional norm of Australia is that the Federal Parliament has power to legislate with respect to external affairs. The norm provides a frame for legislation, but leaves indeterminate very large specifics such as when, why and what.

The question then becomes whether a lower norm falls within the frame provided, not whether it is the only possible norm within the frame, for it is obviously one of many.[37] As Kelsen says, '... one cannot get correct statutes out of the constitution by interpretation'.[38] Even more to the point is Kelsen's view that 'one cannot get correct judgements out of statutes by interpretation', by which he appears to mean that it is not possible for the judgement to be determined in advance by the norm or by an interpretation. Many different judgements may be possible within the scope of the norm. Thus, judgement is not a theoretical or logical process, but 'a function of the will' or of frame-filling. Judgement is an act of norm-creation, giving precedence to one of the meanings within the frame of the norm.

Kelsen is here rejecting the formalist view that where indeterminacy appears to exist in the law, it can be rectified by proper interpretation, exposition, extrapolation, or 'cognition' of the law. A method of correct frame-filling cannot be determined intellectually, as many theorists suppose, but is inevitably an act of will reproducing the political beliefs of the interpreter. As Stanley Paulson points out, Kelsen would therefore invalidate most of the theories about interpretation currently endorsed by United States constitutional commentators, who argue for 'the *right* view of interpretation, the *constitutionally mandated* view, contending that to adopt any other view would be a mistake'.[39]

'Indeterminacy' for Kelsen therefore does not mean that a decision cannot be made, but rather that the making of a decision, or the filling of the frame is of necessity underdetermined by the norm, and requires an act of will or of application. Kelsen follows Kant in arguing that judgement or subsumption under a rule (or principle) can not be determined by mere understanding of the rules.[40] Subsumption is not a cognitive, but rather a willed, process, and is therefore also fundamentally political. Kelsen unequivocally characterises theories which attempt to elaborate a 'correct' view of interpretation as theories about legal policy – what interpretations *ought* to be adhered to, not simply of understanding the determinate aspects of the positive law.

The distinction which is fundamental to Kelsen's view of interpretation – that between mere cognition of the positive law and creation or interpretation of it – maps on to the is/ought and theory/policy distinctions. Cognition of the positive law, which is the task of positivist legal theory, involves understanding the position of the frame, and the various possibilities which fall within it. Interpretation and creation, which are the tasks of legislators and judges, involve filling in the frame – making a policy-based choice about which of the possible contents of the frame to choose. A theorist might describe where the frame lies, what is inside it and what outside. The legal instrumentality will need to have understanding of the position of the frame, but in making a decision must exercise its will, not just its cognitive faculty.

In effect, what this would mean if carried to its logical conclusion, is that no 'description' of an actual positive legal system is possible, and that the pure non-political theorist must be relegated to the abstract articulation of the metaphysics of law, which is itself, as I have argued, a political exercise. This is because in describing where the frame lies, a theorist will need to make a decision about the interpretation of a higher norm, or higher frame. Otherwise the system becomes for the theorist a hierarchy of frames, not norms. In other words, if every norm is indeterminate in some way, no description can be made of any norm which is not also an intervention in the normative order. Kelsen was obviously trying at this point to avoid recognising the politics of description, since the consequence of doing so would undermine the whole notion of a 'pure' theory of law. However, it is clear that there is considerable tension in Kelsen's work (at least of this period) between the cognition of a structure of positive norms, and the political acts that take place in relation to that system. It is only by maintaining as absolute distinctions which are in fact not at all clear that Kelsen was able to persist in defending the 'purity' of his approach.

'The Good, the True, and the Beautiful'

Indiana Dworkin needs little introduction. He is a juristic adventurer of international fortune and fame. Full of cosmopolitan dash and derring-do, Indy never shirks or ducks a challenge: He is a Man for All Legal Seasons ... In his own version of The Greatest Legal Story Ever Told, Indy finds himself in a procession of tight corners, close calls, and near-misses, which he manages to survive by dint of his own ingenuity and imagination.[41]

Ronald Dworkin has the distinction of being one of the few liberal legal theorists in recent times to espouse the view that there is a single correct decision in any litigation.[42] In doing so, he has not taken the route described by Kelsen as representing the traditional approach to interpretation: that by mere detailed cognition of the formal law right answers can be obtained. Instead he has taken a circuitous path via community standards, eventually transferring the locus of interpretive certitude from texts to social and legal institutions. It is not just the law, but the law in its social and political context which provides the basis for a 'correct' interpretation.[43]

Dworkin agrees that meaning is contextual but limited by the obvious or clear cases. Such cases are not contextual but agreed upon, although Dworkin does not seriously examine how and by whom. The central is just the central and the clear is just clear. Interpretations must fit the central cases, unless they conflict, because these are the things which are most beyond challenge.[44] Dworkin says that 'paradigms anchor interpretations', which is not to say that they are there for all time, just that an interpretation must account for them as part of the current context. My problem with this is not just that Dworkin recognises that paradigm cases exist, since obviously they do, being part of the persistent structure of meaning in the world, but that he gives them a particular role and value in his account of how interpretation *ought* to be practised, thus entrenching, rather than questioning them.

Dworkin does not want his theory of interpretation to be one view among many. Being one of the multitude of interpretations which account for the paradigm cases is not good enough for Dworkin, if only because such a position would offer little guidance on how to get the correct result in a case, and makes of law an incoherent and contradictory mass of details, rather than a perfectible, cogent and integrated method of fairly resolving disputes. Thus, not only does Dworkin want to say – 'this is what judges actually do' – or – 'this is the range of possible decisions which a judge could make' – but rather – 'this is what an ideal judge would do'. Having said that law rests upon the making of constructive interpretations, Dworkin simply relocates the position of certainty in interpretation, removing it from the text, and enshrining it instead in what literary theorists might refer to as an 'ideal reader' – one who is perfectly integrated with the requirements of social context and sensitive to the limits of the text itself.

So rather than simply leaving interpretation and decision in the hands of the judges (admittedly a totally inadequate way of pursuing one's political ideals) Dworkin aims to prescribe to judges what is in fact the best way to interpret law. This is the method practised by his hypothetical superjudge, 'Justice Hercules' or – to demonstrate his cultural sensitivity to the British reader – 'Lord Hercules'.[45] Although the text of law does not proclaim its own unique meaning there is nevertheless a meaning which claims priority over all the others because of the inherent virtues of the view of the world to which it is attached. In this way the judge with complete clarity of insight will not only know what is the best law for the instant case, but will also have a sense of the underlying principle of communal coexistence which lies behind the present law and forms the basis of the future law. Law's *telos* is the dream of its pure self. Law as it is works gradually towards the realisation of law as it ought to be. The teleology of law is this revelation of its immanent existence. In this way Dworkin returns to the belief in an absolute signified, 'real' law, which is the objective measure of the judicial process.

Judges, however, although they might know what is best in the present apparently do not have sufficient insight to determine what is best for the law in the future:

> The courts are the capitals of law's empire, and judges are its princes, but not its seers and its prophets. It falls to philosophers, if they are willing, to work out law's ambitions for itself, the purer form of law within and beyond the law we have.[46]

In a spirit of liberal tolerance and free enterprise Dworkin does not deny that there will be some healthy competition between philosophers wishing to provide law with a vision of its future self, with this qualification: all philosophies, if they are to qualify as explanatory of law in the right way and therefore be a part of meaningful philosophical dialogue, are subject to Dworkin's own grand vision, the king of philosophical principles, the sovereign law of law and philosophy – integrity.[47] The moral implications of the term are unavoidable. Being subject to integrity for Dworkin means ultimately being subject to values like the coherence and continuity of the legal tradition, its inherent goodness, and the common cause and shared values of the community generally.

The point about shared community values, and the integration of future dreams with community history and custom seems dangerously complacent, if not downright ignorant, about social differences and inequalities. By grounding his view of the best, integrated, interpretation in community values, Dworkin does nothing more than entrench existing hierarchies: the marginal remains marginal, and the centre remains powerful. By making social consensus and legal history such powerful determinants of moral and legal justifications, Dworkin simply ignores their historically oppressive roles.[48] Dworkin does not apparently understand this point because it is not only his Constitution, but also his idea of law and society generally which, in the words of Sanford Levinson, 'turns out to contain only the good, the true, and the beautiful'.[49]

What is missing from mainstream accounts of interpretation is any understanding of the way that systems of power influence and authorise the acceptable readings, and marginalise or delegitimate readings which are critical or which attempt to transgress the conventionally acceptable boundaries. Although Dworkin, for instance, accepts that interpretations are 'political', the politics he has in mind seems to be related to questions of what would ordinarily be termed social, economic, or national policy. Such questions are those played out as debates among reasonable men and those who are forced to buy into the terms of such debates in order to further their cause. Such a 'politics' starts from the assumption that the ideal of basic freedom and equality is not only an ideal, but actually exists, or from the equally ridiculous assumption that if we make out in our theories that our ideals exist, they will eventuate. Thus, as I have indicated, the political implications of starting from established 'central' cases are ignored in Dworkin's work, because he sees them as neutral and commonly accepted. Dworkin's 'politics' concern matters of detail – exactly where to draw the boundaries in any case, for instance. He does not trouble himself by asking how the central gets to be central, who is keeping it there, or who is thereby excluded from its certainty. He does not bother to ask himself whose interests 'social consensus' protects, or wonder about whether in fact such a thing exists except as an ideological system which helps to maintain oppressive structures.

The Differend

I have written about several different sorts of interpretation in this chapter: interpretation of facts, practical interpretation of the substantive law, and theoretical 'descriptions' of the law in general. In each case, it has become evident that the dominant paradigm requires interpretations to be 'grounded' or to correspond to its object, but tends to erase the process of construction involved, and thereby to erase the politics, and the contingency of interpretation itself. A description of 'facts' must be grounded in *the* facts: that such a description is grounded in a version of the facts which accords with legal orthodoxy is not made explicit. A pure description of the law is supposed to correspond to *the* law, and becomes 'political' only if the law's misogynist, racist, or class-based foundations are exposed. In itself it is neutral. A theory of law is idealised as a description of what the general characteristics of law are, without participating in the political structures which maintain law. Self-reflection has not been a strong point of orthodox legal theory, which tends to assume that it can proceed objectively with the language of reasonableness without interfering in anybody else's political struggles.

The important point here is not a critique of the idea that interpretations should be grounded in something, or should correspond to something. My critique is of the idea that there is *one thing* that an interpretation can correspond to – one set of facts, one true description of the law, one account of the nature of law, one true theory of interpretive practice. By emphasising the singular nature of the object, and not recognising that the maintenance of a singular vision simply eliminates all other possibilities, mainstream legal thought proceeds by appropriating or erasing the other, and by maintaining the (hierarchical) differend at the centre of its practice.

For the moment I will leave the question of language here: the next chapter deals with different sorts of foundations – those which are assumed to ground legal institutions. In Chapters 4 and 5 my argument will return to the question of language and its structural relationship to the idea of law.

3
'Before the Law'

INTRODUCTION: THE LIMIT, THE ORIGIN AND THE ESSENCE

> What remains concealed and invisible in each law is thus presumably
> the law itself, that which makes laws of these laws, the being-law of
> these laws. The question and the quest are ineluctable, in other words,
> rendering irresistible the journey towards the place and the origin
> of these laws.[1]

In Chapters 1 and 2 I began a critique of the limits of law, concentrating
in particular on the political implications of maintaining such rigid
territorial frontiers in law and legal theory. My aim has so far been to
demystify – to reveal the underlying politics of – the claims of objectivity
and neutrality which have been so crucial to legal thinking. This
chapter and those which follow it attempt what I would term a
'deconstruction' of the traditionally posited limits of law. My intention
is to examine the gaps, logical incoherence and acts of theoretical force,
which are integral to the ideology of positive law. Such an analysis is
closely related to the aim of 'demystification', since it is only by
revealing that the legal logic which has been naturalised is in fact entirely
constructed to protect the authority of law, that it is possible to realise
the full extent of the political force of law.[2]

As I indicated in Chapter 1, the idea of law is conventionally bounded
by myths of legal origins. The law is said to be held together (either
ideally or in fact) by some abstract principle – the rule of recognition,
sovereignty, the basic norm, community values, natural reason. In
Reading the Law, Peter Goodrich makes a useful distinction between
ideational and institutional sources of law.[3] These are the sources
which are identified in legal theory as respectively the theoretical and
practical principles of validation of the complete legal structure. An
'ideational' source is an ultimate principle from which legality as a
concept is derived, an 'external and absolute justification for legal
regulation'.[4] Clearly Kelsen's *grundnorm* is an ideational source of law:
Kelsen's claim is not that the *grundnorm* exists as a concrete legal
institution, but rather that it exists as an idea which in some way allows
certain acts and norms to be interpreted as having validity within a

legal system. Criticism of Kelsen on the grounds that a *grundnorm* cannot be factually identified, or attempts actually to locate a *grundnorm* in an existing legal system, rather neglect the ideational character of this norm. I am concentrating on Kelsen in this context because his work provides an extremely clear and systematic positivist exposition. What is especially interesting about Kelsen, however, is the way in which, as Iain Stewart says, 'his "pure theory of law" fell apart in his hands – under pressure of contradictions that had been present from the start'.[5] Part of this chapter will be devoted to looking at some of these contradictions, and others will be picked up in Chapters 4 and 5.

In contrast to an ideational source, an institutional source is the factually existent institution or complex of institutions which is identified by jurists as the source of law in a particular society. The United States Constitution provides the factually existent framework or foundation for United States law. The Queen-in-Parliament is the factually existent source of the law of the United Kingdom.

Goodrich points out that the idea of a source or origin of the law performs a dual function in legal theory – to keep law together, and to ensure its separation from non-law:

> The two claims, those of unity and separation, have traditionally been closely linked in legal doctrine; law is kept separate and distinct from other institutions and forms of control precisely by virtue of being a unity, by virtue of having an 'essential' characteristic which distinguishes law from all else. That 'essence' or unifying feature of law has been variable in its content but relatively constant in its form: the formal unity of law has traditionally been based upon its derivation from an absolute source or origin.[6]

Law is unified and different from non-law because it has its own particular origin, some paternity which distinguishes it from any other institution, and from any other structure of norms. The limitedness of law, in particular the demarcation of a boundary between law and non-law and the coherence of law as an independent institution, is thus reliant upon the identification or at least postulation of a source which can both separate and bind.[7] This much was clear from the discussion of the limits of law which I undertook in Chapter 1. The object of legal theory, in particular positivist theory, has been to identify the condition of law's existence in some meta-legal sphere which ensures both that law is recognised as law from outside – that is, scientifically – and that from the internal position there is a clear authority for legal propositions.

As I noted, the difference between natural law and positivist theories is in essence a difference in the quality or content, not the form or position, of the ideational source. Whether the ultimate reference of law in a natural law theory is supernatural or simply the natural qualities of an ideal super*man*, the appeal to a transcendent principle of justification remains. Natural law's claim is to a necessary ultimate principle, while positivism relies on the historical and contingent nature of the source of law. Both natural law and positivism attribute the ultimate principle of legal justification to a particular theoretical space which exists before the law, and which inheres in the law as its essence. Posing the question of where law comes from, legal philosophies invariably trace the chain of legal causation backwards to a moment of genesis – the limit, the origin and the essence.

In order to provide a thorough critique of this jurisprudential tradition, I would like to pull together a number of threads. To begin with, I will contrast the positivist discourse of 'proper' law, which has laid the foundations for modern legal analysis, with the tradition of 'common' law. The distinction between the proper and the common has not only a linguistic significance, but also sheds some light on the characteristics of positivist legal thought. Secondly, I will look at the position ꞏbefore' the law occupied not by the conceptual origin of law, but by the liberal legal person, who is assumed to exist before the law, but who in various ways is a construction of the law, and who shares some of the masculine characteristics attributed to 'proper' law. Thirdly, I will look more closely at the notion of the conceptual origin, and elaborate on the inbuilt incoherence of the notion of a unitary origin of law.

THE COMMON AND THE PROPER

One of the characteristics of positivist-inspired legal theory is the search for a legal *logos*, an authoritative source of law which demarcates the boundary between law and non-law, and places the stamp of legality upon everything within its terrain. As I have said, this mode of thought – to propertise and essentialise the law – is a feature of modernist liberal jurisprudence. 'Proper' law, as Austin called it, was law which was authorised by a singular identifiable source and which was different from the individual and from the broader society. At the beginning of the ninteenth century, jurisprudence was striving for the philosophical dimensions of a science, and – like most other disciplines – took on the discourse of science in order to legitimate its status as an intellectual pursuit. As David Sugarman explains, it was necessary for law to be seen as a coherent and ordered structure in order for it to be recognised as a proper object of study, and to distance itself from the seemingly chaotic mess which had been the common law prior to the nineteenth-century legal enlightenment.[8] The scientific approach is to give order to the theoretical object by giving it a law, that is, by laying down certain rules of perception and description, but at the same time to distance the object from the subject by insisting that the law is of the object itself. Applied by jurisprudence to law, the discursive requirements of science necessitated the discovery of the law of law – to give it structure, shape and closure.

It is interesting to contrast the results of the positivist revolution in law to the concept of law which immediately preceded it in the common law tradition. By doing so I think it is possible to appreciate more clearly some of the characteristics of positivist thinking itself. In particular such a comparison enables us to gain a sense of the historically determined nature of concepts of law.

In its classical formulation, the authority of the common law derives not from a single identifiable, remembered, source, but on the contrary from the fact that it is immemorial. It is the fact that the origin of a law *cannot* be remembered which makes it law. Hale distinguishes between laws which have their origin in writing (validated by Parliament) and laws which do not have their origin in writing, which he says, have *'obtain'd their Force* by immemorial Usage or Custom'.[9] Similarly, Blackstone said: '... in our law the goodness of a custom depends upon its having been used time out of mind; or, in the solemnity of our legal phrase, time whereof the memory of man runneth not to the contrary'.[10] Law was good in the sense of authoritative if its origin was beyond memory, and it was good, in the sense of fair or just if it had been tested and refined over a long period of time. According to Hale, legal memory dated from 1189, the beginning of the reign of Richard I.[11]

Far from entailing an understanding of law as an arbitrary and chaotic mess, however, the common law jurists saw the lack of determinate origins as indicative of the coherence of the common law. The tradition of the law and of law making as a gradual, conservative process, was seen to ensure the maintenance of the wisdom and spirit of the law, without compromising its identity or continuity as sudden legislative acts would. Hale explained that the identity of the common law was preserved by the relationship with the past. Although continually changing, the common law was seen to retain its essential abstract spirit:

> ... tho' those particular Variations and Accessions have happened in the Laws, yet they being only partial and successive, we may with just Reason say, They are the same English Laws now, that they were 600 Years since in the general. As the Argonauts ship was the same when it returned home, as it was when it went out, tho' in that long

voyage it had successive amendments, and scarce came back with any of its former Materials; and as Titius is the same Man he was 40 years since, tho' Physicians tell us, That in a Tract of Seven Years, the Body has scarce any of the same material Substance it had before.[12]

In this way the collective reason and identity of the common law was considered to subsume questions about both the nature of judicial innovation as well as the determinate origin of the law. Common lawyers were emphatic that judges do not make law: as Blackstone wrote, they are 'the depositaries of the laws, the living oracles'.[13] Law was rather relayed by the judges through time, from precedent to precedent. The paradox of this form, according to both Pocock and Cotterrell, is that the law was perceived to be 'always already existent' yet 'continually evolving', being reinvented through the succession of cases.[14] In keeping with the view of judges as the oracles of the law or the guardians of its wisdom, true knowledge of the law was not considered to be available to anyone: the scientific disjunction between the subject and the object of knowledge did not crystallise for the common law until Bentham's scathing critique of its obscurity in the hands of the judges. Legal wisdom was not seen as separate from the judges, but nor did they construct the laws individually. Their position was as the receiving and transmitting agents of the tradition of the law, the medium of communication.

One important deviation from the 'mainstream' view of the common law which I have outlined was supported by Edward Coke, who argued that the common law was derived from an 'ancient constitution' dating from before the Norman Conquest.[15] This 'ancient constitution' was the source and template of the law – all valid law was not only derived from it, but was identical to it. In other words, 'true' law had existed from ancient times: legal change was either a degeneration from this true law, or a restoration of it.[16] Coke wanted to give a memory to the common law, traditionally characterised by its amnesia, and to theorise it as a pure non-temporal identity. He was also trying desperately to protect the law from the excesses of parliamentary innovation and from the charge that it was a political instrument of the judges.[17]

Leaving aside Coke's views, the dimensions of the traditional common law mind can perhaps be most usefully understood in the light of a distinction between two types of knowledge made by Jean-François Lyotard, certain aspects of which map on to the pre-modern (common) and modern (proper, positive) legal discourses. The 'narrative' model of knowledge is illustrated by the practice of the Cashinahua Indians in the transmission of particular culturally significant stories: 'Every narrator presents himself as having first been a narratee: not as autonomous, then, but, on the contrary, as heteronomous. The law of this narrative, if I can speak of law in such a case, is a law that it has received.'[18]

Only at the end of the story does the narrator attach his[19] own name to it, this being the name that will be carried into the next version of the story. Each narrator is thus narrated both by the narrative process itself, and by the name-giving community to which s/he belongs, as well as being the narrator of an original version which is no mere imitation of the story, but rather a reinvention and reanimation of it. The narrator does not have an autonomous identity: s/he has the identity given by the narrative context. Most importantly, the origin of the narrative is forgotten in the ongoing life of the narrative: the tradition is always a relay and never reducible to a static content or an original all-encompassing authority.

Lyotard contrasts this 'heteronomy' of a tradition which moves through time to the modern Western attitude to tradition which is 'to keep things from being used up by time, and to reject the new'.[20] The Western impulse to 'think identity without difference' and to 'preserve, acquire, and accumulate contents'[21] is an attempt to rediscover and retain the origin, and thus to confine the tradition to a limited, autonomous, non-temporal space. In a similar vein, in *The Postmodern Condition* Lyotard explains the difference between narrative forms of knowledge and the modern scientific approach as a difference manifested in attitudes to self-legitimation and proof: while 'narrative knowledge does not give priority to the question of its own legitimation and ... certifies itself in the pragmatics of its own transmission' the 'game of science' rests upon conventional procedures and standards of self-verification.[22]

The narrative model then, does not rely upon the idea of there being an identifiable and fixed origin to which any manifestation of the narrative must conform. Nor does it rely upon a separation of the subject of the narrative, the narrator, from the narrative itself. In contrast, the modern Western 'scientific' approach is to look for some authentic justification or criterion of legitimation, and to separate the position of the subject from the object of knowledge (which remains the same no matter who is doing the knowing). This contrast is reflected in the common law approach to law, and the modern 'scientific' positivist approach. As I have explained, the common law was not seen to be authorised by one template, or one frame of legitimacy, and its speaking subjects, the judges, were not seen to be autonomous agents who could originate law, but as mystical oracles or guardians of the law. The law was common, customary, communal, not imposed. In contrast the positivist approach to 'proper' law has been to separate the subjects – judges and people – from the law, to insist that the law is different from its agents, that it can be 'created' by individuals and legislative bodies, but only within the conventional structures of legitimation which provide a boundary between law and non-law. Positivism has never been able to account adequately for the remnants of classical common law thinking in modern legal praxis, in particular the fact that much of the common law escapes the positivist structure of origin, rules and principles.

The point of contrasting classical common law thought with modern positivist thought is to get a clearer picture of the historically contingent dimensions of modern legal thinking. Through the lens of modern thought, common law ideas often appear incoherent and illogical, but this is (at least in part) because the underlying paradigms of law were different from those of the post-Austinian era. In the next sections of this chapter I will consider two of the building blocks of positivist legal thought – the autonomous legal subject, and the notion of the origin of law as its limit and as formative of its identity. I should reinforce an earlier point here, which is that my argument applies not only to self-styled positivist thinkers, but to the paradigm of law which we all tend to utilise at some point or another.

THE SUBJECT *BEFORE* THE LAW

The origin of the law is the thing which is conceptually posited as existing logically before any laws do, or before they can be properly designated 'laws'. The origin is the essence which gives unity to the law. This 'sovereign term' (Constitution, basic norm, rule of recognition, etc.) which exists before the law is the subject of the last three sections of this chapter. In liberal positivist thought however, there is another sovereign subject before the law, who actually reflects the stereotypical masculine characteristics of the law itself. Derrida writes: 'To appear before the law, to answer a summons, means ... to come or be brought before judges who represent or guard the law for the purpose, in the course of a procès, of giving evidence or being judged.'[23]

Derrida is writing of the subject who appears *devant* the law, that is, in front of it. The translation of this phrase into English exposes a paradox, since 'before the law' means both 'in front of the law' and 'prior to the law'. Natural legal persons have traditionally occupied both positions, but it is the before in time which is given precedence in modern positivist thought. In order for there to be law which is posited, must there not already be the individuals who will devise, be subjected to, enforce and adjudicate the law? At the level of litigation, moreover, there must be the parties who claim to have suffered wrong, or who are alleged to have done wrong. Liberal positivism proceeds on the assumption that the law is a human creation: human subjects are not a legal creation.

This linear positivist chronology in which pre-existing human beings create a legal system which is conceptually separate from them and then order their affairs accordingly, neglects the various ways in which subjects appear after or in front of the law as its constructions. To be 'before the law' as Derrida points out, means to be in a subject position which is laid down by the law: this being before the law is in fact the subject-in-crisis of contemporary philosophy. It is the being before/after the law which has so shaken our liberal assumption of a pre-existing human subject, and challenged the notion of rational agreement between subjects. The example of the corporation as a legal 'fiction' is an obvious enough representative of the subject created by the law: corporations obtain legal personality and certain of the associated duties and privileges of legal persons through a legal process. But are those legal persons who also fit the law's description of a 'natural' person any less fictional? Without the law to posit and determine subjectivity, the person who wishes to appear before the law would be unknown to the law. Obviously having 'natural' personality is an insufficient basis, even in these times of supposed equality before the law, to be regarded as a legal person, much less to be accorded the full range of rights and duties which attach to adult white heterosexual men. Even more interestingly, are so-called 'natural' persons also legal constructions of a sort? The twentieth-century philosophical preoccupation with subjectivity as a construct within an economy of representation focuses the interrelatedness of what is traditionally seen as law and non-law in a particularly strong way. For if the subject before the law who is undergoing construction by legal institutions is *already* constructed prior to the law her intervention in the law *must* bring with it those social norms supposedly outside the law.

In fact legal personality is very much a contextual matter: a little thought easily illustrates the way that the law constructs meaningful situations and an assortment of corresponding subject-positions. For instance, not any two people are eligible to be the subjects of a legal marriage. They must be of opposite sexes, able to give consent, and over a certain prescribed age. For this purpose the law begins by constructing people into two opposing categories of sex, and determining what counts as 'consent'. On the whole, a legal guardian can give consent for a six-year-old child to undergo an operation, but not to undergo marriage. Such a young child is not able to consent to sexual intercourse. A fifteen-year-old person or a foreigner in a country can be criminally responsible and liable to pay all sorts of taxes, but cannot generally vote. In most places a woman cannot take a combat role in the armed forces, a traditional marker of citizenship, and can never become a priest in the Catholic church (a legally sanctioned discrimination). A non-aboriginal person cannot make a land claim based on the *Mabo* principles. A corporation can make a multimillion-dollar profit from putting consumers at risk, can pay or avoid the corresponding taxes, and can also protect its executives and other agents from prosecution for manslaughter or other serious criminal charges. A single woman cannot take advantage of *in vitro* fertilisation procedures. A white man cannot formally take advantage of affirmative action legislation. And so on.

A few interesting matters should be noted here. First, apart from a few relatively minor areas designed at least to look as though traditional areas of 'discrimination' (read dispossession, attempted genocide, slavery, rape, etc.) are being addressed, the legal person as a bundle of rights and duties is modelled on the adult white heterosexual privileged and mentally 'sound' man. Despite its claimed separation and neutrality, the institutionalised law reflects and represents the demands of the social law. With a few differences the corporate body also reflects this model of the rational property-owning autonomous agent.[24] This is the person who is traditionally the creator and executor of law, and who enjoys the status of its standard case.

In fact, I would go so far as to say that 'woman' as a concept currently has no place at all before the law. Obviously women as human beings have attained a place before the law, but when the universal, neutralised person before the law is discursively, symbolically, representationally male, there can be no thought of a subject before the law who is specifically a woman. This is a point which has frequently been made by Luce Irigaray in various contexts in arguing for sexed rights, that is, a legal regime which recognises two sexes, rather than just one universal sex which is clearly male.[25]

Recognition of sexed rights may be one useful step in the process of breaking down the male symbolism of the law but, unlike Irigaray, I do not regard it as an inevitable feature of a non-patriarchal legal or social system. As a psychoanalyst, Irigaray believes that there is something necessary about sexual difference as a significant element of human production and reproduction – in *je, tu, nous* she argues that 'Sexual difference is necessary for the continuation of the species',[26] and (somewhat dogmatically) that to 'wish to get rid of sexual difference is to call for a genocide more radical than any form of destruction there has ever been in History'.[27] (Given that sexual difference as it now stands has itself been the cause of so much destruction throughout Western history, this argument is not particularly compelling. Moreover, utopian visions of a world without such sex-based destruction can hardly be compared to events like Hitler's project to eliminate the Jews, or the colonial British success in killing off the Tasmanian aboriginal people.) And it is not just sexual *difference* which Irigaray regards as essential to survival, but the sexual *dichotomy*: it is *two* genders which are necessary, because they are mutually defining, and because reproduction demands a division into two.

These comments appear to be directed at those feminists such as Monique Wittig (who is certainly not a psychoanalyst) who have argued that the social significance of the category of sex must be eliminated.[28] However, in my view the assertion that reproduction relies on the sexual dichotomy assumes that the elimination of the category of sex would entail the elimination of sexual activity of the traditional penetrative type between biological females and males. This is by no means evident to me. As long as penetrative heterosexual sex remains one of the available options, I can't see how the elimination of the significance of the dualistic sexual order would involve the end of the species.

To say that 'woman' has no place before the law is a simple recognition of the universal masculinity of the legal subject. To say that there must be two sexes before the law is a much more contentious statement, and repeats the typical legal gesture of defining and categorising our existences in a way which is perhaps unnecessary in this context. Although possibly strategically useful, I do not think that it can be regarded as by any means a solution to legal oppression which is, after all, itself based on the dualistic (hetero)sexual order. Two sexes are, in any case, as oppressive to those who do not simply identify with one sex or the other or whose identifications do not fit their bodies, in the same way that the archetypal legal man is, broadly speaking, oppressive to women. None the less, the question of what can be done about the masculinity of the legal subject remains a very important one.

Secondly, it is clear that even the standard legal man is a contextual construction. There is no position which is simply that of the absolute legal subject. The rights or duties a legal subject has, and therefore her or his identity as a subject, are a consequence of the legal construction of particular situations. Of course, as I have indicated, people find their legal subject positions constructed in very different ways, according to the view the law takes of their position in society. The notion of equality, that all natural persons are in fact equal before the law, is nothing but a protective measure for the standard case which masks the contextual nature of subjectivity by setting up an ideal of the legal person. This is because the recognition that all natural persons are not in fact equal before the law and never have been, and *can't possibly be* (given the fact that social equality is yet to be achieved) would pose a fundamental challenge to the predominance of the legal man paradigm by making explicit the force which entrenches him in his privileged position. There is now no formal legal or philosophical reason for white male privilege – so how does he retain his privileged position except by force?

Thus, in order to be before the law, to be recognised by it in some sense, you must be after the law: only after it has done its work on you, given you meaning and characteristics, can you appear before the law. You must be propertised by the law, becoming for the law what a proper name is for language – both inside and outside, before and after.[29] Only after you have submitted yourself to the determinations of the law, been forced into its definitions, been named and stamped by the law as a proper legal subject can you have any influence over the law. This is a circle which is characteristic of law's efforts at closure: to exist before the law, to be in a position to change it, make it, abolish it, you must be after the law, made by it so that it will recognise you. At the same time, in the modern Western world it is important that this creation of subjectivity is erased in order to perpetuate the myth that the neutral legal person is an ideal universal natural person, not a reasonable white man. This metaphysics of law is also reflected in legal practice: for instance, only after you have said to yourself or been told by your solicitor 'this is how a reasonable legal person would look and speak' will you be given any credibility in court. Even then, you might have problems being heard, depending on your position within the social hierarchy.

And this is not all. The person designated by the institutional law as 'natural' is already a constituted position in an array of social legal systems, from the norms which order our perception of the world, to linguistic principles, and cultural norms. As I have argued, none of these systems of norms can ultimately be distinguished from the institutionalised law except by theoretical-political force: our legal subject position is therefore a function of a multitude of contextual and historical factors.

THE 'MYSTICAL FOUNDATION OF AUTHORITY'

> ... beyond any apparent beginning, there is always a secret origin – so secret and so fundamental that it can never be quite grasped in itself.[30]

On one level, the preoccupation within jurisprudence with the idea of finding a theoretical or institutional foundation for law seems either very ambitious, or very ignorant. If we look around us at the multitude of laws which shape our thoughts and our existences, even if we look only to what the Realists called legal 'reality', it very quickly becomes evident either that there is no *order* of law (except perhaps force) which will account for everything, or that it lies well beyond our current understanding of the object. Of course, the positivists greatly reduced their task by eliminating from the definition of 'law' everything which did not correspond to what they wanted law to be. The logic of this process of elimination can, as I have argued, really only be understood in relation to the political context of jurisprudence and of the jurisprudes, and makes of their theories an obfuscating, apologetic, and – except for those whose purposes are obfuscating and apologetic – useless act of force. What good is a theory which cannot explain or contain the power differential between judges and advocates? What good is a theory which cannot explain that not only the formal 'law' but the laws of class and of legal language prevent advocates from framing their case in the way they might wish in order to preserve a good working relationship with the judge, in order to build up (usually) his ego, and in order to maintain their professional status? Even so, accepting the positivists' arbitrary limitations and circular definitions, the task of describing some sort of legal order, especially one which is reducible to a general underlying and unifying principle, still seems to be formidable, because of the sheer size and complexity of the object.[31]

Having said that, the positivist project has never been entirely empirical. Whether the claimed method has been to describe existing legal systems in an effort to distil out a conceptual order, or to impose conceptual order on an otherwise chaotic set of norms, the idea has centrally been to reduce law to some sort of underlying system or set of ultimate sources. What I want to look at now are the ways in which this reduction, and in particular the reduction to a basic authority or origin, relies on a silence about the role of what could be called the founding undecidability of law. In other words, the authority or origin of law is necessarily plural, or heterogeneous. More precisely, it is split between law and not-law, and positivist-inspired theory has not only generally failed to recognise the implications of this contradiction, it has often (though not always) ignored it altogether. The recognition that the origin cannot in fact be singular but must be riven by paradox would threaten irredeemably the positivist apology for the rule of law, since the resolution of the paradox can only be through what Derrida calls the founding violence of law. Where the set of contradictions I am about to describe have been analysed by legal thinkers, they are generally regarded as an interesting theoretical 'puzzle' or constitutional antinomy, with logical, not political, consequences.

The Mystery of Sovereignty

The motivation for the search for the origin of law is a simple and inexorable one, yet its unqualified linearity leads it into the mystique of an inexplicable genesis. When we know what makes our present rule valid, we do not simply accept it – the concept of faith is not strong in secular philosophy, though it clearly has its place in legal praxis where we are continually required to accept unquestioningly seemingly illogical, incoherent, unjust and irrational doctrines. Instead, as theorists of the concept of law, we ask what makes a validating source authoritative, and so on, until there can be no further questions, just a limit which halts the infinite regress. Such a process of validation was formalised by Kelsen in *The Pure Theory of Law*, as the conceptual structure of a legal system. The axiom of traditional legal philosophy is that the legal system must be authorised by an exterior source, a source which logically cannot be bound or altered by the system derived from it. The necessity was formulated by Salmond as follows:

> It is requisite that the law should postulate one or more first causes, whose operation is ultimate, and whose authority is underived. In other words, there must be found in every legal system certain ultimate legal principles, from which all others are derived, but which are themselves self-existent.[32]

Thus, we search backwards through our chain of validity in order to find the first reason which is the end of all justification, and the legal rule is characterised as legal only if it is derived from such an unconditional reason.

This final reason is 'unconditional' – because it is the beginning, or end, of all justification, it is thoroughly inexplicable in the terms of the system itself. It is a mystery because its own authority cannot be explained. (This is where faith and force come in.) Wittgenstein wrote that we need a rule to follow a rule, meaning that we can always ask for some more basic explanation or definition to show us how to follow our present rule, or to give meaning to it. And: 'If I have exhausted the justifications I have reached bedrock, and my spade is turned. Then I am inclined to say: "This is simply what I do."'[33] The quest for further and more basic justifications must end somewhere: when it does, that does not mean that we have reached the truth, but rather simply something we take for granted and cannot prove or justify.[34] Derrida has made a similar point in 'White Mythology' in considering the possibility of a 'total metaphorology of philosophy': the idea is rejected in principle because the original imperative would always remain outside the theory which would not therefore be a totality: 'If one wished to conceive and to class all the metaphorical possibilities of philosophy, one metaphor, at least, would always remain excluded, outside the system ... the metaphor of metaphor.'[35] The argument is simply that one term, as author or axiom of the system, lacks the power of complete dominance or complete comprehension because it cannot theorise or comprehend itself. Similarly, theories of law which bind the system within a determinate limit, cannot have anything to say about the *legality* of that limit. It is just a theoretical wall.

In so far as everything legal is purportedly derived from such a fundamental term it is itself the very essence of legality. Yet in so far as it is necessarily prior to any comprehension or determination of the law it must be non-legal. This is to suggest not so much the permeability of the concept of law's frontier, but its undecidable nature, an undecidability which, as Derrida argues, can only be solved by the founding violence of the law:

> Since the origin of authority, the foundation or ground, the position of the law can't by definition rest on anything but themselves, they are themselves a violence without ground. Which is not to say that they are in themselves unjust, in the sense of 'illegal'. They are neither legal nor illegal in their founding moment. They exceed the opposition between founded and unfounded ...[36]

The foundation of authority is 'mystical' because it *exceeds* the system: this is not to say that it is outside the system, but both of it and beyond it. Such a view is also expressed by Peter Goodrich, who writes, 'paradoxically, this ideational source is always a deferred or absent source, it is always in its nature hidden rather than explicit, abstract rather than readily available, past rather than present'. Later, Goodrich writes that the ideational origin of law has always been 'invisible', 'protected', 'hidden' and 'obscure'.[37]

Derrida goes on to say that what this paradoxical and mysterious structure indicates is that law is 'essentially deconstructible'.[38] The mystery of law's origin is explained as a 'silence [which] is walled up in the violent structure of the founding act. Walled up, walled in because silence is not exterior to language.'[39] Conceptually, the silence could be said to take several forms – silence about the paradox itself in the effort to present law's origin as coherent and singular, silence abut the other which is walled up inside law's endless search for the same, silence about the political consequences of this series of silences. Practically, these silences give law the alienating character which I discussed at the beginning of Chapter 2 – for instance through its focus on the Western masculinist discourse of the rational and the reasonable and the impossibility of appearing *as a woman* before the law. Thus, although it may seem extreme to speak of conceptual 'violence', it must always be remembered that the conceptual provides the metaphysical context and support for the violence of legal discourse and legal practice.

I think that it is also important to point out here that the violence in question is not only a founding violence, but, as Derrida explains, also the violence involved in the conservation of the system:[40] silence is 'walled in' and not out, because it is the unspoken or repressed entailed by all legal practices, and which defines and supports them. The founding violence creates the law, but it is also of the law, and appears within it. I will come back to this in Chapters 4 and 5.

The Remarkable Thing About Law[41]

As I explained in Chapter 1, the idea that law is limited rests not only upon the existence of some abstract or empirical legal foundation of the law, but also upon the existence within each and every law of some identifying mark. As Joseph Raz puts it: 'If the thesis of the limits of law is right, there must be a criterion of identity which sets necessary and sufficient conditions, satisfaction of which is a mark that a standard is a part of a legal system.'[42] For instance, the basic norm is at once the fundamental legitimating source of law: as such it is also the mark or criterion of identity which must be represented in a standard if it is to count as law. Any norm which does not carry within it this mark is not part of the legal system. This is the law of the law – that every law 'properly so called' bears the mark of legality. Otherwise it would not be law.

This structure is the basis for the distinction between law and non-law and therefore also for the theoretical integrity of jurisprudence as a discipline. The structure is inherently paradoxical because the closure of law relies upon its openness. The impermeability of law's frontier rests ultimately upon its permeability.

To see how this is the case it is useful to look at the argument made by Derrida in 'The Law of Genre'.[43] Derrida begins by making a similar point to that of Raz about how categories of thought, institutionally defined academic disciplines, and literary genres are defined. For instance, Lyotard attributes the scientificity of science to the existence of a set of criteria against which any proposition must be measured in order to determine whether it counts as a 'scientific' statement.[44] Like law, scientific veracity is legitimated by an institutionalised set of conventions, principles and rules. Similarly, the philosophical nature of philosophy – what makes an argument 'philosophical' – is determined by a certain set of criteria relating to coherence in argument, political neutrality and, perhaps most importantly, the specific philosophical tradition within which any particular argument is made. That there are different philosophical traditions of itself indicates (though this would not count as a 'philosophical' statement) that the history of philosophy may be as important in formulating an acceptable philosophical argument as the more usually cited desire for truth (however it is defined). The existence of different philosophical traditions might even be seen as a little embarrassing for philosophy, which is supposedly universal in its enquiries, utilising a process of natural, or at least common, reason transcending the boundaries of nationality, culture and language.[45]

Derrida makes some general comments about these matters in 'The Law of Genre', by pointing out that the definition of a genre, within which we can include areas of knowledge, or any conceptual separation of one intellectual terrain from any other, depends upon there being some 'mark' or 'trait' which allows us to distinguish or recognise the genre. (I will continue to use the literary term 'genre' here, but it should be read as including any of the sorts of intellectual domains which I have been referring to.) There is then a 'law of genre' – basically that a 'trait' sets the limits of any conceptual territory such as science, philosophy or law, determining what falls within the genre, and what falls outside. As Derrida says, 'This may seem trivial.'[46] It is, nevertheless, remarkable. Derrida calls this mark a re-mark, not only because it is repeatable, but because it is 'always a priori remarkable':[47] it is always noticeable as the formal characteristic of the genre, and it must have this remarkable quality if it is to represent the mark of the genre. It must be possible to remark upon it.

Derrida goes on to explain that there is a paradox which besets the definition of any genre. And the paradox is another law, the 'law of the law of genre', since it applies generally. It is simply that the limit (or 'mark', etc.) which defines the genre, can itself never be either inside or outside the genre. Because it is itself a principle of definition and must inhere in everything which forms a part of the genre, it cannot wholly be outside, yet nor can it be wholly inside, since as a designation it is not itself one of the objects of a genre. Whatever it is that makes a poem poetic, is not itself a poem. Whatever it is that makes a philosophy philosophical, is not itself a philosophy (but rather, in this case a certain set of institutionalised conventions). At the same time every 'poem' must have whatever it takes to be one, so the defining characteristic of poetry is not wholly exterior to the genre.

What this means, in essence, is that there is no absolute 'closure' or self-identification in any genre, or in any intellectual discipline: there is always something other than the genre inside it, and something essential to it outside. The re-mark, since it is situated at the edge of the genre, between its inside and outside, prevents the genre from ever becoming itself. In order to become itself the genre would need to be self-identical, which it cannot be while the mark is present – being a non-generic thing the mark disrupts self-identification, while without the mark there would be no genre to identify with. The mark is therefore the different condition of similitude, the *other* enabling repetition. The process of classification is therefore always imperfect.

If this sounds difficult, that is probably because it is intellectually taxing to regard differently our understanding of, for instance, the (conventionally) mutually exclusive dichotomy between outside and inside. It is hard to imagine that this opposition may not be as clear as we assumed.[48] This is rather like the traditional division of the jurisprudential possibilities into natural law and positivism, anything else being regarded as not quite philosophy, or at least not affecting in any substantial way the territory of the major debate. We tend to think that law must be *either* 'natural' *or* imposed (culturally, legally, socially, and so on). This obviously reflects a basic division in modern thought between 'nature' and 'culture' (or 'society'). The distinction appears to account for all of the possibilities, in the manner of a simple *either/or*, a position which appeals to our senses of logic and coherence. Seeing the possibilities in a different way is very difficult, and one way to begin to do this is to show how the distinction is never absolute, and breaks down at a certain crucial point. This is essentially what is being done with the inside/outside dichotomy in 'The Law of Genre'.

Thus the genre of law, being itself subject to the law of genre, is characterised by this failure of self-identification and closure since whatever it is that makes law law cannot itself be law, though as the law of law, it cannot simply be non-legal either. So law fails to close, self-determine, or self-identify by virtue of the very quality which ordains that it be closed, determined and self-identified. The foundation of law is 'undecidable', meaning that there is a tension or suspense between what might otherwise be seen as absolutes. 'Undecidability' is not merely something like the loose sense of 'indeterminacy' often alluded to in relation to the operation of language, for instance, the indeterminate reference of the word 'reasonable'. 'Undecidability' involves a clash of imperatives: the mark of law is absolutely legal, and it is absolutely non-legal. This is an unresolvable contradiction, a point of 'undecidability' in positivist theory.

A complication here which is also quite remarkable is that while the genre of law must be subject to the law of genre, nevertheless the law of genre must be comprehended within the genre of law. As a genre, law shares the law of genre with other genres. As a law the law of genre is within the genre of law. (Exactly where this leads is not at all evident to me, but I thought I'd mention it anyway.)

A LAW OF PARADOXES

These paradoxes of the legal genesis appear in various ways in theories of law. They also appear on the fairly rare occasions when courts have been called upon to determine the legitimacy of an entire system of social governance, for instance after a revolution or *coup d'état* has resulted in one system being supplanted by another.[49] In this section I want to look at a few examples in legal theory and in the judicial expression of the 'law' on this question. While doing so it is important to bear in mind that although these moments of undecidability have certainly surfaced in legal theory, they have not featured in any critical way: positivist legal thought has been interested overwhelmingly in maintaining the limits of law, and has avoided concentrating too much on any logical aporia which might challenge the theory of law's limitedness. The mystery, violence, or paradox of law's origin has therefore generally been perceived to be marginal to positivist thinking – once acceptance of law is gained the problem of the legitimacy of the entire system is no longer regarded as problematic, and internal matters of legitimacy are seen to flow from overall acceptance. As I will argue in later chapters, however, this erasure of the founding undecidability is yet another act of theoretical force, and is moreover an operation which cannot simply be carried out once: it recurs over and again in the general maintenance of law. In other words, logically speaking it is not only the origin of law which does not fulfil positivist ideals of closure, but laws generally. If law is a limit, it must share all of the two-sided characteristics of other conceptual limits. The significance of this is that the 'founding violence' is itself of the system. I will come back to this point in Chapters 4 and 5.

The Aporia of Positivist Theory

One of the clearest expositions of the formal characteristics of a legal system is that of Hans Kelsen. As I explained in Chapter 1, Kelsen's *grundnorm* (or basic norm) is the foundation of validity in a legal system: anything ultimately validated by the basic norm is law, while anything not validated by it is not law. The last justification in any series of justifications, the first condition of the law, is to be found where there are no more justifications, merely a final norm. Thus the basic norm takes the place of the first and last criterion of law, the limit between law and non-law. But the basic norm is not itself simply part of the legal system: it is not a law in the same sense that other norms are laws because 'it is not created in a legal procedure by a law-creating organ'.[50] Nevertheless, it is part of every law: it is in a sense the *most* legal thing, because it is the essence of law. The basic norm must be at once both internal and external to law, legal and non-legal. In particular, this frontier of law is what makes it possible, for Kelsen, to interpret certain norms as legal: it is the condition of cognition of the law:

> The basic norm is not created in a legal procedure by a law-creating organ. It is not – as a positive legal norm is – valid because it is created in a certain way, by a legal act, but it is valid because it is presupposed to be valid; and it is presupposed to be valid because without this presupposition no human act could be interpreted as a legal, especially as a norm-creating act.[51]

Every legal norm is valid by virtue of the conditions of its creation: legal norms are created and empowered by norms superior in the legal hierarchy. The basic norm, on the other hand, is merely a 'presupposition' or 'hypothesis' which constructs the system as being a coherent one. Since Kelsen is emphatic about the purity of jurisprudence, refusing to theorise law beyond the purely positive system which is derived from the basic norm, the nature of its authority must be beyond question, truly inexplicable.

Because the basic norm, being both legal and extra-legal, is at the heart of what it is to be law, and is reproduced in every law, there is a non-legal dimension of every law. As the remarkable trait which binds laws together into Law, the basic norm escapes law while delimiting it, meaning that the attempt to close law off from its Other (the whole realm of not-law) can never succeed logically. Quite apart from all of the other arguments which I have outlined then, logically speaking the law cannot simply be a closed or self-identifying structure. The impurity of concepts appears in this way in the positivist idea of a legal system: whatever is 'inside' the limit of law is there only because of the mark or 'trace' left there by the 'outside'. In other words, the outside cannot be kept entirely out, and nor is the inside ever entirely in.

Thus the character of the basic norm is entirely mysterious, and this is a crucial part of its theoretical utility. Certain theorists have criticised the idea of the basic norm for being unidentifiable sociologically or legally. For instance, Graham Hughes writes:

> ... we are dealing here with the concept of a functioning legal system, not with a species of geometry, and presuppositions, if they are advanced as reasons for the viability of fundamental concepts, ought to be susceptible to a process of verification.[52]

This seems rather to miss the point about the basic norm's function as a conceptual limit: it is there to provide a semblance or fiction of objectivity and coherence for a system of norms which can find no other ground.

Kelsen did recognise the paradoxical nature of the basic norm, calling it first a 'hypothesis', then a 'presupposition', and finally a 'fiction'. The basic norm is a fiction not only because it contradicts reality (that is, does not exist), but also because it is self-contradictory.[53] It is self-contradictory because it represents an ultimate empowerment of the law, and thus implies that there is an even higher authority. To put this another way, the identity of law is reliant on a general principle, itself neither legal nor non-legal, representing a limit or finality which is, however, always requiring that more questions be asked.

The silence which shrouds the authority of the basic norm is also manifested as a dislocation of its logical and chronological aspects. Kelsen's description of law traces authority backwards in time: there is a chain of Constitutions, each authorised by its predecessor, while the Historically First Constitution gets its authority from the basic norm. The basic norm is before the law in time as the unique and historically first act of positing law: the origin of a legal system is an apocalyptic moment 'before' law as such. Yet while as a matter of theory the basic norm is chronologically *before* the law, it can only be recognisable *after* the law is already in existence. There can be no question of a basic norm if there is no law through which it can be recognised. A revolution may have all the popular support and military strength required to overturn

an existing regime, but until it actually proclaims some law, it cannot
– on Kelsen's account – constitute a rival legal system or represent a
rival basic norm. The basic norm itself is reliant on the existence and
efficacy of law. For instance, if a revolutionary group proclaims a new
constitution and a new legal order which purports to replace an
existing constitution and legal order, only subsequent events will
demonstrate which is the legitimate source of law. If the old order re-
establishes itself before the revolution is 'successful' the new laws will
never have gained legitimacy. On the other hand, if the revolution is
successful, the new laws will be proclaimed to be valid, and presupposed
to have always been valid, even though when proclaimed this may not
be at all certain.[54] Thus the basic norm, though before the law as a
matter of both logic and chronology, must also be after the law.

Illimitable Limitedness

> The point was this, really, is omnipotence able to limit itself? ... Is
> infinity able to reduce itself irretrievably and irrevocably to finitude?[55]

If we turn to an example from classical (pre-EEC) British constitutional
theory we can see (in a different form) a similar phenomenon of
uncertainty evident at the limits posited by theory. The idea of a
highest or sovereign legal term is traditionally located by British
constitutional theorists in Parliament, or more precisely, in the Queen-
in-Parliament which is neither the Queen nor the Parliament nor even
simply the two institutionally combined, but rather the *process* of
determining law within such an institution.[56] As the place where law
is determined absolutely, the Queen-in-Parliament is traditionally
positioned in a space similar to that of the conceptual origin of law
theorised by legal philosophies:[57] the source of its authority is mysterious
– 'undisclosed', 'firmly wrapped in obscurity'[58] – it is outside, or more
usually 'above' the law, and is the origin and end of validity. As
Blackstone wrote:

> It [Parliament] hath sovereign and uncontrollable authority in the
> making, confirming, enlarging, restraining, abrogating, repealing,
> reviving and expounding of laws, concerning matters of all possible
> denominations, ecclesiastical or temporal, civil, military, maritime,
> or criminal: this being the place where that absolute despotic power,
> which must in all governments reside somewhere, is entrusted by
> the constitutions of these kingdoms. [59]

And as Lord Reid said in *Madzimbamuto* v. *Lardner-Burke*, no court has
power to question the validity of British legislation: every legislative

pronouncement of the Queen-in-Parliament is necessarily valid by virtue of that institution's supremacy:

> It is often said that it would be unconstitutional for the United Kingdom Parliament to do certain things, meaning that moral, political, and other reasons against doing them are so strong that most people would regard it as highly improper if it did these things. But that does not mean that it is beyond the power of Parliament to do such things. If Parliament chose to do any of them, the court could not hold the Act of Parliament invalid.[60]

(We must note the significance of this: the *court* has pronounced Parliament to be sovereign.[61]) The United Kingdom Parliament, much more than other national legislatures which are formally limited by a constitution (meaning that legislation is ordinarily subject to judicial review) enshrines the notion of an ideational source of law as a purely creative power rather than as a mere limit of legislative validity or final source of justification.[62] Founded upon a mathematical or scientific model rather than upon an Enlightenment conception of the sovereignty of the human will, twentieth-century positivisms have tended to postulate a source which is an axiom like Kelsen's basic norm (such as a constitution) rather than a boundless creative energy. British constitutional theory, on the other hand, still insists upon sovereignty as a creative principle, and this notion of the limit of law manifests even more marked paradoxical characteristics than those already discussed. In discussing the differences between the views of Austin and Bentham on the questions of illimitability and indivisibility of the sovereign, Raz suggests that because illimitability was essential to his conception of sovereignty it was Austin, rather than Bentham, who first theorised the legal system as a coherent totality: if limitable, the sovereign is not the limit of the system since a higher source of law must be available.[63] Whatever its nature, a limit *is* necessary to the idea of law as closed, and it is one consequence of the approach I am taking that this limit is itself, in some senses, illimitable, though this does not mean omnipotent, but rather irreducible and undecidable.

Because it lacks the formal constitution which would be its own limitation, the United Kingdom Parliament is, as itself constitutive of legislative validity, said to be illimitable in the sense that there are no substantive constraints on its legislative capacities.[64] It can, to paraphrase Blackstone, legislate on anything.[65] But because it is illimitable, and only because of that, it must be limited in the most extreme sense, which is that it cannot have power of domination over itself:[66] As Bacon wrote:

> For a supreme and absolute power cannot conclude itself, neither can that which is in nature revocable be made fixed; … And for the

case of the Act of Parliament, there is a notable precedent of it in King Henry the Eighth's time, who doubting that he might die in the minority of his son, provided an Act to pass That no statute made during the minority of a King should bind him or his successors, except it were confirmed by the King under his great seal and at his full age. But the first Act that passed in King Edward the Sixth's time was an Act of repeal of that former Act; at which time nevertheless the King was a minor. But things that do not bind may satisfy for the time.[67]

Although the sovereign process in British constitutional law is completely comprehensive in its relation to everything external to itself, it must be completely limited to the point of incomprehensibility because of its incapacity to encapsulate its own identity. Parliament cannot legislate to bind itself, it cannot enact unrepealable legislation: it is therefore unlimited in the sense that it cannot be subjected to its own determinations.[68] As sovereign, the Queen-in-Parliament, whatever its empirical existence or identity, symbolises precisely that point in legality which is *not* legality, the union of the absolutely limited and the absolutely unlimited. Neither of these terms can be compromised in the least to resolve the paradox, for it is only by virtue of being illimitable that Parliament is limited. Conversely, if Parliament had power to bind itself, it could not be illimitable.[69]

(This paradox is comparable to that evident in the judicial process. In *London Street Tramways* v. *L.C.C.*[70] the House of Lords decided that it was bound by its own decisions and that any wrong decision could only be corrected by Parliament. In the *Practice Statement* of 1966, however, the House of Lords made it clear that it did not intend to be strictly bound by its own decisions.[71] The paradox implied by these events could possibly be explained away by saying that the court's function is to decide the case, and decisions about decisions are of a different logical order.[72] Nevertheless, they are still decisions and within the ambit of precedent.[73] Thus the superior court's ultimate authority to decide does not extend to limiting itself, but if it cannot limit itself it cannot, properly speaking, *decide*.[74])

I suggested in relation to Kelsen's basic norm that it is theorised within the space opened by a disjunction of the chronological and logical dimensions of the concept of a source. The basic norm is posited as the chronologically first act of positing, yet recognition or construction of it as presupposition can only occur after the system has proved itself, *become* legitimate. In general terms it could be said that the sovereign term is as much the product of law as law is of the sovereign, because it is only through law – by the backwards tracing of justifications – that any single and highest validating factor can be postulated. A similar difficulty is evident in the notion of Parliament as the supreme institution 'before' or 'above' the law, since it is only through the processes of law that the institution can be recognised and its supremacy postulated. The point is made by R.T.E. Latham in his discussion of Kelsen's basic norm:

> Where the purported sovereign is any one but a single actual person, the designation of him must include the statement of rules for the ascertainment of his will, and these rules, since their observance is a condition of the validity of his legislation, are rules of law logically prior to him.[75]

To put it very simply, it may be that the Queen-in-Parliament can legislate on any matter it wishes, and is thus totally unlimited in its substantive powers, but it must *be* the Queen-in-Parliament before it can do anything, and is thus always subordinated to the legal question of its own constitution.[76] Like the legal subject, the Queen-in-Parliament is before the law in the various ways discussed above: it is prior to the law ideologically and (in some senses) theoretically but also after the law or defined by it. Latham advanced this argument to support his claim that Kelsen's notion of the basic norm, more than that of Parliamentary sovereignty, 'provides a general scheme or calculus of the formal validity of law'.[77] As has become evident, however, Kelsen's 'scheme' or 'calculus' resists totalisation, not through its circularity, but because of the apocalyptic beginning of law which is simply the fictional end of all justification, and not an absolute normative ground.[78]

CONCLUSION

These paradoxes which are at the heart of the ideas of an ideational and institutional source of law are, I would suggest, completely irreducible, being symptomatic of the general structural limitations of legality which, as I indicated in the first part of the chapter, underlie its 'essentially deconstructible' character. Whether the sovereign term is theorised on the one hand as simply a limit of legality, a basic norm, or highest reason, or on the other hand as an illimitable and indivisible sovereign power capable itself of positively instituting and altering the legal order, it is necessarily besieged by such difficulties (which do not, however, destroy its conceptual utility). Indeed, as I have intended to suggest, it is precisely because of these gaps, silences, paradoxes, or mysteries that legal unity and self-determination can be theorised:[79] the postulation of any singular, positive, and homogenising criterion of legality must therefore be recognised as involving the repression of the irreducibility of the origin in order that it may be posited as conceptually, if not empirically, indivisible and comprehensive.

This analysis concludes the first part of this text in which I have attempted to present the big picture of legal theory and its associated politics. The next part of the book concentrates on certain aspects of the thought of Derrida, in particular the notion of iterability. My aim will be to look much more closely at the logic and structure of this picture. However, before doing so, I wish to raise, if only momentarily, the problem of the decision, which appears to me to encapsulate the failure of any thought of an absolute legal grounding. The 'Interlude' which follows is intended to highlight the connections between the various dimensions of law which I have so far been examining by showing how they all rely, at some point, on the exercise of agency. It is also intended to facilitate the move into the analysis of repetition and iteration which follows in Chapters 4 and 5.

Interlude

Interlude

The Decision

INTRODUCTION: THE UNIVERSAL AND THE EXCEPTION

> In the course of time one grows weary of the perpetual patter about the universal, repeated to the most tedious extreme of insipidity. There are exceptions. If one cannot explain them, neither can one explain the universal. Commonly one does not notice the difficulty because one does not think the universal with passion but with an easygoing superficiality. On the other hand, the exception thinks the universal with intense passion.[1]

On the whole, jurisprudence is about universals. It is about distilling general principles and discerning what is essential and what marginal. Jurisprudence takes the central case as the universal and theoretically superior one, and proceeds from there. As I argued in Chapter 1, this process of defining what is essential, or what is universal, is one of the ways in which the privileged position of the philosophers is written into their conceptual systems, giving it a clear theoretical and therefore political advantage over any case which is regarded as different. The whole liberal tradition has been one in which the central case of the human being has corresponded to the central case of the man. Not only has this provided a safe place for privileged white men to be, it has also given them a vantage point from which they can with immunity practice objectifying and arrogant modes of perception,[2] disguised all the while as 'reason'. The practice of thinking solely in terms of universals, rather than in terms of the specificity of particular situations and relationships, casts everything as a variation on the same set of standards, and perpetuates hierarchy in our modes of being and knowing. The central case is the theoretically and politically superior one, followed by the deviation or marginal case, which remains, however, closer to the truth or the centre than that which is totally different or other. This is not to say that some ideal of knowledge must be abandoned but rather that the ethical and political dimensions of knowledge need to be more thoroughly understood, rather than erased by a scientific mentality.

Kierkegaard's statement that we tend to think the universal with an 'easygoing superficiality' takes on a particular significance in this

91

context. The position of the universal is taken for granted, and anything which does not quite fit can be simply explained away by the central/marginal dichotomy. 'On the other hand', says Kierkegaard, 'the exception thinks the universal with intense passion.' It is quite an easy and safe thing to ensconce oneself in the universalising modes of thought, and to disregard or reappropriate within one's own point of view that which would appear to be other. It is quite another thing to try to think from the position of the other, a project which involves subordinating one's own certainty and personal boundaries to a different set of norms, experiences and expectations. Clearly, such an attempt can never be totally successful because total success would involve the erasure of our own history as subjects: I cannot simply step out of my own history, though by recognising its situatedness and the contingency of my own boundaries, I can at least use my imagination to try to step into someone else's. What is important here is that understanding of the other does not come without some sacrifice to the self. This is the necessary consequence of interactions on a subject-to-subject basis, rather than on a subject-to-object basis.

White Western men have objectified practically everybody with their universal reason. However, the centre and the margins are themselves of course relative to one's position in the social hierarchy, meaning that white middle-class straight feminists have also thought the exceptions of other (lesbian, working class, Third World, racially oppressed, etc.) women with this easygoing superficiality. Those who think the exception for one set of relationships may still practice the easygoing superficiality of universalising objectifications for other matters. At the same time, the passion involved in thinking the universal from the position of the exception is more than adequately borne out by the history of feminism, of neo-colonial challenges to Western imperialism, and of critiques of the racism of predominant modes of thought. The position which is marginal, or outside cannot as a matter of survival ignore or avoid the universal in the same way that the universal can ignore or placate its other.

One of the ways in which this focus on the universal is manifested in legal theory is by its neglect of the material side of law. This neglect is part of a general effort to maintain the ideal of law as a closed set of norms with an abstract existence, and whose contact with reality is through their application to cases. Clearly the norm here is the central case of law, while the process of making a decision, and the decision itself, are regarded in legal theory as philosophically secondary. The fact that law can only imperfectly be conceptually separated from its practical existence has not been particularly well dealt with by legal theory. This has a whole range of consequences for legal thought: one consequence which is particularly marked is the resulting neglect of any notion of judicial responsibility. 'Ethics' is seen to exist at the level of the (abstract) law, not at the level of decision making, and judicial responsibility is downgraded from a respect for justice to a duty to articulate and apply the law. Justice is thus conflated with law.[3] Attempts are made by legal theorists to minimise the status of the decision so that it really occurs only in marginal and infrequent 'hard cases' or even so that such 'hard cases' can themselves be decided by the proper application of hidden legal or extra-legal principles. Ronald Dworkin's principle of 'integrity' for instance is an effort to reduce the notion of decision making to application of rules, principles and standards: although these may, in Dworkin's view, exceed what is formally considered to be law, their effect is to constrain the judicial process to a particular set of norms in order that the unique correct decision may be reached. I will return to this theme in Chapter 4.

DECISIONS AND THE DECISION

In this interlude I want to look more broadly at the nature of the decision as a legal event, and in particular, as an event which is formative of the law itself. It is possible here to speak of the decision in two senses. In the first place, the more obvious 'decision' is the judicial decision and, by extension, all of the other administrative, political, or personal actions which take place 'within' a normative order. (This position 'within' will also be questioned in later chapters.) Such decisions are traditionally presented as being subordinate to 'the law' (understood as normative abstractions), but the clear implication of recent thought on this matter is that this subordination is yet another metaphysical mystification, which can be challenged by careful attention to the relationship between the 'law' and the 'decision'.[4]

Secondly, there is a sense in which it is useful to speak of the founding moment of a legal system *as if* it were a decision. Clearly it is not possible to say that every legal system has been founded by what we would factually call a decision: in particular, English law has no clearly identifiable moment when an exercise of the will formed it as a legal system. On the other hand, it would be possible to say that, like many other similar cases, United States law was founded by the collective decision of the revolutionary leaders, coupled with a successful revolution, or that Australian law was founded by the decision of Britain and the separate Australian colonies to create a legal order. This is not the sort of decision I am interested in here: what I want to look at is the conceptual event which puts an end to the endless speculation about the source of law, and aims to resolve the type of paradoxes associated with legitimacy which I outlined in Chapter 3. The idea of the social contract as a myth of political, social and legal origin is a representative of such a 'decision' (one which remained circular).[5] In other words, it is useful to speak of there being a founding 'decision' as a way of understanding the closure of the legal system. This 'decision' certainly has its empirical correlates, for instance in the collective foreclosure of certain questions by lawyers and philosophers – a continuation of the act which delimits the law to begin with.

To put the problem another way: I have discussed in some detail the idea and original mysteries and paradoxes of the legal order. In doing so I have outlined the traditional terrain, and raised some questions about what is frequently not articulated or explored in legal theory, in particular the erasure of the political dimension of traditional thought. What needs to be considered at this point is the event or act which in some way arrests the endless generation of theoretical complexities by virtue of its own force, yet which cannot resolve them. This event or act could be expressed as the (legal) order which initiates the legal (order).

This 'order' which initiates the 'legal' is in effect an exclusionary act separating law from non-law. The decision is an end to reasons, or an 'exclusionary reason' as Joseph Raz puts it – 'to make a decision is to put an end to deliberation'.[6] What I am referring to here then, is a decision or an originating crisis which delimits and defines the 'legal' by creating and removing an 'other', perhaps like the process of division and repression which, according to Freudian theory, forms the conscious and unconscious parts of the psyche.

The force and effect of such an event is no less than that of the Decision postulated by Michel Foucault in *Madness and Civilisation*: the Decision discussed by Foucault is traced to Descartes' exclusion of the possibility of madness from the domain of reasonable doubt, and represents a moment of rupture in epistemological continuity.[7] This Decision is the foundation for the Enlightenment concept of reason, for in one blow it creates and divides reason and madness, and excludes madness from the interior of reason's domain. It is the order which creates the rational. Derrida writes of this Decision:

> ... the silence whose archaeology is to be undertaken [ie. the archaeology of madness] is not an original muteness or nondiscourse, but a subsequent silence, a discourse arrested by command ... The issue is therefore to reach the point at which the dialogue was broken off, dividing itself into two soliloquies – what Foucault calls, using a very strong word, the *Decision*. The Decision, though a single act, links and separates reason and madness, and it must be understood at once both as the original act of an order, a fiat, a decree, and as a schism, a caesura, a separation, a dissection.[8]

Described in this way as the act which founds reason, the decision is not necessarily a deliberate or willed action: it cannot even be said to be literally an action, being more of a recognition, a retrospective alienation of madness from the legitimate interior of reason. If we wished to write the history of the legal consciousness, or – to use Foucault's term – its archaeology, a similar moment could possibly be located in the establishment of the 'science' of law which began with the division of law from other bodies of knowledge, and the exclusion of non-law from the heart of 'proper' law.

Derrida continues that he would prefer to use the term 'dissension' – 'to underline that in question is a self-dividing action, a cleavage and torment interior to meaning in general'.[9] For the time being I will stick with 'decision', while flagging the question of the place of dissent within a decision as a crucial matter to be considered later. Dissent arises not only as the wayward opinion of a judge in a majority decision, but also as that struggle internal to law's meanings which precedes any attempt to reach a decision. Dissent, in other words, precedes the decision: the decision closes off dissent, in the need to achieve at least for that moment, some certainty.

SOVEREIGN DECISIONS

What can be made of theorising such a decision? Even raising it as a question seems to me to be somewhat dangerous in that it is potentially productive of huge misunderstandings. So let me try to be absolutely clear about this. As I will explain in a moment, certain theorists – notably G.W.F. Hegel and Carl Schmitt – have been quite blunt about the ultimate authority of a 'sovereign' to define the legal order through its decision-making capacity, and have made of this a central element of their theories of the state. Schmitt in particular attempted to develop an authoritarian approach to law, and has been duly ignored for most of the twentieth century because of his complicity with the Third Reich in this endeavour.[10] On the other hand, modern jurisprudes in the Anglo-American tradition have conveniently either erased altogether or glossed over the question of power in the determination of law. This has been part of a general effort to defend law as it more or less is: we can tinker with details and theorise it endlessly, but must take the whole for granted. So we are left with sanitised mystifications like the rule of recognition, the 'fiction' of the basic norm, sovereignty of the people, the 'basic goods', or the wisdom of the founding fathers, all of which are in their way lovely theoretical statements and ideals, but which neglect power as a foundation for law. Just who is it who gets to recognise law, who is it who gets to construct the fiction of legitimacy, who are these people who are sovereign (if not those who are already empowered), who gets to say what is 'good', and what is so natural and right about the outdated opinions of a bunch of privileged men? Who 'owns' the discourse of rationality? In effacing such matters from legal theory, which is again part of the effort to make it scientific-sounding, the law is immunised against fundamental challenge.

My purpose in speaking of the decision as a formative moment of the law is not to provide a theoretical defence of 'decisionism' – the position which would prioritise the decision as the legitimate foundation of authority. It is, however important not to neglect the decision, and the concomitant understanding of power, by enthusiastically emphasising norms and the 'rule of law'. My aim is in the first place to highlight continually the theoretical arbitrariness, and institutional and political character of the limits of law in order that they may the more effectively be critiqued.

To get back to the point then: Carl Schmitt wrote in his work on sovereignty, *Political Theology*, that 'all significant concepts of the modern theory of the state are secularised theological concepts', explaining that 'the omnipotent God became the omnipotent lawgiver' and that 'the exception in jurisprudence is analogous to the miracle in theology'.[11] From theology, political theory takes the notion of an omnipotent sovereign who has the ability to perform extra-ordinary, extra-natural, or extra-legal, deeds. The sovereign, declares Schmitt in the striking first sentence of *Political Theology*, 'is he who decides on the exception'.[12] The foundation of law, on this view, is a decision of the sovereign, and this remains the defining characteristic of law – that which delimits it:

> After all, every legal order is based on a decision, and also the concept of the legal order, which is applied as something self-evident, contains within it the contrast of the two distinct elements of the juristic – norm and decision. Like every other order the legal order rests on a decision and not on a norm.[13]

Schmitt's thought is thus quite openly based on the idea that the sovereign defines law through the decision on the exception. Such a view of the sovereign power to decide perpetuates a totalitarian account of the relationship between the sovereign and the law, since the decision and the sovereign occupy a position simply *outside and before* the law. At the same time, the decision is on the *exception*, and is therefore already inflected with the determination of the law.

In contrast, Hegel's monarch, also formulated through its power to decide, cannot be reduced to a simple position outside or before the law. In true Hegelian style, the 'power of the crown' is said to enshrine 'three moments':

> (α) the universality of the constitution and the laws; (β) counsel, which refers the particular to the universal; and (γ) the moment of ultimate

decision, as the self-determination to which everything else reverts and from which everything else derives the beginning of its actuality.[14]

The final moment of sovereignty for Hegel is the power of 'ultimate decision'. The monarch is the actual (concrete and personal) power of decision which forms the State into a self-determining totality. Yet – as Jean-Luc Nancy explains – the monarch enshrines a 'tremendous contradiction'.[15] On the one hand, the monarch is merely formal – the position which completes the unity and totality of the state, the entity which, in a sense, signs and seals the law, so that it can be recognised as such. The monarch cannot simply make arbitrary decisions, but as Hegel explains in the addition to §279, 'is bound by the concrete decisions of his counselors'. And, in the same addition, 'he has often no more to do than to sign his name. But this name is important. It is the last word beyond which it is impossible to go.' As Nancy comments, the monarch's function is 'only the naming of right'.[16] The monarch is the pinnacle, limit, or point of completion which adds no substance to the law. On the other hand, the monarch's decision is absolutely essential in that it gives a concrete will, an *'I* will' to the law.

Thus, 'the decision itself is infinitely undecidable: it adds nothing, and it adds itself'.[17] Nancy goes on to explain that what is crucial about this is the recognition that jurisdiction is 'juris-*diction*' – the speech of the law. Law becomes law through the performative utterances of the monarch, and at the everyday level, through juridical performances. It is worth quoting Nancy's exposition at length:

> This very simple, but obviously very formidable, general constraint [the formality and performative necessity of the decision] rules the position of the monarch. We must recognise in it the homologous constraint **(and perhaps homogeneous one)** which the theoreticians of 'decisionism' stress in the law (*droit*): the necessity for the juridical act in general always to contain an ultimate residue that established, prepared, written or deliberated law does not contain, and which is the performative of this law, the decision that law should make right, that it is effectively *gesetzt*. The constraint of enunciation, as a general constraint of the *existence* of discourse, is just precisely the constraint of juris-*diction* ... And this constraint **(which moreover is perhaps not just an isolated case, that of juridical discourse, but which on the contrary makes jurisdiction in general the constraint of every discourse, of the whole order of discourse)** always requires the existential posit of a *judex*, of a unique individual who says the right, and who is not unique because he takes this power to himself (he must be legitimated: the monarch is legitimated by the Constitution), nor

because people have decided to give it to him (for then it would be this decision, taken by others, which would be the real decision, the paradoxical decision of giving up one's power to decide), for it is not properly speaking a question of a 'power.' But the judex is unique because *only a single individual can speak.* (Emphasis in bold text added)[18]

There is much of interest here, especially within the parentheses. Note first that Nancy suggests that the position of the monarch in relation to the state is not only homologous to but homogeneous with the position of the judicial act in relation to laws. The decision of the monarch is not just *like* the decisions of judges or comparable to them, it is perhaps of one and the same order, in that both are the performances which make law of the law. Both are the articulations which exist at the frontier of law, and not, as positivist idealists would have us believe, usually inside the law. The inescapable theoretical implication therefore is a picture of law as a performance, not as a static set of norms. Moreover, Nancy indicates that this contradictory constraint which is juris*diction* – submission to a law which one is in the process of defining and articulating – is the constraint of all discourse. The speaking subject's discursive jurisdiction is defined by the re-creative event of enunciation – the speaker is at once subject *to* and subject *of* the discursive law.

To cut what is a fairly long and detailed story brutally short, as the person who is archetypally in this position in relation to the law, the monarch – although one and indivisible as the pinnacle of the state – is none the less divided, as a speaking subject is 'already divided when it enunciates [itself]'.[19] Divided as being essentially of the state and separate from it. As Nancy comments, these contradictions and paradoxes associated with the sovereign power of decision are raised in the Hegelian account in a way which is not evident in the 'decisionist' emphasis on the indivisibility of the sovereign.[20] The position of the Hegelian monarch is defined by this undecidability, which is nevertheless given certainty by the act of deciding.

CONCLUSION

Positivist theory has tended to foreclose radical questions about decisions: the law is seen to be the primary theoretical object, and decisions are simply moments of legal expression, acts undertaken in accordance with law, or, less frequently, the occasion for creating new law on a particular point. Thus the decision is thought of as being generally 'within' or occasionally creative of, a static set of norms. As I have suggested, this 'normativism' is one of the ideological conditions which allow the abdication of judicial and official responsibility: action 'in the name of the law' effaces the agency of the individual.

Adding emphasis to the decision as a limit question, on the other hand, indicates that the individual is never subsumed by the law, and can never abdicate her responsibility simply by reference to the law. Put simply, the decision either to abdicate or to follow the law mechanically is still a decision which cannot itself be totally determined by law. The decision not to decide or to apply the law mechanically is still a decision, the 'residue', perhaps of law's determinations. Interestingly, movements in twentieth-century philosophy have not only challenged the notion of the autonomous agent who is ontologically separate from external laws, they have also blown wide open its cover as a participant in the political structures which efface the other, and finally clarify its – our – position of responsibility. No longer can it be defensible to hide behind the law's systems of exclusion and repression and claim that we remain all the while objective, free, non-political, neutral, non-sexed and non-racial persons.

Now, what I have discussed so far is primarily the notion of the decision as something which exists in the same place as the sovereign term as the founding moment of law in its distinction from non-law. Whether or not we identify the sovereign term with the ultimate power to decide, like Schmitt and Hegel, the point is in my view clear enough: the ideational or institutional source of law, as I argued in Chapter 3, is exceptional to the law, and essentially undecidable in its relation to the law. It is only by the work of a decision, or something analogous, that this undecidable moment can possibly be the basis of law as a conceptually closed system. This decision on that which is first and foremost law's exception – its source – is the 'founding violence' of the law. Violent, because it forms a logic of sameness, division, exclusion and repression.

At one end of the conventional jurisprudential hierarchy, this decision is manifested in the philosophical limitation of law to a particular variety of institutionalised norms. Kelsen, for instance, specifically refuses to theorise law beyond the limit which he has posited, deliberately foreclosing in the name of legal purity the possibility of jurisprudential enquiry into the non-legal, the pre-legal, or even the proto-legal (that is, the nature of the presupposition of the basic norm). Austin *determines* the province of jurisprudence as laws 'properly so called', and Hart draws a circle which collapses in on itself around 'recognised' rules. The positivists have been followed in this positing of legal limitations by others: Finnis buys into an arbitrary cultural distinction between the practically reasonable and the practically unreasonable, and Dworkin reinscribes judicial interpretive possibilities into an idealised and equally limited integration of conventional social values. This collective philosophical decision – as an act which attempts to remove contingency and more importantly heterogeneity from law – has effectively also removed the decision: and with the decision also the exception, the particular, the practical, the ethical and the other.

Yet this philosophical decision is not only at one end of the conventional jurisprudential hierarchy. This decision to erase the decision from the philosophical terrain of the law and to reduce law to the notion of abstract principles, rules, or whatever, is none the less repeated throughout law – although the decision generally speaking can be erased from the ideology of legal thought as non-normative, the decision to do so leaves its mark on the resulting law and must moreover be continually reasserted in order that the proper limits of law are observed.

This is what I would make of Nancy's observation that the founding decision of the sovereign is *homogeneous* with the juridical decision which, I would argue, is not just the judicial decision, but any decision effected in relation to the law – which is to say, any decision. In other words, the decision which founds the legal system, which establishes its limits and coerces conformity, is, paradoxically, not a unique decision. It is not the *only* decision, for it must continually be repeated in order for the limits of law to be maintained.

Part Two

Part Two

4
Repetition

When the Greeks said that all knowledge is recollection they affirmed that all that is has been; when one says that life is a repetition one affirms that existence which has been now becomes. When one does not possess the categories of recollection or of repetition the whole of life is resolved into a void and empty noise.[1]

INTRODUCTION AND RECAPITULATION

To commence this chapter, I think it is time to summarise, at least in a schematic chapter-by-chapter form, the argument which has so far been presented in this book.

In Chapter 1, I examined the limitations which are definitive of both law and legal theory. In particular I considered the nature of the distinction between law and non-law, which defines the terrain of jurisprudence as an academic discipline, and provides the foundation for a view of legal analysis as a process which is distinct from its 'other' – in particular, ethical, social and political conventions. At this point I also provided some preliminary critique of the notion that law is limited as a system, outlining some of the basic indeterminacies of legal 'judgment' and the necessarily political nature of any characterisation of the limits of law. This analysis was repeated at the level of the norm, which has also traditionally been characterised as a limit. Finally, I offered the view that legal oppression is a result of an ideological (and perhaps procedural) incapacity to question the limitedness and singularity of law: conventional understandings of law do not provide us with any way to submit law to external reconstruction. In our current regime change can only occur by the careful and gradual reduction of the other to the proper realm of legal meanings, a process which is always carried out strictly by those who are already recognised and empowered by law.

These matters were taken up in relation to the question of legal language in Chapter 2. One of the most important issues in the analysis of law as a system of power, relates to the establishment of differends between legal discourse and non-legal discourse. The major focus of that chapter was therefore to look at the conventional understanding of legal language and interpretation, including the distinction between prescription and description, and the way these views have entrenched the exclusive nature of legal thinking.

In Chapter 3, after looking briefly at the differences between the traditional common law theory and positivist-inspired thought, I approached the matter of the 'before' of the law on two fronts. In the first place, the liberal-positivist assumption of the pre-legal natural subject was considered in relation to the twentieth-century philosophical 'crisis' of subjectivity. Secondly the idea of a single unifying limit of law was analysed in more detail, and several structural indeterminacies or paradoxes of the idea of an ultimate source of law were related to the notions of legal unity, coherence and validity.

The Interlude presented some observations about the theoretical place of decisions in law. This analysis will be continued in this chapter: my aim from now on is to look at the ways in which the resolution of the indeterminacies or gaps in legal thought are in fact reliant on certain terms which have traditionally been marginalised or relegated to the other in legal metaphysics – the fact, the decision, the act. I have suggested that although the decision represents a break with the legal context because it puts an end to legal questions even as it regenerates them – and is thus a silence within normativity, an exception, a non-concept – none the less only its repetition *as* a repetition of the original authority of law, a repetition of otherness *and* of the founding violent exclusion of otherness, can account for legal validity.

None of this at all leads to nihilism, nominalism, rule-scepticism, or decisionism, but it does lead to a reformulation of the relationship between the law 'properly so called' and the political events which constitute the law. What I have offered is primarily a critique of the institutionalised conventions of legal thought and of jurisprudence, and a set of arguments about the embedded, masked, politics of those conventions.

In 'Plato's Pharmacy' Derrida writes '... law is always a law of repetition, and repetition is always submission to a law'.[2] Repetition is essential to the idea and the practice of law, but this is not something which has been explored in any detail in Anglo-American jurisprudence. Where repetition as a theme has featured in legal thought, it is generally in the context of the process by which the law reproduces itself in new contexts – for instance the relationship of one case to the line of precedents which has preceded it, or the process by which a norm is legitimated by a prior set of norms and conventions. Even at this point, there is a great deal more which can be said about the temporal and causal aspects of law as repetition, but there are also other areas which can be opened up as well.

The importance of this questioning cannot be underestimated. An analysis (and strategic use) of repetition can, as both Irigaray and Derrida illustrate in their different ways, be an extremely powerful critical tool, and is one of the crucial elements of the 'postmodern' challenge to certain central traditional understandings of identity, the ideal/material and central/marginal dichotomies, and – in the context of law – the distinction between norm and decision. Unpacking these matters in the various contexts in which repetition occurs in law (that is, everywhere) is no easy task, but it is one which I see to be extremely important.

To simplify the project, I want to focus in the first place on two questions. In the first place, what is it that is repeated in law which is or ought to be important to an understanding of it as a system? Why is 'law always a law of repetition' and how are the various repetitions organised so that they form a system? In other words, why are the pragmatics of repetition important to the concept of law? Secondly, what is the nature of repetition? Why is 'repetition always submission to a law'? Most importantly, I want to look at what it is about understanding law as repetition which can disrupt our conventional notions of law as a self-contained abstract identity. This 'deconstruction' of the concept of law should also be understood in the context of the reinstatement of the decision which I wrote of in the Interlude.

'law is always a law of repetition'

In the first place then, why is 'law always a law of repetition'? What repetitions are at stake in the law and specifically in the positivist notion of a legal system?

Most obviously, the idea of law as a universal entails repeatability. A law is not a singular event, but a statement of a universal or an idea which can be applied in different situations. The law, or what is essential in the idea of the law, recurs in a multitude of contexts – in this way what is crucial about say, two sets of facts, is that they are considered to be legally the same. It is the law, though, and not anything essential about the set of facts, which makes this determination. In Australian law, for instance, it is possible to regard it as the same offence (manslaughter) when a man kills a woman because of jealousy as when a woman kills a man because he has been violent towards her over a long period of time. What is the same about each event is the law, which – depending on the circumstances – categorises them as the same for the purposes of determining a criminal status. As the example shows, the law is a very powerful means of entrenching inequality by mere definition, although I should also point out that it is only recently that this similitude has arisen in the law, and it remains controversial not because jealousy is regarded as a dubious basis for a partial defence to murder, but because women have to prove they were suffering from a 'syndrome' even to benefit from the partial defence of provocation when they have been abused over a period of years.

Traditionally jealous men could be convicted of manslaughter, while abused women were generally convicted of murder.

When an event occurs which does not fit neatly into the pre-existing classifications, or cannot be squashed in, or for political reasons is seen to fall outside, the work of the law is to say whether and to what extent it is the same as the situations which have preceded it, or indeed whether some different idea or law ought to be attached to the set of facts. By definition, such a new idea is itself from its outset also repeatable. It is premised on the assumption that it may recur as the same in a new set of facts. That there may never be an actual repetition is irrelevant: it is the possibility of repetition which is fundamental. In 'Plato's Pharmacy' Derrida said of the idea (*eidos*) which is law: 'The *eidos* is that which can always be repeated as *the same*. The ideality and invisibility of the *eidos* are its power-to-be-repeated.'[3]

As ideas about the world then, the law must be repeatable: the notion of an idea, or element of thought, entails nothing less than its having the power to occur more than once. In this way law is a set of ideas about the world, which orders it into particular categories and determines what is the same and what is different. In other words, the law delimits what counts as the same, while it is also that within a particular situation which *is* the same. The law delimits and polices itself as that which is the same, even as it produces endless differentiations, distinctions and exclusions to categorise within this economy of the same that which it defines as different.

I should mention here as an important complication that the definitional acts which laws perform, also compel repetition of action in legal subjects. Laws are there to determine what counts as acceptable and unacceptable behaviour, and therefore have the basic role in ensuring that people are, in what it considers to be the relevant respects, the same: we drive on the same side of the road, tend to arrange ourselves into heterosexual couples, can wear frocks or pants, or just pants, depending on our sex, fill in tax returns, and so on. Laws of all kinds are directly expressed in the behaviour of individuals, compelling us to act repeatedly in the legally same way (or take the consequences). If we think only about the positive institutionalised law, THE law, it may seem that we have a great deal of residual freedom to behave how we want. If we are thinking, however, of the laws which order thought, our cultures, our sexual beings, our social existences, our understanding of our place in the world, then finding an unconstructed residue is somewhat more difficult. This is certainly not to suggest that we have no agency, just – as Judith Butler argues – that we will have to find it in a different place than in the traditional liberal notion of the rational autonomous individual whose liberty is restricted only by positive laws designed to ensure that he does no harm to others.[4]

But I digress. This repeatability which is essential to the idea of a law, or to law as an idea, is one part of what I think law is all about. It is not possible, in my view, to think of law without repeatability, although the nature of that repeatability can make a great deal of difference to what we think about law, as I will explain in the next section. It is immediately evident, for instance, that to think of law as repeatability is to think of it as a process which can never be reduced to a static system of norms.

Beyond this minimal understanding of what a law is logically, however, positivist thought draws into its picture of law several other repetitions which systematise law – selecting and excluding laws so that a closed legal system can be theorised. (As I have said, the closure is never successful, even at the analytical level. Practically speaking, it is not possible for the legal system to determine its own changes, its own interpretations of itself and of facts, or its own decisions. On the analytical level it is not possible for a legal system – or a theory of law for that matter – to be self-grounded.)

As I explained in Chapters 1 and 2, the idea of the rule as a limit or frame is repeated in the modernist thesis of the limit of a total system (a rule of recognition, God, reason, a basic norm), in the nature of legal interpretation as a process of limiting texts which is itself subject to the limitations drawn by a theory of interpretation, and moreover in the understanding of jurisprudence as limited to a particular sort of norm. The form of law as limited is repeated throughout our general understanding of what law is and how it must be applied. The determination of different sets of facts as legally the same because they 'fall within' a norm, is repeated as a form in the idea of the law itself, that is, that some norms are laws 'properly so called' and the same in the sense that they belong to the one system.

So there is a repetition of the form of law as limited. I have already commented upon the political dimensions of this repetition as it exists in modern Western legal thinking, and in particular the way in which it allows a particular perspective to be written into the law, as the law itself. More specifically, however, the systematic aspect of positivist thinking is grounded in the repetition of the law of the law in every law. The specific thing that limits law (and is therefore the law of the law) is repeated in each component of the legal system. What does this mean? In positivist thought, the ultimate ideational or institutional source of law must be a part of *every* law in order for it to be law. The one and indivisible sovereign, for instance, is the plural and divided essence of each law *as* law which distinguishes it from non-law.

This is a rather complicated way of saying that in order for a law to be a law, in the positivist thesis, it must carry within it the mark of its legitimacy, which is that it owes its being to whatever it is which is thought of as the ground of law. (As I have indicated, this 'whatever it is' is basically what Peter Goodrich called the ideational and institutional source of law.) What is the *same* about each law then, is the law of the law, or the law of the genre of law. Not only must the ultimate source or sovereign term of law be repeated in the law in order for individual norms to count as law properly so called, it must be repeatable, so that law can continue to be applied. The authority of every decision is derived from this source, the decision itself is thought of as a lower repetition of it, and without such authority no *legal* decision could be made.

As I have said, repeatability as a form is what law essentially is. There can be no thought of law (or none that I can think of at the moment) which does not involve the possibility of recurrence: that is, that the law can come again to define as the same something otherwise new and different, and that the law tends to compel repetition as conformity to a set of standards. Of course, exactly what repetition entails is very much a question of theoretical and political focus, as I will explain shortly.

The repeatability of the sovereign term of law is an altogether different thing. It exists in modernist thinking about law as a way of ensuring the hierarchical nature and systematicity of law. More specifically, the ideological function of the notion of the repetition and repeatability of the ultimate source is to guard the boundary between law and non-law which is so important to the style of positivist totalitarian thinking which filters life through the law's singular lens.

'repetition is always submission to a law'

All this is highly abstract without consideration of the nature of repetition. In this section I wish to look at the logic of repetition, and at its potential as a subversive, rather than conservative, idea. Exactly how this flows into thinking about law as a process will not be considered in detail until the final section of this chapter.

My framework for thinking about repetition as a governing feature of the concept of law is not (for once) only Derridean, but also drawn from the work of Irigaray. This framework has three 'moments', to use a Hegelian terminology, that is 'the same', 'the other of the same' and 'the other of the other'. Irigaray is useful in this context because she highlights the limitations of Derrida's work for breaking through the barriers of patriarchal law. In other words, Derrida may be useful for exposing and negotiating patriarchal 'certainties',[5] but does not help a great deal in bringing out the potential of that which cannot simply be translated into, or understood as a facet of, the patriarchal arena. Margaret Whitford has interpreted Irigaray in a schematic way which is exceptionally useful here. In her commentary upon Irigaray's reading in *Speculum of the Other Woman* of Plato's cave scene, Whitford says this:

In her [Irigaray's] interpretation of Plato, the realm of the Idea or
the Form is designated as the realm of the Same, or the Self-Identical.
The world is described as 'the other of the same', i.e. otherness, but
in the sense that it is a more or less adequate copy. The cavern then
becomes the 'other of the other', i.e. it does not, in its materiality,
figure in the other two worlds at all, it is not a copy or a semblance
or a likeness of the Idea or the Same.[6]

Plato's pure realm of Ideas, Forms, or truth which is represented by
the sun, is the Same; the world, including the shadows and representations evident in the cave, is the 'other of the same'; as the 'other of
the other', the cave itself is not representable. To follow the schema
through allegorically, in what follows, the conventional conceptualisation of law in jurisprudence is in the realm of the Same, as an endless
search for law's self-identity, and the Derridean approach to law is in
the realm of the 'other of the same' because it brings an understanding
of the other into our concept of legal similitude, while itself being post-
traditional (that is, owing its terms of reference to the tradition, while
moving in some ways beyond it).[7] A legal 'philosophy' which is
motivated by the need to reach beyond the current system, however,
needs also to focus on the promise, however provisional and
unsatisfactory, of something which is neither the same, a variation on
the same, nor an interrogation of the same from the position of the
other.[8]

'all that is has been': the same

Philosophical emphasis on the notion of law as an idea has, as I
indicated above, been on the essence or repetition of that which is the
same in different material circumstances. The concept is that which
may be abstracted as being the same for different cases: the concept
of 'rock' is what makes all rocks in one essential sense the same thing.
The concept of 'law' is that which makes all laws in one essential sense
the same thing. The notion of identity has traditionally been predicated
on some such notion of self-sameness at the core of a being, as has the
notion of truth, which is always the same thing because it does not
owe anything to particular subjects of knowledge. It is, after all, central
to the notion of repetition that something of the same recurs, otherwise
it would not be repetition at all, but a rock and a law (for instance).

Traditionally philosophy has concentrated on sameness – the central
case, the essence – and on the notion that some sort of philosophical
purity or truth can be derived from this method. As Irigaray comments,
philosophical 'discourse sets forth the law for all others, inasmuch as
it constitutes the discourse on discourse',[9] and furthermore, 'this
domination of the philosophical logos stems in large part from its power
to *reduce all others to the economy of the Same*'.[10] The reduction of all

others to the economy of the Same is more than a philosophical 'method' or law for several reasons: it is therefore necessary to bear in mind the way that the laws of philosophy operate ideologically.

For a start, as I explained in Chapter 1, what counts as the same, or as the central case, is very much a political act of inclusion and exclusion: exactly who gets to say what is the same and what is marginal or different determines the conventions on these matters. Politically speaking, there may not be a great deal at stake in many definitional acts: personally I am not very concerned about who or what is excluded from the category of 'rock'. That, however, is not really the point. The point is that the ideology of sameness as self-identity, truth, essence, and so on, is reproduced in our sociopolitical categories, giving rise to an economy of sameness, that is, an economy which discriminates on the basis of whether something fits easily into its system of categorisation or not. Law is an 'exercise in purity' because it tries to separate out clear categories of existence, rather than recognising the multiplicitous and interweaving strands of being and doing.[11] In law, that which can be easily identified or comprehended by the law and by the law's system of values, is immediately given value within legal processes: it is heard and responded to as a recognisable event. That which does not so easily fit into the established system of differences is either neglected or appropriated: that is, translated, analogised, into the conventional structure.

In Irigaray's terminology this realm of the same is a homosexual economy, because it involves speech by and amongst men.[12] More specifically, it is 'reasonable' speech by and amongst privileged Western men about what is object to them – women, the Third World, indigenous populations, and so on. (And in this 'and so on' do I not reveal my own prejudices about the 'other' – who is visibly other and who is relegated to 'and so on'?) Most crucial for feminists has been the recognition that this homosexual economy involves a reduction of sexual difference to one sex – the male: the feminine is constituted only as a reflection of or deviation from the masculine.[13] In this sense the discourse of jurisprudence has been almost entirely within the space of this homosocial, homosexual discourse: as a conversation almost entirely between men, and almost entirely ignorant of the concerns of any but the reasonable man set, in their positions as the adjudicators, administrators, legislators, theorists, and typical subjects of law. This obviously goes well beyond the empirical observation that it is men who run the law: there are reasons why it is relevant to feminists that men are in control which go beyond a mere desire to be included. In other words, the economy of the same in law is not simply a question of its empirical homosociality, though this is one irreducible aspect of it. What is in issue is the 'masculine' as a model for legitimacy, the patriarchal figures (such as the correlation between 'paternity' and 'legitimacy') which order legal thinking, the boundaries of propriety and the proper which monitor the frontiers of legal thought, and the ideology of sameness which ensures the reproduction of this system of relations.

The philosophical valuing of sameness then, is not a politically innocent focus, and the way that it has been played out in Western culture is all too familiar. Repetition as repetition of the same, conserves frameworks in a static sphere of self-identical 'being', which refers to the past in the present, rather than to the future in the present.

'existence which has been now becomes': the other of the same

However, this economy of the Same, with all of its philosophical and political power to reduce otherness, contains within it an otherness which – at least theoretically – opens up the possibility of transgression. This is because the same is never purely the same, but also other. As Derrida explains, to be repeatable implies not only an essence of sameness which can recur, but also the *other* which enables differentiation: for something to be repeatable means that it cannot be unique or pure. The 'repeatable' is more properly 'iterable' since there is always a residue (*iter*, other) which is not reducible to the ideal of the purely repeatable:

> Iterability supposes a minimal remainder (as well as a minimum of idealization) in order that the identity of the *selfsame* be repeatable and identifiable *in, through*, and even *in view of* its alteration. For the structure of iteration … implies *both* identity *and* difference. Iteration in its 'purest' form – and it is always impure – contains *in itself* the discrepancy of a difference that constitutes it as iteration.[14]

On a microscopic scale this is similar to Derrida's argument about the 'law of genre' which I explained in Chapter 3. There is some thing constituting sameness which is not itself the same, but different. As Derrida goes on to explain, this difference constituting sameness occurs merely on the level of the iterable thing: the difference between identities which constitutes them as such (as per Saussure's arguments about linguistic terms) is a different difference, so to speak.[15] In other words, identity is constituted by the differences between things, and is always marked by the others which constitute it. Identity is also constituted by its repeatability or iterability, and is therefore always marked by the difference which allows the same to reproduce itself. Repeatability always implies such a difference in sameness and is therefore iterability.

It is perhaps in the light of these considerations that we can read Kierkegaard's enigmatic statement that 'repetition is the *interest* of metaphysics, and at the same time the interest upon which metaphysics founders'.[16] The repetition, in other words, without which the category of the metaphysical would be impossible ('a void and empty noise') is nevertheless the event which exceeds the metaphysical in its reaffirmation of particularity. The repetition is the gap in metaphysical continuity, within which the possibility of practical freedom and justice appears, and without which the metaphysical myth collapses. What is important here is not only this paradoxical structure of containment and excess which constitutes the repetitive moment, but also that for Kierkegaard it is only repetition which can open the space where individual freedom manifests itself.

So Derrida said (to go back a few paces) that 'the *eidos* is that which can always be repeated as *the same*' and that 'law is always a law of repetition, and repetition is always submission to a law'. As repeatability is always iterability, so must repetition be iteration. Repetition is always submission to a law, but there is something about a repetition which is *not* submission to a law. The concrete fact of a repetition is not reducible to the same in repeatability: the repetition is different not only from all cases which have preceded it, but also from the idea, concept, or law which made it possible – otherwise it would not be a repetition. In other words, the repetition is the conclusion of law, the end of the *eidos* (the other, the fact, the decision) even as it constitutes it. (Where would ideas be without actual expression of ideas?)

This is most clearly seen in the context of a case. For a case to be a case of law, in which the law speaks, has something to say, and is repeated in some way in the decision, there must be some relationship of similitude between it and the idea of law. The case is played out first and foremost within law's economy of the same: at every point through the process of law, it is reduced to this economy in order that it will be recognisable as a case of law. However, in order for any of this to happen, the case is already necessarily differentiated from the abstract realm of law as an individual litigation. As a repetition of the law the case must already be other to it: the repetition is submission to a law, but is also iteration, since it is always in itself distinct from the law. At the same time, the abstract realm of law must always contain the possibility of the difference which occurs in the case: otherwise it would not be law. All this is not quite the same as saying simply that every case is novel in its materiality and therefore different from all the others, a point which is obvious and hardly new, but which is still underestimated in its theoretical importance.

Where does the decision come into all of this? As I have said, the decision is that which is formative of the law in its (theoretically) closed state, because the decision continually concludes questioning about the law so that its processes may continue. The decision is unique as a reason because it is an event (not purely speaking, to be sure) rather than a norm: the decision puts an end to norms at the same time as it is a beginning of norms. In the first place it demarcates and distributes the rights and wrongs of a case in a single act or order which – at that point – prohibits further argument. And, in the common law at any rate, it is also the site of the construction and reconstruction of norms, having this authority precisely because it is not an academic disagreement or abstract opinion, but the concrete determination of a dispute between legal 'persons'. The decision is therefore the critical moment which escapes the law but which is utterly bound to it: it would not, after all, have any authority, nor would it even exist, were it not for the law. (Of course, to repeat myself here, I am not merely talking of the unique judicial decision which concludes a case, but all of the decisive moments which have preceded this decision and flow into it.)

If we accept that in the way outlined above the decision is always other to the law (the 'other of the same' in Irigaray's terms), and, moreover, that it is here that the opportunity to read the law reconstructively arises, then it also seems obvious that this is the space where the question of justice is at its most critical. At least this is where a 'justice' which is not simply an abstract expression of rules within the realm of the same but a re-reading and reconstruction of the law in the particular case entailing a decision that would remain recognisable to law, must arise. Derrida made this point very clearly in 'Force of Law: The "Mystical Foundation of Authority"':

> ... for a decision to be just and responsible, it must, in its proper moment if there is one, be both regulated and without regulation: it must conserve the law and also destroy it or suspend it to have to reinvent it in each case, rejustify it, at least reinvent it in the reaffirmation and the new free confirmation of its principle. Each case is other, each decision is different and requires an absolutely unique interpretation, which no existing, coded rule can or ought to guarantee absolutely.[17]

A 'just decision' does not flow automatically from a 'just law'. In fact on this analysis, a law can only be *rough justice*, since it cannot foresee its application to every single case. The law is only there to provide the backdrop, the context, the guidelines, but not the absolute determinant, for the decision. We could go so far as to question whether even a decision can be 'just' since the laws are invariably embedded in it, including laws which run so deep in our society that they cannot be unpacked in a moment. The process of reading the law which leads to the decision must stop somewhere – in fact part of the structural power and instability of the decision lies precisely in the fact that at every step of the process pre-decisions are being made about what to include and what to exclude which foreclose the possibility of an *absolutely* just decision. I should also concede that it is possible that the 'just' is by definition not absolute and that the ideal of an 'absolute justice' is nothing more than the myth conditioned by a metaphysics of totality and completion. These are matters beyond my present concerns. Let me assume for now that if anything has the capacity to be 'just' it is a decision which is based on a reconstructive approach to the law and an understanding of the otherness of the case.

As a statement about the relationship of the 'just' decision to the law this is very appealing, theoretically useful, and helps us to escape the endless repetition of the same in the law which a neglect of the other leads to. Or does it? Yes and no. On the one hand, it is useful to appreciate that the law as a process (a becoming rather than a being) is always being submitted to these transgressive reconstructions: as a statement which repeats the common law's self-justifications Derrida's comments about the process of reading and reconstruction in the search for a just decision seems quite apt. On the other hand, the 'law' which is being read and reconstructed here is itself critically indeterminate. As I have argued throughout this book, although there is an ideology of a singular 'law' which pervades legal thinking, there is in fact a multiplicity of laws, both within this apparently unique 'law' (that is, in its sedimented layers) and in the social and cultural laws which are its context and which flow into it in unspeakably complex ways. So '*the* law' is 'essentially deconstructible', but as with all cases of deconstruction, the process entails a certain selection of threads or strands: at a basic practical level, this selection becomes especially critical where a decision has to be made in a context which is not theoretical or abstract, but involves a (hopefully) self-reflective judge in a position of simple hierarchical superiority over the (usually) self-interested parties. The 'laws' will at some point become far too complex for any judge, no matter how responsible, to untangle. There is an extremely delicate and none-too-clear boundary here between a simple unreflective affirmation of the law (which is bound to happen somewhere in the process) and the free decision made on a responsible re-reading of the law for the otherness of the case.

To put this another way, the re-reading of the law and the making of a decision will inevitably involve crossing the line between law and non-law, and the exposure of this as an arbitrary barrier to decision making. However, a decision which is of the law in the sense that it is formulated in the context of the law will also always reaffirm this frontier, if not formally, then at least implicitly by accepting some hierarchy of laws. Common law judges have been all too willing to reconsider over and again the minutiae of (for instance) the doctrine of privity of contract, while accepting uncritically as common truths stereotypical views about women. For decades commercial law evolved while the courts maintained the fiction that Australia was uninhabited in 1788 when the first fleet arrived, meaning that a developed body of land rights law is still a long way off. Given that any system which has the power to declare itself *the* law will practice such hierarchisations and partial appropriations of the other, how can it be possible for it ever to set the conditions for a 'just' decision?

As Derrida says then, justice is in the future, *à venir*, to come.[18] It is not in the future which simply re-presents the present, but is rather something yet to materialise, and will remain so, like deconstruction, which is never complete, never quite there, but always on its way.

The process of reconstruction and reformulation of the law which justice demands therefore involves some degree of response to the other, but in so far as this remains a *legal* response, it takes the form of assimilation, appropriation and integration of the other. In so far as it is a response which exceeds the legal sphere, the possibility of an ethical subordination of the law to the other may arise. However, if the law is to remain the law such an excessive response will be only partial and momentary, because the other must become part of the sphere of the same which the law enshrines. The other must be representable by the law if it is to have its effect on the law, but in becoming representable it loses its otherness.

Reformulating law as iteration rather than repetition brings Irigaray's 'other of the same' into our understanding of law. The other is recognised, but only in its relatedness to the same. The analysis and reformulation can be incredibly detailed and even transgressive but it always takes place in and around the traditional scene. As Whitford explains, for Irigaray this 'other of the same' is the position of women in patriarchal-defined systems:

> The 'other of the same' now comes to refer to women in patriarchy. This too is the realm of the Semblance, of appearance, the realm of woman (or women) within the masculine economy, of woman (or women) as she is (or as they are) for men.[19]

Submission to any law, whether it is the laws of philosophy, the institutionalised laws of the state, or the social laws which construct sexuality, is submission to the patriarchal order. This remains the case even where the 'other' is foregrounded as an important theoretical element of legal thinking. At this point the homosexual economy takes on a heterosexual aspect,[20] because women as an other are brought into the domain of thought, but only in their relationships with the male-defined tradition. The same is disturbed, confronted, challenged, through its relationship with alterity, but never destroyed or even dismantled.

'a void and empty noise'?: the other of the other

I think this is where deconstruction in its relationship to the tradition, and as itself a masculinist tradition in the process of becoming, is only ever one of a multitude of possible feminist strategies. Although deconstruction teaches that we may not be able to think, theorise, or express an outside or absolute alterity, it is none the less important for feminists to attempt to imagine it – at some point to refuse negotiation in favour of separation (lesbian separatism being only the most obvious form) or of the thought of some unimaginable other. For instance, Gayatri Spivak's unimaginable 'other' woman is the 'gendered subaltern':

> Incanting to ourselves all the perils of transforming a 'name' to a referent ... let us none the less name (as) 'woman' that disenfranchised woman whom we strictly, historically, geo-politically *cannot imagine*, as literal referent. ... Today, here, what I call the 'gendered subaltern', especially in decolonised space, has become the name 'woman' for me.[21]

And Irigaray asks, envisaging another such space where being a woman is not reducible to the patriarchal name of woman: *'But what if these "commodities" refused to go to market?* What if they maintained "another" kind of commerce, among themselves?'[22] Indeed. What of the expectations, desires and communications *between* women which are irreducible to the economy of masculine representations? Are they nothing more than a 'void and empty noise' because they escape the repetitions and recollections of metaphysics, or do they establish their own rhythms and the prospect of what might be called – to distinguish it from the homosexual and heterosexual realms which have preceded it – a lesbian economy? Of course such a label carries too many references to the current conventions (the category of sex, the notion of an economy) to be anything more than the suggestion or anticipation of an other space which can never quite be reduced to any patriarchal description.

The question I want to leave hanging at this point, for I think it is of immeasurable importance to jurisprudence, is whether the law is stuck forever in the same and the other of the same. Can law escape its own iteration compulsion, that is, its focus on the same and that which can be reduced to the sphere of representation of the same? Can law ever face the other without reducing it, or would it self-destruct in the attempt? Would it be possible, for instance, for the law to submit itself to the conceptual mysteries of a body of aboriginal customary law, instead of appropriating and recognising it where convenient? Would it be possible for the law to take the point of view of a woman who has suffered violence rather than pathologising her perspective and actions as a 'syndrome' because she departs from the model of the reasonable man? Would it be possible for the law to listen to conversations between women, rather than assume that any conversation must have a man in it? More importantly could the law not only listen, but *be* a conversation between women in certain respects? Would it be possible, as a partial measure which would none the less go further than most in place today, for the law to adopt double, or triple, or multiple standards, instead of just one?

ITERABLE LAW

Just in case you were wondering, or hoping, I am not about to answer these questions, though I expect to raise them again in the conclusion of the book. Right now it is time to wrench ourselves back from these difficult and seemingly unanswerable questions to a somewhat more pragmatic look at what an understanding of iteration as the undecidable movement between the same and the other can bring to an analysis of legal theory. (Did I say 'pragmatic'? Trust me.)

Acts and Norms
The work of Kelsen is useful in this regard because of his thorough analysis of what he called legal 'dynamics', that is, the processes by which the law replicates itself through repetition, and the way that this repetition consolidates laws into a unitary system. In his major early works Kelsen made a distinction between legal 'statics' and legal 'dynamics', which are, broadly speaking, respectively the study of 'the legal order only in its completed form or in a state of rest'[23] and the study of the way that legal validity is reproduced throughout a developing normative system.

As I have already mentioned, Kelsen thought of law as a system of norms. In the modernist tradition in law this is hardly a controversial characterisation, so it provides a useful starting point. There is a hierarchy of norms, those at the bottom gaining their validity from those at the top. The validity of a norm, in Kelsen's view, can *only* be derived from another norm. But exactly *how* does this happen? How can validity just move from one norm to another? Something must be connecting them in order for this to occur, because otherwise we would just be looking at two isolated norms. Something must be connecting the council by-law to the Constitution, and it is not only all the intervening norms, because these are equally abstract, static and isolated. In the end, how can the basic norm reproduce itself?

In order to explain validity as a dynamic process, Kelsen introduced the notion of the legal act. The act is for Kelsen the principle of dynamism itself: it is the mediating agent between norms which is at once the creation and application of laws. Without the act, no reproduction of the basic norm, or any other norm, could ever occur. The presupposition of the basic norm is theorised as purely creative, but every lower stage in the legal hierarchy, apart from the very last, is simultaneously creation and application of law:

> ... every act is, normally, at the same time a law-creating and a law-applying act. The creation of a legal norm is – normally – an application of the higher norm, regulating its creation, and the application of a higher norm is – normally – the creation of a lower norm determined by the higher norm. A judicial decision, e.g., is an act by which a general norm, a statute, is applied but at the same time an individual norm is created obligating one or both parties to the conflict. Legislation is creation of law, but taking into account the constitution, we find that it is also application of law. In any act of legislation where the provisions of the constitution are observed, the constitution is applied. The making of the first constitution can likewise be considered as an application of the basic norm.[24]

Every creation is an application, and every application is a creation: though absolutely distinct analytically, these two aspects of normative dynamics are welded into a single normative act. Kelsen deflects the obvious conclusion that it is therefore the *act* which is the source of validity rather than the norm by saying that the act is 'determined by a legal norm'. And, the 'legal quality of an act is identical with its relation to a legal norm'.[25] Acts are determined by norms.

Despite its circularity (acts determining norms, norms determining acts), this sounds like a convincing enough account of legal closure. Certainly to survive law must repeat itself, and in particular the basic norm must live on in every other norm if law's systematicity is to be maintained. Kelsen has recognised, however, that the norm itself is never purely repeatable, and that there must be something which is other to the norm, that is the act of repetition (as application) which establishes the conditions for further repetitions (as creation). Kelsen thought to contain the otherness of the act by insisting that it was only ever defined in relation to a norm. The norm therefore remains the superior term.

However, the norm would be nothing without the act. It would, in fact, be non-existent, since the norm in an account of law as posited must be created. Every norm must be created: moreover, there would be no norms without the possibility of application. Rather than say that the act is determined by the norm then, shouldn't we say that the norm is only an abstraction from the act? An effect of the act, perhaps in the same way that we can say that what we think of as subjectivity is an effect of system of relationships between people. After all, acts can only be recognised as legal or non-legal retrospectively, by further acts, through the filter of a norm (which is still created by an act). The (applying/creating) act is other to the norm which it repeats, since otherwise it would be a norm, not an act. Without this otherness, the system would not be dynamic at all but simply a set of norms derived from somewhere. (Where indeed?) The system therefore must be primarily a play of acts,[26] a doing rather than a being, despite the privileged position attached to the norm.

Moreover, in its creative aspect, the act is always a repetition of the presupposition of the basic norm, which is pure creation, and as I have noted in Chapter 3, undecidable in its relation to the system. The basic norm is repeated in each law because it is the condition of each law's validity, meaning that the basic norm must be continually re-created by an ongoing series of acts. This leads to an interesting moment in Kelsen's description of the dynamic infrastructure of law, since he is absolutely rigorous in insisting that 'the source of law can only be law'.[27] However, it is precisely that rigour which leads to this play of acts within the system, and to the necessity of a presupposition, described unambiguously as an act, as the condition of the basic norm.[28] The ultimate condition of law, in other words, can only be an act, a presupposition, (a decision).[29] We could call it the basic act. This presupposition is one of two acts described by Kelsen as 'borderline cases' because it is not an application of anything. The other borderline case is pure application, that is 'the execution of a coercive act'.[30] Does Kelsen therefore implicitly reveal that the hierarchy of law is bounded by acts rather than norms?

As if that were not enough, the basic act must be repeated continually for the dynamism of the system to be maintained. Legal acts cannot be simply acts within norms which have been established by one singular apocalyptic act, because the demand for validity is an ongoing process, not a singular event. At every moment in a legal system there is only the *is* of past recognition, which cannot be translated into the *ought* of present and future obligation without some reassertion of the basic act.[31] How does the judge come to the conclusion that she should apply white Australian law rather than aboriginal law to a case even if the latter seems more appropriate? By her assumption – a repetition of the basic act of presupposition – that white Australian law is valid, applicable and exclusive. The decision itself is a repetition of the basic assertion of validity, even as it escapes, in its nature as an event, all of the law which has preceded it. What this shows, incidentally, is that the basic act is never *only* an act because it too is repeatable throughout the legal system.

There is a struggle here between the metaphysics which is constantly returning to the same and the otherness which is the condition for the same, but which has always been theoretically marginal. Even where the 'other' is only that which is the subordinate term in a binary built into the system, such as the norm/act distinction, the conflict of holding each in its proper place is marked. In Kelsen's case the struggle is between the expression of the principle of normativity (the basic norm) in every norm, and the ongoing legal performance which makes this abstraction possible. The myth of closure breaks down at certain points, taking with it the whole edifice of normative certainty. As I have mentioned several times, Kelsen went some way towards recognising the undecidable nature of the basic norm when he finally characterised it as a 'fiction', because it is self-contradictory.[32] The self-contradiction he was referring to was, however, its position as an unquestionable authority for all norms, a stopping place for all questions about validity, which ought, however, itself to be subject to such questioning. As I have argued, the undecidability of the basic norm goes well beyond its problematic bedrock status: it is not only repeatable, but *must be* repeated, and must be repeated as undecidable through a series of acts which both exceed and are contained by law.

To return to an earlier theme then, the founding violence of law can never be *only* a founding violence. It is repeated violence, aimed at holding in place a certain set of legal relationships.[33] The mystery of authority which it attempts to resolve is also never only a founding question, but one which threatens continually the 'proper' character of legal truths. In my view this system of violence is not only a theoretical or abstract matter, but very obviously expressed in the hegemony of the legal system. A 'law' which was neither systematic nor hegemonic *may* well escape the structure of violence built into the hierarchical systems currently in place in the West, but this is a matter for further speculation.

Rule Cases and Hard Cases

Legal philosophers traditionally distinguish between 'rule cases' and 'hard cases'. Rule cases are said to be deductively decidable from an existing legal rule, while a hard case is one for which no clearly ascertainable rule which fits the relevant facts is available. The hard case has at times looked like an obstacle to positivist thinkers. In particular Ronald Dworkin argued that if there is no rule to fit a case then it must be determined on the basis of non-legal criteria.[34] This argument has been quickly and easily rebutted by positivists who reappropriate the hard case by arguing that law is not only composed of rules, but also of less specific normative guides, and that in any hard case the judge has discretion *within* law to decide according to generally evident legal principles.[35] My own view is that within the traditional matrix of legal thought, the fact that there is not always a clear rule to apply to a case is really only a problem for old-style positivist formalists, who tended to think of law as a thoroughly calculable process – this type of formalism, which should be distinguished from the new formalism of (for instance) Ernest Weinrib,[36] was based on the idea that there is always a deductively available answer to a legal conflict, which could be discerned through correct interpretation of existing rules.

Now, this division between rule cases and hard cases may seem to be a fairly benign distinction. Given a rule, and even without it, some cases will simply be easier to decide than others. Some cases will just seem to fall nicely within the rule and appear for all intents and purposes to be the same as previous cases. Others may be somewhat different, but not different enough to fall outside the norm. Yet other cases may be so different that no one could possibly say that they are within the ambit of the rule. So we have easy cases, borderline cases, hard cases and various degrees of difficulty in between.[37] As a description of how rules get applied to sets of facts this is fairly unobjectionable.

However, the distinction gives rise to several matters which I think are important in this context. In the first place, there can be no pure distinction between rule cases and hard cases. The idea behind the rule case is that the same is repeated in a factual situation and that this similitude is evident to the legal decision maker, who therefore has nothing more to do than apply the rule. Yet if repetition is always iteration, and can only proceed on the basis that there must be something other to the same making the same what it is, even this apparently obvious similitude takes on a constructed character. To say that something is essentially the same involves filtering out all of the factual differences, meaning that the decision on the same is in fact always also a decision on the differences. In order to be able to say that this case is the same as the one which preceded it, the judgement must already have been made that its differences are not relevant. Similitude does not just leap out from facts, but is the effect of pre-existing legal and social constructions.

This does not make every rule case a hard case, but it does mean that the decision in any case cannot be reduced to a mathematical deduction. It also means that there is something always other to the 'formal' or simply legal processes of law at stake in the making of any decision. Positivists have generally been keen to minimise the decidability of law: that is, they have wanted to argue that on the whole cases either fall within a rule, or do not, and that judges therefore on the whole do not have to create anything, but simply apply the law without recourse to any other criteria. What this view neglects of course is the whole 'falling within' process – which is an ugly way of saying what I have been saying all along, that the similitude of facts does not magically appear from nowhere, but is the effect of the process of ongoing decisions and exclusions.

The rule case/hard case distinction therefore serves not only to reinforce the economy of the same upon which the modern philosophy of law has been built, it also minimises for the majority of cases the role and responsibility of the judge: after all, if all the judge has to do is to apply a rule she escapes the moral consequences of actually deciding it. My argument on this point can be summarised as follows: in the first place, the decision actually to apply the law is irreducible to the law itself, and therefore involves an ethical responsibility extending beyond mere application. Secondly, decision making in even the most clear case is predicated upon a continual process of characterising the same: there is never simply one decision, but a whole series of actions, exclusions and determinations which feed into the decision which is called for in a particular instance.

5
After the Law

An automobile in bad repair can be a noxious physical object, but no one can call it an opaque bottle containing a reputed snail.[1]

INTRODUCTION

The limit of the legal system is the origin or ideational source which binds a designated set of norms within its circumference, delimiting the essence, identity and similitude of law as a function of its own sovereign authority. Yet authority determined in this way is never simply singular, identifiable, whole or present: it can be construed as such only in so far as it is in its essence as a limit also paradoxical, divided and absent. Its validating power does not flow unencumbered through an otherwise empty or static system, but is conveyed by the repeated punctuation of acts or decisions in the structure of universals which expose its formal systematicity as necessarily disrupted, discontinuous, delimited.

The limit of the case is the rule or complex of rules, standards, or principles which bind within their delimitations the universalised facts of the case, conferring upon it an essence, identity and similitude shared with other cases. The case is never 'in itself' a case: it is a case *of law* delimited and determined by the idealisations which give it its being as a case.[2] As I have been saying all along, the limited and exclusory nature of law pervades the positivist project on *every* level: it is not just a question of the legal system being limited (though this is the central thesis of positivism) but of a certain proprietorial conception of laws in general, which pervades legal thinking right 'down' to the construction of facts and the interpretation of legal texts. These various elements of law 'properly so called' are mutually reinforcing: in particular the thought that the law as a whole is limited, in its turn limits the scope of available legal interpretations and perspectives. The ultimate limit is reflected in the local limits, preventing much (or any) thought of the other beyond the law.

To this extent, the structure of the case 'within' the rule repeats that of the law 'within' its origin: the limit determines an inside and constructs the essential sameness which binds together the interior, generating through that mechanism the elementary system of legal meanings. The question which now arises is fairly obvious: if the metaphysics of the 'proper' law pervades legal thinking beyond the thought of the 'proper' limit of a legal system, and if the frontier of law is in any case always permeable in the ways I have described, how does this dynamic get played out at the level of the individual litigation or other legal action? In this chapter – continuing the project begun in Chapter 2 – I will examine more closely the relationship between the rule and its consequences in the context of the process of reading and applying the law. More specifically, I will look at the separation of the real from the ideal in law, and raise the prospect of a material approach to legal thought.

This will lead to a further characterisation of the decision as the end and formative moment of the law. As I have suggested, in any of its manifestations, the decision is irreducible to the law, and in fact can be seen as the material basis of any norm. Rather than subordinate the decision as an event to the realm of legal abstraction, my aim has been to emphasise its ambivalent place in both holding the law together and disrupting the continuity and unity of law. The decision is an iterable iteration: it is other to normative abstraction, and able to be reinscribed in the narrative of law's continuity. It is in this moment, I think, that we find an ethical dimension in law. This is not to say that the law is ethical in so far as its judicial officers make decisions which are at once constrained and unconstrained by law, but rather that it is here, not in the formal content of legal prescriptions, that the possibility, and indeed necessity, of what Cornell calls an 'ethical relation' arises. The importance of this for the critique of traditional conceptions of law is that it reveals the political basis of any claim that decisions are not being made: the attempt to deny agency in the process of law and to insist that it is law which is supreme is an avoidance of responsibility for the injustices which law condones. If we think of law as a performance, like Judith Butler's notion of gender as a performance, rather than as a static thing, it is not possible so easily to erase the politics of law and legal theory. This is something I will be exploring later in the chapter.

BEFORE THE DECISION

To begin with, as a way into this problem, I want to look at a matter which seems peculiar to the common law – the *ratio decidendi*. As I explained in Chapter 2, the question of the *ratio decidendi* in common law thinking is a very specific aspect of the process of reading the law which appears as a quest for the law itself, for the law which exists behind materially existent facts and words. In this sense the question of the *ratio decidendi*, the *reason* for the decision, its determinant, justification, origin and condition, repeats the question of the law itself: what is it that makes law of this (act of) law? What is it about the decision which justifies it and carries it into the future?

In fact the problematic of the *ratio* is not as focused in legal interpretation as it once was: in interpreting previous decisions courts tend to look more broadly at whether something said in the course of a judgment was on or off the point, and what implications it had for the point (whatever that was). Rather than looking for a unique *ratio* then, there is an altogether justifiable tendency to look more broadly at the process of reasoning used, and any principles which can be distilled from this process. Whether we are referring to a *ratio* in the traditional sense, or to a set of reasons which founded the decision, however, the thought which grounds what is called 'legal continuity' is that there is an abstract level of any decision which makes it a *precedent* rather than a one-off act. Bearing this in mind, I will continue to use the terminology of the *ratio*.

The 'ratio of the ratio'[3]

The *ratio* is the law of the decision, that which exists logically *before* the decision, but is recoverable only *after* it, to be reflected upon and applied in future cases. The *ratio* is central to the case, and determinative of the decision, even where the case and the decision have appeared before any thought of such a reason has been articulated.

But this is not all. Not only is the *ratio* the reason for a particular case, it is the dynamic principle of the common law itself, as Julius Stone has said:

> In the stream of time in which the common law is assumed to unfold from its own pre-existing resources to govern a changeful society, the *ratio decidendi* would be the indispensable organic link between generations both of men and emerging legal precepts.[4]

The *ratio* is the organic link between the generations, the seed perhaps, or DNA, which ensures continuity between one case and its successor, one man and his (legal) progeny. Connecting the old action on the case with the modern law of negligence is a series of decisions and their abstracted reasons, which tell of a gradual evolution from one thing to the other. Connecting Fortescue with the pre-eminent common law judges of the twentieth century, say Denning, Dixon, Cardozo, are a long line of other men who have achieved legal greatness, or at least had it thrust upon them. The *ratio* or *reason* of the law is also here the indispensable link between the law and the men of the law: they are themselves of the law, its progeny or 'oracles' to use Blackstone's term.

Thus the demands of continuity, logic and masculine homosocial reproduction require that there be some connecting *ratio*, that the decision is within reason, even if no such reason had ever been articulated chronologically before the decision. At the same time, the simple recognition that this *ratio* or reason can be recognised as determinative of the decision only *after* the process of legal interpretation has itself reached some conclusion, already begins to erode the purity and priority of legal reasons. Even in the most simple case, there is always a question of the scope or level of generality of any *ratio*, a question which is only resolved by future readings. In the most difficult case, several judges may have come to the same conclusion for very different, even conflicting, reasons. The predominant interpretation of such a case will also only arise in the *ex post facto* readings of the case which supplement its inability to read itself.

The necessity of subsequent interpretation in determining a *ratio* suggests an inversion of norm and decision because the norm of the case (the *ratio*) is a reason constructed as existing *before* the decision (since without it there could not have been this decision) at some stage *after* the decision is reached. In other words, the *ratio* can only exist after the decision: it it realised *as a ratio* in the process of interpretation undertaken by a subsequent judge. Only in this way can it provide the necessary link between the first case and its successor. Yet it is also necessary that in being realised as a *ratio*, the norm of the case is taken to have existed *before* the original decision. The decision becomes prior to its own *ratio*, in that the *ratio* is discernible only through the medium of the reality and presence of the decision and the case.

Given that decisions have reasons, given that there is always a presupposition that there is something 'before' the decision which justifies it,[5] the project of legal theory and practice has been to attempt to recover that 'before' and to formalise it as a proposition of law. Indeed two dimensions of the idea of the *ratio decidendi* – the fact that there is a reason for the decision, and the urge to discover exactly what it is – have appeared to be inseparable in orthodox thought on the matter,[6] as have the idea that 'law' exists as a separate system of norms and the quest for the absolute source of the system's unity and validity.

The various tests which have been devised for ascertaining the *ratio decidendi* have (at least) one thing in common: the thought that there is one or several reasons which are essential to the decision and are of the order of the 'law' rather than of the concreteness of the case. For instance, to take only one of the most famous tests, Arthur Goodhart proposed that a *ratio* could be determined by taking the facts treated as material by the judge and combining them with the decision reached upon those facts.[7] In opposition to Goodhart's thesis, Julius Stone pointed out that the category of 'facts treated as material' is infinitely indeterminate. As an example, Stone distinguished nine 'fact elements' of *Donoghue* v. *Stevenson*, three of which are as follows:

(a) Fact *as to the agent of harm*. Dead snails, *or* any snails, *or* any noxious physical foreign body, *or* any noxious foreign element, physical or not, *or* any noxious element.

(b) Fact *as to vehicle of harm*. An opaque bottle of ginger beer, *or* an opaque bottle of beverage, *or* any bottle of beverage, *or* any container of commodities for human consumption, *or* any container of any chattels for human use, *or* any chattel whatsoever, *or* any thing (including land and buildings).

...

(f) Fact *as to plaintiff's identity*. A Scots widow, *or* a woman, *or* any adult, *or* any human being, *or* any legal person, *or* any potential legal person.[8]

Clearly the category of facts treated as material is indeterminate in even the simplest case. If facts have anything to do with it, at the moment of decision there are therefore a number of potential *rationes decidendi* rather than a single authoritative reason, meaning that the subsequent judge is compelled to make a number of choices concerning the previous case, limiting it to her own ends.[9] In his earlier work Stone seemed to suggest that later cases gradually define the scope of a precedent, making it less indeterminate.[10] This style of argument is reminiscent of Dworkin's chain-novel scenario which was so effectively discredited by Stanley Fish.[11] In his last book Stone completely opened up the realm of legal interpretation by arguing that 'the more judgements, the more discourse – the more discourse, the more words', and therefore the greater the range of potential interpretations.[12] At the same time, Stone argued that the process of finding a singular and determinate *ratio* was a viable act of construction performed by a subsequent court, but one which meant that the precedent is necessarily moulded to the requirements of that later court. In other words, the precedent never really precedes a case in any simplistic fashion, but arises in the act of construing a decision so that it has meaning in another context. The precedent is subsequent to the case to which it attaches, but as I have said, *constructed* as prior to both it and the case in which it is resurrected for reconsideration. This is yet another instance of a point at which law's story about itself cannot be closed, but requires an act of interpretation to fulfil its own logic.

Universal Reasons
Notwithstanding Stone's arguments, it is generally assumed that it is possible at least to uncover a reasonably accurate idea of the reason(s) upon which a decision was based, and that this reason is abstract and ideational, like the 'law' itself. Indeed, the common law doctrine of *stare decisis*, that previous decisions are authoritative, requires at least this potential of continuity between cases, for it is only as a decision

within reason that a case can be said to have any future authority. The question I am interested in relates to the nature of this 'within reason': what is the logic of the decision made within reason, and what is the political function of maintaining the mythology of reasons and reasonableness? As I have indicated, the continuity presupposed by the very idea of precedent is itself hardly linear: there is no clearly discernible system of influence or evolution which just flows through decisions, but rather repeated reconstructions of cases (or statutes for that matter) designed to bring their 'meaning' reconstructed as past, into the present context.

Neil MacCormick writes that in common law systems the idea of the *ratio decidendi* is necessary to the decision, as its primary justification. The decision must be justified, it must have a reason, if it is not to be totally arbitrary and meaningless.[13] It is clear enough that as far as the dispute between the parties is concerned there must be some reason if the decision is to be justified. However MacCormick means by 'justification' not a solution which is justifiable as between the specific parties, but a universalisable reason which logically precedes the instant case as its major premise, and which can be repeated in any materially similar case. This possibility of repetition (which is always also iteration) is in fact the essence of the doctrine of precedent: the precedent exists as such only in so far as it has this ideal dimension of being able to reappear in the characterisation of a future case. The authority of *Donoghue* v. *Stevenson*[14] resides in its capacity to return to the legal arena in an idealised form, as it did in *Grant* v. *Australian Knitting Mills*,[15] and hundreds of subsequent cases. Of which we could perhaps say, paraphrasing Stone, that although an automobile in bad repair is not an opaque bottle containing a reputed snail, a new overstarched undergarment is.[16] Or at least, there is some same thing, which would be part of the reason for the decision whatever that is, which connects the case of injury rapidly sustained as a result of consuming a bottle of ginger beer containing a (reputed) snail, and injury slowly sustained as a result of wearing for a week at a time two sets of new long johns containing chemical irritants. A clear case of alterity in repetition, I would say.

The logic of repetition which I outlined in Chapter 4 is particularly pertinent here, so I will repeat, or rather iterate, a couple of points. First the subsequent case is in its materiality different from the precedent. It is not, to state the obvious, the same case. Such an indisputable difference in repetition seems to be trivial, the point about the repetition of the same in altered circumstances which grounds the notion of legal continuity being that an idealised sameness returns as the *essence* of the new case, thus marginalising materiality. There is something essentially the same about the reputed snail in the opaque bottle and the chemical irritant in the long johns. It is their common property which was repeated, not their uncommon differences. Yet again to state the obvious, it was only in the subsequent case that this common property was revealed, or should I say constructed, as common. The difference of a subsequent case must be an essential difference for the simple reason that a decision is required to resolve the case and reinforce its similarity to that which it constructs as its precedent.

The case may be identical in all material particulars, but it can never be identical in its materiality or particularity, meaning that a decision is required to connect the 'essences' of the two cases. The instant decision stands between precedent and subsequent case as the author of their identity and the indelible mark of their difference. Although identity may be more or less common-sensical (by which I mean discursively constructed as clear) and decision may be more or less mechanical, the logic of this identity and machinery requires the inscription of a decision.

Secondly, the repeatable must have the capacity for self-differentiation, even as it defines itself as pure. The ideal attains its existence only through its repeatability, meaning that it can never be purely self-identical. Thus, the condition for the universalisability of reasons is not (only) the possibility of repetition, but also the necessity of difference within that possibility.

THE IDEAL AND THE REAL

To say that the law is *iterable* immediately challenges the basis for the metaphysical separation of the universal and the particular, or the ideal and the physical, which has been so crucial to legal philosophy and legal discourse generally. It is evident from the attempts to articulate the underlying generalities of cases which I have outlined that the thought of law is indeed this thought of the separation between the ideal and the physical. The law is seen to exist clearly in the realm of the ideal, and is made manifest in the concrete examples which it governs. This separation between the law as ideal and its applications or manifestations as concrete is a discursively entrenched, or perhaps discursively *produced*, feature of legal thought and practice.

What would it mean to say, as against this assumption of the ideational quality of law, that law is – like Judith Butler's reconstructed concept of gender – a performance?[17] What would it mean to say that law is a process of materialisation in relation to which 'the law' as we understand it in its abstract sense is only ever an effect? Perhaps this would be like saying that the subject has no essential being but is a set of material discursive relationships and is continually under construction, and that the sense of a subject as a separate independent unit is the effect of that set of relationships. Or it would be like saying that the same thing which seems to be meant by an original and its translation has no independent existence but is the effect of the linguistic relations which conditioned the translation in the first place. Or, it would be like saying that the signified has no independent conceptual existence, but is the effect of the system of differences between signifiers.

To say that 'the law' as the signified of the ongoing performances of legal subjects, including judges, police and other officials, is the conceptual effect, rather than the cause, of legal actuality, would be to invert the ordinary pattern of influence assumed by legal orthodoxy which is based on the primacy of the normative structure which gets 'applied' in practice. Laws constrain practice, and conversely, we could argue that practice determines laws. But perhaps speaking of a cause and effect here is too simple: can we really just argue that in performance causation is inverted? Or are cause and effect here really just a conceptual separation of two sides of the one process?

My argument to this point has made various inroads into these questions. For instance, in Chapter 4, I offered a reconstructed view of the conventional understanding of the relationship between norm and decision, where the decision (or any legal act) is said to be primarily an application of the pre-existing norms. By emphasising the reliance of the norm on its repeatability and actual repetition, it is possible to see this as only one version of the story (the version which, not coincidentally, suits legal hegemony). In this chapter I have unpacked the notion of precedent, indicating in particular the paradoxes of reading and reconstruction which are inherent in the idea of the *ratio decidendi* (which is only one example of the idea of a legal 'before' to a decision). It is clear enough that the processes of reading the law and applying it occur as two sides of a single event. The arguments I have put forward have been intended to demystify the space 'before' this process occurs, which has always been taken to be filled by the abstract, universal law which precedes interpretation, application and decision.

What I want to do at this point, to conclude this analysis in what I have always seen to be its formal aspect (another arbitrary, but useful, distinction) is to generalise a little. This will involve looking in the first place at the relationship between the 'real' and the 'ideal' in law, and secondly, at the possibility of thinking of law as a performance in which the constraints are not prior to action in any simple sense, but always under reconstruction through the iterative practice of law (and often being made up as we go along).

Facts and Laws

As I have indicated, conventional and common-sensical thinking about law tends to assume a distinction between law as a conceptual system (the 'brooding omnipresence in the sky' idea) and law as a practical activity (the Realists' law). The practice of law is thought to be the day-to-day expression of the deeper structure, an expression which is at times instrumental in the formation and development of the conceptual system, but which is on the whole subordinate to it. In this way 'law' is generally taken to refer to an ideal substratum. The term 'ideal' here is used in opposition to the 'real' or 'concrete' aspect of law, not to refer to an ideal or utopian realm of laws. Thus legal theory has emphasised the principles, doctrines and rules, taking, as I have pointed out in various contexts, a very specific (limited) approach to the distillation of these norms.

In the first place, it is necessary to think about how the 'reality' of this larger and deeper legal process is 'expressed' through the medium of repeated cases, and perhaps most critically, in the facts which make up the case. Like the sign, the case and its facts are never simply an event, never a unique and discrete moment with its own irreducible spatial and temporal substantiality. This may seem surprising, but just as the signifier can only ever function because it it repeatable and thus has an ideal aspect as well as a physical substance, so too can the *case* of law only be characterised as such because of its place within an iterative system. Although there undoubtedly is an event – a certain conjunction of people and occurrences resulting in litigation – such a conjunction does not constitute in itself the case, which is a repeatable and significant materialisation of facts. What is 'material' in the case is not its physical dimensions but rather that which is meaningful within it – it is only that materiality which accords to the case its identity and dignity as a legal artefact.

There are several aspects of this materialisation or conceptualisation of the case, which is precisely its case-ness, its being as a case. In the first instance, the case as a unit is authenticated by appearing in a specifically legal setting: the scenario is a court and the personae are the judge(s), the lawyers, the plaintiff or prosecutor, sometimes witnesses and a jury, and various other minor characters, all of whom *materialise as characters* – are characterised – within this particular forum. Each has her own particular role, is given a part to play which is an iteration of past performances. The setting is itself repeatable, being a sign and necessary condition of the case.

Repetition of law is not, of course, a *sufficient* condition for the existence of the law itself, for mere enactment cannot preclude the possibility that such a courtroom drama is staged, a fiction. The law can be imitated, a possibility which we should always take seriously. In 'Limited Inc. abc …' Derrida considers the case of a 'fictional' performative utterance, such as a promise, and points out that the standard case, defined in speech-act theory as 'literal' or 'serious' is constituted as a paradigm by the exclusion of the non-serious or non-literal.[18] The possibility of an 'imitation' in a fictional medium is comprehended within the central or serious case, by its very exclusion.

Thus we could say that central to the law's seriousness is its potential for self-mimicry. And if we were not being so serious about the law all the time, we might even say that this potential is most perfectly realised *not* in *L.A. Law* or films like *Witness*, but in its own performances, which are at once deadly serious and inexplicably self-parodic – the ultimate in drag, perhaps?

But it is not only the case that there is always the potential for fictions of the law (like *L.A. Law*), in addition to legal fictions (like the 'personality' of a corporation), but also that the law itself maintains various meta-legal fictions in order to preserve its integrity, and in fact is perhaps nothing more 'real' than the sum of those fictions. This fictional configuration of law could be characterised in various ways, for instance in the desire for purity which involves the filtering out or repressing of multiplicity and difference. Or, the fictional quality of law's reasons could be seen as part of the Western mythological base. In *The Mythology of Modern Law*,[19] Peter Fitzpatrick argues that Western legal thought is based on the mythology of the denial of myth. He explains that Western culture is based on the thought that it has transcended the realm of mythology with the institutions of science and history, but that this is no less of a mythology than those 'primitive' world views which are thereby excluded: it is, in fact, the perfection of mythology because it manages to efface its mythical status in its totalistic narration.

What about facts? Aren't they the particulars of the case, and irreducibly non-ideal? Again, yes and no. As I noted in Chapter 2, facts have always had the reputation of being extra-discursive and objectively discernible, a feature of practical legal thinking which has helped to entrench the perspective of the socially and legally powerful. However, clearly facts can be constructed as meaningful only within the discursive structure of law. Evidence is presented in a case, but only as a representation of alleged prior historical occurrences, and as a representation to the court that these facts are meaningful in the context of the dispute.[20] Evidence cannot be evidence of anything unless it is already a sign and representative: this is recognised by the fundamental principle of evidence law that evidence must be relevant to the issue. Irrelevant submissions are not evidence. The 'facts' are determined in evidence as significant, material, or relevant, and therefore repeatable and ultimately in need of interpretation.[21]

Such a view of facts and evidence erodes the more usual assumption that facts are just there, and judgement is a giving of meaning to the facts. In the *Cartesian Meditations* Husserl distinguishes between judging and the presentation of evidence. Judging, he argues, is 'meaning' or grounding which is 'correct' or 'agreeing', an adequacy of the judgement with a state of affairs. Evidence, on the other hand, is a having of something which is present itself, it is an unmediated 'experiencing' which is the foundation for a striving for scientific grounding and apodictic truth. Evidence is 'a grasping of something itself that is, ... with full certainty of its being, a certainty that excludes every doubt'.[22] Interestingly, Husserl continues by saying '... it does not follow that full certainty excludes the conceivability that what is evident could subsequently become doubtful': certainty excludes every present doubt, but it does not exclude the possibility of future doubt (which is surely a present doubt in itself). Leaving aside this complication, it is none the less clear that if evidence is to be meaningful, (that is, evidence *for* something), it must pre-empt judgement: evidence is already a judging in that it represents a state of affairs as leading to or supporting a chain of reasoning suggesting a certain juridical outcome.[23] Evidence and judging, in other words, are formed from the double mimetic process of truth in presentation and representation, which is the subject of the next section.

Like phenomenological reduction, the determination of materiality or relevance involves the negation of that in the facts which is physical and irrelevant: a relation of exteriority is supposedly established between the material particular and its own particularity, which is irrelevant. (It was something universalisable about the snail in the ginger beer, not its particularity, which had meaning for *Donoghue* v. *Stevenson*, even though it was clearly the particularity of the snail which made the plaintiff sick.) Yet even irrelevant matters do not exclude themselves: they are isolated as irrelevant by the law of the paradigm and are immaterial in their repeatability as such. 'Irrelevant' matters are significant as irrelevant, and therefore cannot be wholly exterior to relevance. If the fact that Donoghue was Scottish did not have some materiality or repeatability precisely in its essential immateriality or irrelevance to the case, how could we be so certain that such a fact has no bearing on the decision? In other words, that which is immaterial in the sense of being irrelevant originates in a legal exclusion – a drawing of limits determinative of materiality – meaning that the particular itself is inflected with the trace of the ideal against which it is defined: if a 'fact' is immaterial in the present case, then according to the law by which it was determined as such, it ought to be repeated as immaterial in a materially identical case, subject, of course, to the possibility that in a different case it may become material.

Conversely, that which is material in the sense of being relevant or perhaps essential to the case can always become marginalised in a subsequent case. Although it is only ever material because of its significance, that is, because it re-presents something as essentially repeatable, that significance, centrality, or essence, exists only as an exclusion of the insignificant, marginal, accidental and other. The hierarchy of matters which are relevant or irrelevant is not self-evident (as I have pointed out, nothing evident is simply *self*-evident, but the product of a reflection and representation) but rather originates in an exclusion and a normalisation: an exclusion of irregularities in the process of finding the norm of the case.[24] Derrida makes precisely this point in 'Limited Inc. abc ...' when he writes:

> The determination of 'positive' values ('standard', serious, normal, literal, non-parasitic, etc.) is dogmatic. It does not even derive from common sense, but merely from a restrictive interpretation of common sense which is implicit and never submitted to discussion.[25]

A dogmatic determination of centrality in which our understanding of what is same and what is different is never questioned, 'never submitted to discussion', is the norm in legal discourse. As I have indicated in Chapter 4, the question of the other which is dogmatically excluded is barely ever raised, except in so far as it can be appropriated by reasonable legal thought.

In this way, if the case is to have any meaning at all in the context in which it appears, it is through its structure of repeatable essences and differences. What is immaterial is subject to the structure of repeatability, as are the 'facts' determined as material, and as is any proposition of law or any reason for the decision which is finally extracted from this preceding situation. Each of these moments in the case is the result of an exclusion, dogmatism, or decision – a political act ordinarily disguised as obvious or the mere application of common sense.

Legal Performance

As I have indicated, the normal assumption is that law as something abstract is applied in cases, and that where there is no immediately evident rule or doctrine within which to place a case, that judges create one by analogical or policy reasoning. The distinction between applying an existent doctrine and creating a new one preserves the supremacy of law in its abstract realm, and maintains the ideology that judges and other legal actors are mere functionaries whose one responsibility is to this transcendent legal system.

I would rather say, drawing on Judith Butler's use of the term in *Bodies That Matter*, that the law *materialises* in cases: it is at once – to go back to the discussion of Kelsen in Chapter 4 – both created and applied, in an ongoing iterative practice. However, whereas Kelsen distinguishes creation and application as moments of legal *acts* as opposed to norms, I would prefer to say (indeed am compelled to say, at this point), that this distinction is a symptom of positivism's idealistic metaphysics, and that as a material process, the abstract and the physical moments of law can never be absolutely separated: in fact abstract law itself becomes only the necessary effect or reduction to similitude of legal practice.

Leaving aside for the moment the prospect of a more radical response to current legal thinking (which would perhaps move well beyond it in its understanding of the other), what this view of law involves is an appreciation of the decision as at once inside and outside the law: the decision is both an original and a legitimate act, as well as the term mediating the identity of the law and the case, and the precedent and subsequent instantiations. It is the decision in this sense that Derrida associates with 'the possibility of justice': the decision reinvents, re-inscribes, and reforms the law in the process of applying it. The decision as a reflective reinvention of law is a necessary, not a sufficient condition of justice. It will not do merely to reformulate the law: reformulation must at a minimum be carried out as a reflective response to the law's practices of exclusion and marginalisation. Only when law happens having regard to its own history, ideology and hegemony, can the *conditions* of justice be said to have been produced.

The decision in this sense would therefore be the necessary condition for justice, but as I have argued, it is also the necessary condition of law: this is not to say that it provides the logical grounding for law, but rather that as the term which, like the sovereign term, exceeds the law in its formal sense, the decision of a particular case re-establishes the legal system, and provides the basis for future iterations.

In this context it will be interesting to look at another of Derrida's texts, 'The Double Session', in which he presents an allegory of the moment of a repetition, in this case, the repetition involved in *mimesis*. Ordinarily, *mimesis* is associated particularly with the relationship between literature and truth, or between the imitation and the original, and it is these matters which Derrida is particularly concerned to examine. As usual, however, Derrida's text disseminates itself in multiple directions, and it is possible to think the connection between the precedent and the subsequent cases, and between the abstract law and its application as a mimetic relationship.

Derrida explains that the metaphysical structure of the mimetic relation rests upon the assumption of an original centre or truth, which is subsequently writted, materialised, supplemented, or diluted by an act of repetition, reproduction or reflection. The classical idea of *mimesis* proceeds from a simple presence – object, ideal, or *eidos* – to its duplication in the mimetic reproduction:

There is thus the 1 and the 2, the simple and the double. The double comes *after* the simple; it multiplies it as a *follow-up*. It follows ... that the image *supervenes* upon reality, the representation upon the present in presentation, the imitation upon the thing, the imitator upon the imitated. First there is what is, 'reality', the thing itself, in flesh and blood as the phenomenologists say; then there is, imitating these, the painting, the portrait, the zographeme, the inscription or transcription of the thing itself.[26]

The classical concept of imitation is that there is a simple real object, an objective precedent or presentation which is subsequently doubled or represented. The original is the prior, 'anterior and superior' artefact and the image its subsequent representation: the truth of the original has an *a priori* existence, while the truth of the latter is only determinable *a posteriori* – by referring back to the original. One of the most obvious ways in which this metaphysical system has appeared in philosophy is in the correspondence theory of truth – that the truth or falsity of a proposition rests on whether or not it 'corresponds' to some existent state of affairs. As I explained in Chapter 2, the defence of such a theory on the philosophical level (as opposed to our daily existence, in which we generally assume some sort of correspondence theory) rests on the radical separation of the 'real' from language – that the real appears before language or before any representation.

Derrida goes on to say that 'this order of appearance is the order of all appearance, the very process of appearing in general. It is the order of truth.'[27] Whether or not art has the capacity to break free from nature and thus in some sense supersede it (as various literary critics have argued[28]), Derrida points out that the 'order of appearance' is metaphysically stable. The imitated is always in a position of temporal anteriority, it exists *before* the imitation, while the imitation arrives afterwards, simply to represent. This relation between the imitated and the imitation itself has a double dimension, the two sides of which are never entirely compatible, but which are merged in the one act. In the first place *mimesis*, like the 'process of truth' signals an unveiling, revelation, or presentation of the origin, a bringing of the origin into the present, in order that it may appear 'as it really is'.[29] Secondly, *mimesis* is adequation, and its value is measured by its success in representing a prior reality: 'A good imitation will be one that is true, faithful, like or likely, adequate'.[30]

In so far as it is the reproduction and revelation of a primordial event or idea in a repetitive act, *mimesis* in its classical formulation describes not only the process of truth, but also the process of law (often represented as the process of truth). Of course, the process of truth has an obvious place within the process of law: the object of giving evidence in the course of fact-finding is to re-present the truth, to reveal or unveil a previous state of affairs, and to reproduce them within the context of the law. However, there is more to the story of legal *mimesis* than that. The very idea of following any law involves, as I have said, the compulsion to repeat an acceptable standard of behaviour. In this sense, we are always as legal subjects imitating the standards laid down by law within an acceptable range of variations. This process defines our truth and our being well beyond the constraints of institutionalised law. From the point of view of interpreting facts, cases, and the law relating to them, the question is always to what extent they are a version of some prior standard, whether they 'fall within' the law as generally understood. By a double movement of interpretation – an unveiling of prior meanings – and decision – by which we judge or adequate the present case in its relation to a prior act or Act – the process of law would seem to reproduce that of metaphysical truth: every instantiation is measured against a subsuming and pre-existent principle.

Against the classical exposition of mimesis, Derrida proposes a reading of a text by Mallarmé, *Mimique*, which renders in a not entirely fictional context the philosophical ordering of truth and representation, posing in particular the question of the relationship *between* truth and literature. Derrida's text also mimes that relationship, situating itself between the genres of philosophy, literary criticism and fiction.

Mallarmé's *Mimique* describes the action of a mime which, Derrida explains, has been reduced in traditional criticism of the work to mere reproduction of the classical form of *mimesis*. Although the mime is not imitating any thing or physical event, it is traditionally understood as 'imitating (expressing, describing, representing, illustrating) an *eidos* or idea'.[31] Behind the layer of representation, the story goes, there must be some original meaning. In contrast, Derrida's reading of the text emphasises the *originality* of the mime, which remains, nevertheless, a mime: 'There is no imitation' but '*There is* mimicry.'[32] The mime imitates itself in an event which is already a double, and returns to no precedent:

> We are faced then with mimicry imitating nothing; faced, so to speak, with a double that doubles no simple, a double that nothing anticipates, nothing at least that is not itself already double. There is no simple reference. It is in this that the mime's operation does allude, but alludes to nothing, alludes without breaking the mirror, without reaching beyond the looking-glass.[33]

In this way the mime – Derrida's reading of Mallarmé's mime – breaks out of the traditional 'order of appearance' (the 1 and the 2, the simple and the double). Or rather, it does not exactly break out – since that would imply that it originated within a metaphysics from which it has subsequently escaped – but is the undecidable which connects and separates the simple and the double.

Without some such term the 1 and the 2 would be simple discrete events: something is needed to enable the original and the imitation to be recognised as belonging to the same logical order, that is, as being a variation on the 1. Derrida presents the original mime as a sort of allegory for this connecting and separating term: between the original and its representation lies something which is neither, and both. A pre-condition for thinking the simple and the double, the mime's act is therefore prior to the orders of appearance and truth, being the condition which relates the original to the imitation:

> this imitator having in the last instance no imitated, this signifier having in the last instance no signified, this sign having in the last instance no referent, their operation is no longer comprehended within the process of truth, but on the contrary, comprehends *it*.[34]

The metaphysical determination of likeness, that is, the determination which ordains that the imitation is 'like' or re-presents an original, is therefore preceded by the pre-logical mimetic action.

The applicability of this order of events to law may be obscure, so let me try to spell it out, since I think that the process of law is nothing more or less than such a performance. In the first place, the structure of the mime appears in the nature of evidence: as I explained earlier in this chapter, evidence as a presentation of facts is also a re-presentation. In so far as evidence is there to represent a prior or existing state of affairs in the legal context, it performs the traditional function of returning to an origin. It doubles the simple truth. As such, evidence is nothing at all, it has absolutely no meaning. There was a snail which injured a person, we are told. So what? we answer. However, in so far as evidence is there to perform its major function of being evidence *for* a particular chain of reasoning, it represents as it presents, fashioning the truth in its own image, and for its own purposes.

The mime's act is also recognisable in the nature of precedent, and in the process of reading/applying the law, which never merely involve a case of a 2 following a 1, never just a doubling of a simple origin. A leading case on a point of law is often regarded as original in the sense that it generated some new understanding, was decided by a court of high authority, and serves as an example upon which future decisions can be based. Michael Detmold writes that 'Norm and example are incompatible: if I turn an example into a norm I lose the example.'[35] Now, it is certainly true that if I turn a decision into a precedent I lose the particular decision, which was, after all, otherwise of significance only for the litigants: as a precedent rather than a one-off decision a case is inscribed into the legal text, at least for the time being. But an example cannot function as an exemplar, an original, without already being constituted as an instance of that for which it allegedly provides the model: it must first be understood as the exemplification of the exemplar. An event cannot stand by itself as an example because before anything can be an example some value must be attached to it, and some understanding must be reached as to what constitutes following the model. Like the mime, the example or precedent must be already instantiation and original model, both imitation and imitated: it is always an exemplification of itself as an example.

Whether or not an 'original' case is taken up as a precedent, it enshrines this structure where the original and the secondary are never practically or analytically distinguishable. It might be thought therefore, that the case which simply follows or applies the precedent, is a mere doubling of it, mere repetition. But as I have argued, there is no such thing as mere application of a law: there is only re-reading, re-creation, or reconstruction of a norm for a particular case. The would-be imitation is also irreducibly original, a new materialisation. As the repetitive acts which are the condition for law, decisions punctuate its systematic aspect, thus repeatedly breaking its unity at the same time as they are – as the iterable vessels of creation and application – formative of the possibility of the system. Like the mime's act, a judicial performance (or any 'legal' act) is never a simple imitation of a precedent or legislated norm, never merely a rehearsal on a different stage, but at once unique, original, final, and as itself imitable, always an imitation, at least of itself. It is in this sense that the decision can be thought of as existing at once inside and outside the law. It is important to note, at the same time, that although there may be no such thing as mere application, there *is* an unreflective judicial attitude which would minimise its political role in re-entrenching the status quo every time a decision is made automatically on the ground that the law requires it.

APPREHENDING THE LAW

'And after that,' asked Blowbath, 'how do you pronounce judgement, my friend?'

'As you other gentlemen do,' replied Bridlegoose, 'I pronounce in favour of the party to whom fate first awards a good throw of the judiciary, tribunian, and praetorial dice.'[36]

It is by now perhaps commonplace to observe that on its textual level, law is indeterminate. The 'textual' dimension includes not only its written manifestations, but the whole dynamic of legal significances which are at stake in litigation. On this level, the idea of a 'momentary system' proposed by Raz, a snapshot of the law in its present form, a synchronic understanding of law, is unthinkable, not only because of the practical problems in finalising interpretations and discovering what the content of law is on any particular issue. More to the point is that the condition for freezing law in this way is the theoretical repression of the system of deferrals to the future, referrals to the past, and decisive actions, which make up the material existence of law. The desire for a finite and stable content merely hypothesises an autonomy which even an ideal law could not have. Such is the undecidability of deciding what right is (as well as what is right) in advance. Law can never, as Drucilla Cornell explains, be totally justified in advance: justification is never complete because law projects justification but 'never can catch up with its projected justification'.[37]

The undecidability of the structure of law does not negate our responsibility, it rather increases it. As Cornell concludes: 'We cannot be excused from our own role in history because we could not know so as to be reassured that we were "right" in advance'.[38] In the practice of law everything turns on its decidability: the making of a decision is unavoidable and final in so far as it settles the issue between the parties, and constitutes a truth regarding the matter. The decision establishes a certitude which immobilises in that instant the pre-decision uncertainty of legal relations: it apprehends the dynamic of relationships between litigants in finally comprehending them, which is also its comprehension of the law.[39] Yet the moment when law stops, when it is apprehended and comprehended by the decision, immediately gives way to a reinscription of the decision back into law, and into the play of reflections, identifications, reasons and limits which constitute it.

Conclusion

Conclusion
The End of the Beginning

I had learned a strange lesson: walls are laws to some people, and laws are walls to others.[1]

INTRODUCTION

To conclude, I do not wish to attempt to close off the arguments which I have presented in this book, but rather to look at a few of their implications for legal thought. (A summary is available in the Introduction.) I have been concerned to examine classical notions of the structure of normativity, highlighting in particular the tensions involved in the attainment of legal 'certitude' in decision and in the construction of a logically closed theory of law. I have tried to make the arguments as broad as possible and to express the relationships between them as explicitly as possible, at the same time retaining a sense of their applicability in particular fields. I have therefore included not only an analysis of the supposedly meta-discursive theories of systems of law, but also the normativity involved in signification and, to some extent, the institutionalised processes of philosophy. This approach has been useful because of the complicity of each area in the construction of the norms of normality. As I have pointed out, my aim has not been to destroy these institutions, nor simply to criticise their content or self-idealisations. Rather, by focusing on those notions upon which the possibility of formal law is grounded – their origin, validity, rationale, justification, repeatability and identity – I hope to have clarified some of the terms, assumptions, and in particular the politics of traditional legal philosophy.

In this context I have not attempted to develop a sustained argument about the specific politics of law, but rather to show the inextricable nature of law and power: in particular the power to decide the law, and to decide that it is different from other modes of social regulation, enforces a closure in the idea of law which, however, brings with it all of the instabilities associated with any attempt at theoretical closure. In other words, the positivity which is legal certitude – determination of law within a finite idealised structure of rules, principles and connecting justifications (whether naturally based or imposed) – can be the founding principle of practical legal reason only in so far as some non-transcendent exterior acts upon it. At one end of the system that event could be called 'sovereign' and at the other 'decision' – but the point of my analysis has been to demonstrate the mutual subsumption of the theorisation of these terms and in particular their necessary implication in the structures of normativity traditionally formulated as closed.

This, as I will emphasise yet again, is not to say that these structures must at the present time be simply rejected in favour of something different. Nor is it to claim that the structures are unchangeable. All I have offered is a different way of conceptualising normativity which is, nevertheless, necessarily critical of the jurisprudential tradition only in so far as it is reliant on it.

The argument does not, moreover, imply a mere replacement of the norm – which at least is regulative, predictable and safe – with an arbitrary act of sovereign or judicial will as the motivation for the decision. If that were the case there could be nothing to law. (As the most extreme realists thought.) So although what I have argued does implicate the will – and therefore freedom, morality and justice – into the very ideality of law, it in no way implies a subordination of the Rule of Law to freely constituted acts of will. (The distinction Rule of Law/arbitrariness, in other words, cannot be absolute in any theory.)

The event of the decision is rather *at once* the effecting of a transgression *and* the confirmation of the rule *vis à vis* the normative boundary. Julia Kristeva writes: 'The moment of transgression is the key moment in practice: we can speak of practice wherever there is a transgression of systematicity, i.e. a transgression of the unity proper to the transcendental ego.'[2] That is, although the unity of the legal ideal is a closed conceptual ideal, it is inaccessible in practice, inaccessible even to its own expression, or to its own thought, because the practice, expression, or thought imposes finitude upon the ideal (just as the ideal destroys the particularity of the practice, expression, or thought). Practice is that decisive event classically theorised as reliant deductively on the general system but which always escapes its static controls at the same time as it re-forms them. The decision is necessarily transgressive in the sense I have emphasised: it crosses the limit constitutive of legality yet is never simply 'outside' or 'inside' the law.

Just as an 'outlaw' is by definition a person outside the law, but is necessarily inside the law – comprehended by and subjected to law – in order to be so defined, so the 'decision' is transgressive in all the senses which I have described, but can only be transgressive in so far as it is caught by the system, that is, in so far as the decision catches the system. The movement of the decision is never simply *in*gressive or *e*gressive – never simply coming or going – but specifically *trans*gressive – coming and going – or at least crossing the limit in an unspecifiable direction, thus nullifying the limitedness of the limit. So, as Foucault writes, the limit which is the theoretical ideal is dependent for its existence on the transgressive event:

> The limit and transgression depend on each other for whatever density of being they possess: a limit could not exist if it were absolutely uncrossable and reciprocally, transgression would be pointless if it merely crossed a limit composed of illusions and shadows ...
>
> Transgression contains nothing negative, but affirms limited being – affirms the limitedness into which it leaps as it opens this zone to existence for the first time.[3]

'Limited being', being that is meaningful, is comprehensible only because of the space of infinitude which opens inside the limit. The idealised structure of limits against which the transgressive dynamic of practice is directed is in this way transmitted from the internal/external orientation of classical thought to an endless plane where our preferred positive terms are coextensive with the possibility of their opposites. The major difference is that now, instead of having concepts of law and linguistic structure which are antecedent to decision and enunciation, authorising a deductive sequence determining the shape of novel instantiations, a normative limit is conceptualisable only as being continually at war with the material it objectifies, and with the subject defined within it.

'LAW' AND 'MORALITY'

The arguments I have advanced in this book have been concerned mainly with the idea of normative structures and their political implications, on both a macroscopic and microscopic level. I have considered the theoretical conditions which are necessary for the classical theorisation of normative systems, of the application of norms to particular cases, and of the construction of significance, attempting to relate the philosophical issues which are attached to each of these dimensions of the analysis. I began with a statement of the concepts which appear to hold the structures of normativity together – limitedness, continuity, identity, validity, justification, unity, centrality (etc.) – and proceeded to unpack the structure of these notions. Broadly speaking, it has become evident that it is not logic, or any other ideationally pure form, which is the condition of law's coherence. If law is coherent, it is only because its structures fail at some point to satisfy their criteria of self-determination, a point of failure which is invariably masked by some force, violence, or dogmatism serving to re-establish the proper limits of law.

The question which must now arise is this: having concluded that the world is not flat (that is, having realised that an action of going beyond needn't precipitate our philosophical obliteration but is the condition for 'rational thought') have I merely and at last come to the realisation that the world is round – meaning that after a tedious circumnavigation I am merely back where I started? (Though older and wiser.) Just because science tells us that the world *is* round doesn't mean that we can't imagine it to be otherwise; however by proposing a view which is not rule-scepticism but in part an explanation of the universality of norms, do I merely retreat into the traditions from which I started? The question is a difficult one because it opens on to the whole problem of what it means to be in the world at all. And if we start talking about *not* being in the world do we therefore return to a flat earth view? (That is, the inside or outside alternative.) Further would this return mean on the meta-theoretical level that the world is round? (and so on). So far I have encountered merely paradoxes. This is a worse obstacle, being a paradox within a paradox – a paradox constituted in the space which should offer a resolution of the original paradox.

This is, of course, not merely a personal philosophical crisis – it names the crisis of philosophy in general. As Rodolphe Gasché has pointed out, the philosophical moment is itself constituted by the rejection of tradition, which implies a return to tradition.[4] To claim a 'break with tradition' is perhaps philosophically the most traditional gesture. And not only that, but haven't we learnt by experience that philosophical claims to novelty or original thought invariably become situated in a continuous meta-philosophical narrative which reduces them to 'idealism', 'positivism', 'nihilism', 'existentialism', 'medievalism' and now 'post-structuralism'? Is it all not a variation on the old Greek theme? (Here we could ask what 'variation on a theme' implies – i.e., everything I have been considering.)

In one sense I think that the answer to that question *must* be affirmative for precisely those reasons concerning the construction of limits which I have been emphasising. Philosophy is about the world and if there were no limits, or different ones, then we wouldn't have a world, or at least not this one. (We might have the same oceans, trees and mountains, but these are not the objects of our present philosophy.) But in another sense, and for those very same reasons, we must recognise that in the duplicity of this movement there is a space which is irreducible to either its historical or theoretical components.

That this can be so is demonstrated by the movement which is most inappropriately reduced to an -ism, that is, feminism. In my view, feminism is characterised by a simple tension – between the necessity of conciliating, negotiating, or arbitrating our way into a more advantageous position within the current patriarchy and the need to envisage what the world would be like without this and other systems of oppression. All the logic in the world can be mustered against the possibility of actually formulating such a vision, but personally I am not about to abandon it. And of course, to say it is strictly speaking impossible to think in a radically exterior way to patriarchal structures does not at all imply that thought *cannot* be transgressive in the way I have outlined above. The spaces outside are also within. Unlike theories which are played out in a largely academic space, the thing which will keep feminism and other emancipatory movements from being caught within a static mode of thought is the personal/political consciousness which drives it, and the daily necessity of having to face patriarchal institutions.

I wish to unfold briefly what I think are some of the consequences of the sorts of arguments I have been making, after which it will, I hope, be apparent that the business of flatness, roundness, or otherness of the world is – if we are interested in it at all – completely unresolvable. (But if we decide we are not interested that still brings us back to an otherness which remains 'inside' the problematic.)

What then, of the relationship between law and morality? At this late stage I am not going to rewrite the old arguments about law and morality, about, for instance, whether natural law theories involve a fundamental confusion of logical categories or whether positivism is based on a sterile mechanical metaphor which is of limited utility since it completely excludes the necessarily human dimension of law. All I wish to do now is indicate briefly why I think such debates, when they purport to appear in a philosophical context, are largely misguided. My comments do not, however, exclude the possibility of such a debate being conducted on, for instance, an empirical or sociological level.[5]

In *The Unity of Law and Morality* Michael Detmold argues something which is frequently either overlooked or underestimated in legal thought: that the moral identity of law is a necessary feature of the giving of judgment in a case.[6] Even if the judge has a rule by which she is formally bound, she must still make a decision as to whether or not to apply the rule. If the rule is considered to be wrong generally, or wrong in its application to the particular case, then the judge is faced with a difficult choice, which may be resolved by the determination of the rule as wrong in the strong sense (wrong all things pertaining to the case considered) or wrong in the weak sense, meaning that something like the mere weight of *stare decisis* is sufficient to justify the application of the rule.[7] Of course the judge is not able to declare that such a rule is universally invalid, merely that it cannot apply to her present case.

Now, it is often thought that judges do not have this choice: to be 'bound' means that there is no choice, that one *must* apply the rule. As I have argued, however, the quality of this 'must' – the logical imperative of law – is always and necessarily conditioned by the particular event of 'application'. The 'must' exists as such only because of the application.

Such an argument is difficult to comprehend fully (even though its formulation is so simple) especially by those who conceive of morality as a natural and formalisable set of rules or goals. If what is natural or moral about law had to appear as a necessary correspondence of two differently theorised prescriptive orders, then of course the unity of law with morality would be a very difficult, if not impossible, argument. (It is only this relatively crude version of natural law theory which positivism succeeds in rejecting – for instance when Kelsen argues that the *is* of natural law cannot be converted into the *ought* of positive legal obligation.) Detmold's argument does not, however, concern some vague correspondence of legal and moral orders but rather their utter indissociability – which is strictly *unity*, not union – manifested at the crucial point of the particular legal event. The significance of this insight should not be underestimated, though to many it may seem to leave open the problem concerning the relationship of our idealised structures of law and morality. I will return to this point shortly.

In *Limited Inc.* Derrida makes a similar, but not identical, point about the inescapability of the 'ethical-political' dimension of normatively 'determined' decisions:

> A decision can only come into being in a space that exceeds the calculable program that would destroy all responsibility by transforming it into a programmable effect of determinate causes. There can be no moral or political responsibility without this trial and this passage by way of the undecidable. Even if a decision seems to take only a second and not to be preceded by any deliberation, it is structured by this *experience and experiment [expérience] of the undecidable*.[8]

The space of the decision – like the 'mystical foundation of authority' – is that which *exceeds* any formalisable normative structure. The decision, in other words, is properly placed in a location which is not simply contained by law, and can never be totalised or absolutely determined. There is no 'moral or political responsibility' without the necessity of decision. And the decision is necessary simply because of the formal uncontainability of the event within the metaphysical structure of determination. Therefore the ethical dimension is situated not as any formalisable set of rules, nor as anything contained by its own finitude, but rather as the appearance of a certain *particularity* in decision which is not reducible to prescription, which is not finitely explicable, and which negates the possibility of avoiding moral responsibility.

Several matters may be noted about this structure. The first is that although it necessarily implicates morality in law and establishes a space in which an ethical practice must be located, it by no means favours the natural law view (this is notwithstanding the fact that most of my examples have been directed against positivism). All I would say is that an ethical moment is always and inescapably inscribed into the decision, and that the freedom and responsibility attaching to that moment cannot be moderated or qualified by turning for justification to a system of rules or hierarchy of authority because that system and that hierarchy necessarily underdetermine the act in its particularity. The refusal to reflect upon this, and in particular upon the force that holds law together is a refusal to admit responsibility. Moreover abstract norms stand in a relation to the particular act which is yet more conclusive of this moral element of law than mere underdetermination, which is that the system and the hierarchy of authority, are themselves only ever realised in their quasi-ideal identity through the decision which addresses them. This is very far from taking a natural law position – its implications are, rather, that instead of talking about 'natural morality' and 'positive law' our terms have changed to the 'ethical' and the 'calculable', which are realigned *within* the dynamic of decision.

What, exactly does this mean? First, regarding positivism, I would argue that its attempted delimitation of law is always and necessarily deformed by the logical impossibility of totalising the sources of law – both the 'ideational source' as Goodrich calls it (i.e. the hierarchical origin) and the source of law's actuality (the 'material' dimension realised in the decision). I do not here claim too much for positivism in order the more easily to cut it down – the crucial argument is that there is always, *a priori*, something about law which is not-law and that the decision is the only bringing into being (a highly equivocal being) of this structure. Secondly, regarding natural law, we cannot say that the recognition of an ethical moment in the decision supports 'natural' law theory because that would assume rather too quickly an equation of 'natural' and 'ethical'. The argument is not that the term entitled 'natural' is constituted simply as that which, either as excess or priority, is not law, but which is nevertheless inscribed into law, being formative of it. As I have said, that place is certainly occupied by the ethical term but it is inevitably non-natural in so far as 'natural' designates an expressible stratum or modality of normativity, or a state of affairs chronologically prior to the imposition of law. More centrally, the ethical moment is reliant on the normative system for its own being, and cannot be said in any way to pre-exist it. If law is 'natural' in the sense that there can be no strict delimitation between social norms and those prescribed by legal institutions, or if law is 'natural' in the much stronger sense of deriving its unconditional justification from a 'natural' source, then we merely witness an expansion of the idealised normative structure which similarly fails to contain the moral or ethical moment necessary in decision. All we can say in this limited context is that it is 'natural' that we have law, by which I mean nothing more than that without normativity we would not have language, or knowledge, or social relations, or in fact *any* concept of relation. Existence presupposes normativity, and the 'natural' is a product of this structure.

I return, then, to the relationship of law and morality, which remains problematic in precisely the same way that the relationship of law and decision is problematic. This does not necessarily imply an equation of 'decision' with 'morality', merely – which I have already stated – that the decision is an ethical event. Not ethically determined nor determinative of an ethic, but *in so far as it is not motivated* by the law (and at some point, as we have seen, it loses its 'legal' motivation), the decision is ethical. Now, on the one hand this would seem to imply a disjunction of law itself and the necessarily ethical dimension of law. I cannot argue that law and morality are simply *unified* (though there is a sense in which this must be true), because I have problematised the relationship of law and the decision, and – to a certain extent – defined the ethical as existing in a space undetermined by the law. In this sense the ethical term is strictly the Other of law, and law is always the same which the decision escapes. Law is law precisely because it excludes this Other, continually reaffirming the legal by returning its meanings to the institutions of legality. If the decision is an ethical event and if it subsequently becomes inscribed in law, then this mutually exclusive definition of law and morality would mean simply that the law finds itself, or exists as itself, as *law*, only in so far as it can appropriate the ethical event, inscribe its Other into itself, while defining itself *against* that Other. Law and morality are different and separate, but law adopts morality in the very movement by which it excludes it.

On the other hand, although the decision is ethical only in so far as it is *not* motivated by law, the opposite is also true. The ethical event – the decision – is itself conditioned by law because it (as Derrida writes) 'comes into being in a space that exceeds the calculable program that would destroy all responsibility'.[9] The ethical space is reliant for its existence on law because it appears precisely as that excess which is uncontainable by law. At the same time, as I have argued, the law itself is reliant for its own ideational existence on its material realisation: its refusal of an ethical characterisation therefore fails at its own source.

It should be concluded then, that according to the argument I have advanced, just as the decision is never simply inside or outside law but is rather both inside and outside at once, law can never be characterised simply as either exclusive of an ethics or inclusive of it (or even identical with it) because the very movement which would exclude every ethical dimension is predicated upon both an inscription of the ethical moment into law and – prior to that inscription – the decision itself as an ethical event. (It should also be noted that the difficulty of writing about this relationship precisely is symptomatic of the necessary impurity of the terms 'law', 'ethical', 'moral', 'decision'.)

THE END OF LAW

I have written at some length about the beginning of law – about its conceptual origins, reasons and precedents – and so it seems at this stage appropriate to make a few observations about the end of law. Indeed the beginning and the end have been coextensively treated under the general theme of limits, but it is the originating aspect of the limit which I have been emphasising, the crucial point being never to forget that the limit is also always an end.

This coextension of beginning and end can be demonstrated by an argument concerning law, politics, ethics and philosophy in general which – in its application to law – would be stated something like this: the end of the law is the end of the law.[10] This is not (only) a useless tautology, although of course there is one sense in which it *is* (as in a=a). The argument could be expanded in the following manner. The end of the law which is its *telos*, or its underlying rationale (for instance the world view on which it is based) would, if realised, necessitate the end of law. For instance if the end (*telos*) of law were simply that all people should have equal rights in society, and if this aim were realised so that all people actually *did* have equal rights in society, then that would mean that the necessity for law would have vanished. And it is not only the *necessity* for law which would have vanished but also its *possibility* because – as I have explained – the possibility of the theorisation of law is predicated upon the idea of a certain resistance to law (the possibility of transgression) and upon the possibility of the materialisation of law in the decision (which presupposes resistance or conflict regarding the law). So if all people were equal in society and if this were the *only telos* of law, no law could exist because we wouldn't need law and we couldn't conceptualise the need for law. (Something like this is the rationale underlying Marx's argument that the end of the historical dialectic would be the withering away of the state. Perhaps what he didn't realise was that this limit/end/beginning is where necessity and impossibility meet.) Similarly, if the end (*telos*) of philosophy is Truth, and if we attained Truth, then the possibility of philosophy would cease to exist. In fact, Truth would also cease to exist, since it has conceptual value only in so far as it is measured against error or falsity. Though its applications are manifold, the argument is hardly surprising. For an end is an unconditional end only insofar as it implies some sort of perfection or completion (otherwise it is not an end but a means). Thus Aristotle argued that the end (*telos*) of life is happiness or the supreme Good, and that this end is attainable only at the end of life, that is, in death. A happy person must be happy not momentarily, but 'throughout a complete life'. The end of life is the end of life because happiness is 'an *end* in every way final and complete'.[11]

To put the argument in terms of the positivist theorisation of law which I outlined in Chapter 1, we could say the following: the end (*telos*) of the positivist conception of law is, rather than some unidentifiable moral fantasy, the self-determination of law. That is to say that the object of positivist theories is the complete delimitation of law and its separation from non-law. But the mere postulation of this end as attainable would necessitate the end of the theorisation of law because the object (law) would disappear from cognisance: in other words, the determination of the object by theory is one 'non-legal' dimension which positivism can never account for while retaining its object. The end of positivism is the end of positivism. We note here though that the end is the impossibility of law – the *telos* cannot be realised because its realisation is its destruction. Nor can the limit be *known* because in approaching it we merely recognise the undecidability from which it is constituted. The limit is thus never attained. The end of law *would be* the end of law – logically, if reason followed its normal course – but the end of law in which law actually finds itself is the perfect non-realisation of law.

Even in this formulation, the paradox is extremely interesting, but a little further elucidation can expose yet further aspects of its application. *In De Natura Boni*, St Augustine said this:

> ... what is properly called by men corporeal corruption, that is, putrescence itself, if as yet there is anything left to consume, increases by the diminution of the good. But if corruption shall have absolutely consumed it, so that there is no good, no nature will remain, for there will be nothing that corruption may corrupt; and so there will not even be putrescence, for there will be nowhere at all for it to be.[12]

The end (*telos*) of putrescence, in other words, is the end (finish) of putrescence (and of the body). The end of corruption is the end of corruption. Thus, Augustine argues, there is no pain without good – evil is only the negative of good, and God must enshrine the possibility or principle (though not the realisation) of both good and evil. The end (both *telos* and finish) is here the finitude contained in the beginning. (Infinitude is thus also constituted – as excess – out of this play of alpha and omega.) The beginning itself can be conceptualised only on the basis of this finitude or end. The beginning (of law) is the end (of law). (Beginning(s) implies delimitation and therefore end(s).)

The *telos* would therefore appear only as the (suppressed) evaluation of beginning and end running through law.[13]

A cause is an origin, the 'before' of an effect. It is an end or *telos* in the sense in which we believe in or fight for a cause. In both senses it is the reason or condition – without which we would not have an effect, would not fight. It too then, is constituted by its negation or possibility of ending – by the possibility of being 'without' it. The end (finish, effect) of the cause is the end (beginning, *telos*) of the cause. This possibility of 'being without' must also be the very impossibility of the cause – for it cannot *be* (within, itself) *and* be 'without'. The possibility/impossibility of 'being without' is the constitution of the 'being within'.

The end (finish, *telos*) of the cause is the effect. The effect is the end of the cause. The cause no longer obtains when it has turned into effect. (Cause and effect are mutually exterior.) Yet the cause *qua* cause obtains *only* when it has turned into effect. And the effect is only an effect if it has been caused. The effect is the beginning of the cause. The effect is the cause of the cause. And a cause can only be determined as the motivation of an effect. Without an *effect* it cannot be a cause. The cause is the effect of the effect. (Cause and effect are mutually interior.)[14]

What has this to do with the book? As I have indicated, traditionally, the first cause of law is its origin, its unconditioned reason. Its last effect is judicial decision. This, as we have seen, is only one side of the story. The beginning of law is distinction, differentiation, delimitation, and is thus coextensive with its own end. The ends of law – for instance its traditional attempts at closure, and the necessity for decisions to be made – are contained in a finite yet inexplicable and forceful beginning, which is continuously repeated at every stage of legal processes: the freedom of the ethical decision is constituted as a sort of uncontained excess out of this play.

Endnotes

INTRODUCTION

1   (1990) 11 *Cardozo Law Review*.
2   J. Derrida, 'Force de loi: le "fondement mystique de l'autorité"' (1990) 11 *Cardozo Law Review* 919.
3   D. Cornell, 'The Violence of the Masquerade: Law Dressed Up as Justice' (1990) 11 *Cardozo Law Review* 1047.
4   D. Cornell *et al.* (eds) *Deconstruction and the Possibility of Justice* (New York: Routledge, 1992); D. Cornell, *The Philosophy of the Limit* (New York: Routledge, 1991); D. Cornell, *Beyond Accommodation: Ethical Feminism, Deconstruction, and the Law* (New York: Routledge, 1991). See also A. Young and A. Sarat (eds), *Beyond Criticism: Law, Power, Ethics* (1994) 3(3) *Social and Legal Studies*. This special edition contains various articles on the theme of law and ethics.
5   See C. Douzinas and R. Warrington, 'The Face of Justice: A Jurisprudence of Alterity' (1994) 3 *Social and Legal Studies* 405, p. 412. See also D. Cornell, *The Philosophy of the Limit*.
6   Ibid.
7   See also M. Davies, 'Feminist Appropriations: Law, Property, and Personality' (1994) 3 *Social and Legal Studies* 365, p. 369.
8   M. Davies, *Asking the Law Question* (Sydney: Law Book Company, 1994), chs 7 and 8.
9   D. Cornell, *The Philosophy of the Limit*, p. 93.
10 The term is taken from Peter Goodrich, *Reading the Law* (Oxford: Basil Blackwell, 1986) and is explained and used in Chapter 3 of this book.
11 See Chapter 1.
12 D. Cornell, *The Philosophy of the Limit*, p. 93.

CHAPTER 1

1   'This book first arose out of a passage in Borges, out of the laughter that shattered, as I read the passage, all the familiar landmarks of my thought – *our* thought, the thought that bears the stamp of our age and our geography – breaking up all the ordered surfaces and all the planes with which we are accustomed to tame the wild profusion of existing things, and continuing long afterwards to disturb and threaten with collapse our age-old distinction between the Same and the Other. This passage quotes "a certain Chinese encyclopaedia" in which it is written that

"animals are divided into: (a) belonging to the Emperor, (b) embalmed, (c) tame, (d) sucking pigs, (e) sirens, (f) fabulous, (g) stray dogs, (h) included in the present classification, (i) frenzied, (j) innumerable, (k) drawn with a very fine camelhair brush, (l) *et cetera*, (m) having just broken the water pitcher, (n) that from a long way off look like flies". In the wonderment of this taxonomy, the thing we apprehend in one great leap, the thing that, by means of the fable, is demonstrated as the exotic charm of another system of thought, is the limitation of our own, the stark impossibility of thinking *that.*' M. Foucault, *The Order of Things* (London: Tavistock Publications, 1970) p. xv. See generally M. Davies *Asking the Law Question* (Sydney: Law Book Company, 1994), pp. 7–8.

2 See M. Davies, 'Pathfinding: The Way of the Law' (1992) 14 *Oxford Literary Review*, p. 107.

3 In particular, see H. Cixous, 'Sorties' in E. Marks and I. de Courtivron (eds), *New French Feminisms* (Brighton: Harvester Press, 1981), pp. 90–1; and J. Derrida, *Positions* (Chicago: University of Chicago Press, 1981).

4 M. Wittig, 'The Category of Sex' in *The Straight Mind and Other Essays* (London: Harvester, 1992), pp. 1–8.

5 M. Foucault, 'A Preface to Transgression' in D.F. Bouchard (ed.), *Language, Counter-Memory, Practice: Selected Essays and Interviews* (Oxford: Basil Blackwell, 1977), pp. 34–5.

6 See generally, J. Austin, *The Province of Jurisprudence Determined* (London: Weidenfeld and Nicolson, 1954).

7 K. Gray, 'Property in Thin Air' (1991) 50 *Cambridge Law Journal* 252.

8 C. Douzinas, R. Warrington, and S. McVeigh, *Postmodern Jurisprudence: The Law of Text in the Texts of Law* (London: Routledge, 1991), p. 25.

9 H. Kelsen, 'The Pure Theory of Law: It's method and Fundamental Concepts, Part 1' (1934) *Law Quarterly Review* 475, at p. 477.

10 Ibid, p. 477.

11 H. Kelsen, *The Pure Theory of Law* (Berkeley: University of California Press, 1967), p. 71.

12 Ibid, p. 4.

13 This matter will be considered in some detail in Chapter 2.

14 M. Lugones, 'Purity, Impurity, and Separation' (1994) 19 *Signs* 458.

15 Ibid, p. 476.

16 Ibid, p. 463.

17 See Davies, *Asking the Law Question*, Ch. 3.

18 Ibid, pp. 71–5.

19 J. Raz, *The Concept of a Legal System* (Oxford: Oxford University Press, 1970), p. 1.

20 See Douzinas *et al.*, *Postmodern Jurisprudence*, p. 25; N. MacCormick, *Legal Reasoning and Legal Theory* (Oxford: Clarendon, 1978), p. 62.

21 J. Finnis, *Natural Law and Natural Rights* (Oxford: Clarendon Press, 1980), p. 11.

22 Ibid.

23 H.L.A. Hart, *The Concept of Law* (Oxford: Clarendon Press, 1961), pp. 89–95.

24 Finnis, *Natural Law and Natural Rights*, p. 18.

25 Ibid.

26   Ibid, p. 22.

27   Hart, *The Concept of Law*, p. 89.

28   Ibid, p. 90.

29   Hart slips between talking about a single rule of recognition which is the highest rule in a legal system and rules of recognition, an inconsistency which is not entirely accounted for by his discussion of simple and more complex legal systems. One way of explaining the relevant passages would be simply to say that there are various subordinate rules of recognition, and one governing rule.

30   Ibid, p. 107.

31   Ibid, p. 98.

32   Davies, *Asking the Law Question*, p. 80; M. Kramer, *Legal Theory, Political Theory and Deconstruction* (Bloomington: Indiana University Press, 1991), p. 115–24.

33   J. Raz 'Legal Principles and the Limits of Law' (1972) 81 *Yale Law Journal* 823, 842.

34   This is the reason offered by Raz in *The Concept of a Legal System*, p. 200.

35   Raz, 'Legal Principles and the Limits of Law', 851.

36   Raz, *The Concept of a Legal System*.

37   Generally explained in H. Kelsen, 'Nomodynamics' Chs X and XI, *The General Theory of Law and State* (New York: Russell and Russell, 1945), and in 'The Dynamic Aspect of Law', *The Pure Theory of Law*, Part V.

38   Ibid, 115.

39   Ibid, p. 111.

40   H. Kelsen, *General Theory of Norms* (Oxford: Clarendon Press, 1991), p. 256.

41   cf. N. MacCormick, *Legal Reasoning and Legal Theory* (Oxford: Clarendon Press, 1978), pp. 60–2.

42   This is perhaps not unusual: as the boundaries of what constitutes a proper theoretical object for any discipline alter, so too must the boundaries of the discipline.

43   Michael Detmold comments: 'The world is mysterious and difficult to live in, and its difficulties are compounded by the fact that we must live in it with others who can be expected not to see it quite like we do. So we try to make it simpler, more obvious, more settled, and more public. One result of this, the main one, is that we minimize the incidence of hard decisions by making rules, whose logical character is calculated towards simplicity ... This simplification is rightly thought to be important by legal positivists, and they mark this importance by insistence upon the thesis of the limits of law as the limits of that public settlement which people may look to as they set more confidently about their business.' M. Detmold, *The Unity of Law and Morality* (London: Routledge and Kegan Paul, 1984), p. 147.

44   Kelsen, *Pure Theory of Law*, p. 4.

45   MacCormick, *Legal Reasoning and Legal Theory*, Ch. 2. The case used by MacCormick to illustrate his point is *Daniels and Daniels* v. *R. White & Sons and Tabard* (1938) 4 All ER 258.

46   Ibid, 67–8.

47 Ibid, p. 100.
48 Ibid, p. 120.
49 Ibid, p. 233.
50 Ibid, p. 65.
51 Ibid, p. 64.
52 I. Kant, *Critique of Pure Reason* (London: Macmillan, 1929), Transcendental Analytic Book II, A132/B171.
53 Ibid, A138/B177.
54 Detmold, *The Unity of Law and Morality*, p. 147.
55 J. Bentham, *An Introduction to the Principles of Morals and Legislation* (London: Athlone Press, 1970), p. 301.
56 Raz, *The Concept of a Legal System* Ch. 4; Raz 'Legal Principles and the Limits of Law'.
57 Ibid, pp. 831–2.
58 L. Wittgenstein, *Philosophical Investigations* (Oxford: Basil Blackwell, 1958), §47.

CHAPTER 2

1 L. Wittgenstein, *Philosophical Investigations* (Oxford: Basil Blackwell, 1958), §225.
2 H. Kelsen, 'On the Theory of Interpretation' (1990) 10 *Legal Studies* 127, 132.
3 J. Lyotard, *The Differend: Phrases in Dispute* (Manchester: Manchester University Press, 1988), p. xi.
4 Ngaire Naffine has argued that in many rapes there are conflicting realities operating, which are fostered by different cultural conditioning and expectations for women and men. Thus there is a differend between the victim and the offender, which has traditionally been resolved by the law taking the side of the offender. See N. Naffine, 'Possession: Erotic Love and the Law of Rape' (1994) 57 *Modern Law Review* 10.
5 H. Astor 'The Weight of Silence – Talking About Violence in Family Mediation' in M. Thornton (ed.), *Public and Private: Feminist Legal Debates* (Melbourne: Oxford University Press, 1995).
6 E. Laclau and C. Mouffe, 'Post Marxism Without Apologies' in E. Laclau, *New Reflections on the Revolution of Our Time* (London: Verso, 1990), p. 100.
7 J. Derrida, 'Différance' in *Margins of Philosophy* (Brighton: Harvester Press, 1982), p. 9.
8 Frege's condition of a perfect language is that 'every expression grammatically well constructed as a proper name [ie. operating as a noun] shall in fact designate an object': G. Frege, 'Sense and Reference' in P. Geach and M. Black (eds), *Translations from the Philosophical Writings of Gottlob Frege* (Oxford: Basil Blackwell, 1966), p. 70. Ambiguity is eliminated by the fact of direct reference, but such reference can only be hypothesised on the basis of some conceptual identification between the sign and the object.
9 Wittgenstein, *Philosophical Investigations*, §96.

10 S. Kripke, *Wittgenstein on Rules and Private Language* (Oxford: Basil Blackwell, 1982) p. 71.

11 [1932] A.C. 562, 580.

12 D. Hume, *A Treatise of Human Nature* (Harmondsworth: Penguin, 1969) p. 521.

13 See the extracts from Natural Law Party material reproduced in M. Davies, *Asking the Law Question* (Sydney: Law Book Company, 1994), pp. 73–4. The Natural Law Party is a political party which has stood for elections in Australia and the UK, advocating, among other things, the use of transcendental meditation as a cure for the problems of modern society.

14 J. Finnis, *Natural Law and Natural Rights* (Oxford: Clarendon Press, 1980).

15 P. Goodrich, *Languages of Law: From Logics of Memory to Nomadic Masks* (London: Weidenfeld and Nicolson, 1990), p. 117. The Latin phrase in the last sentence is from Coke *Reports* (1777) III, C7b, and means 'in reading, not the words but the truth is to be loved'.

16 W. Blackstone, *Commentaries on the Laws of England*, facsimile of the first edition (1765–69), (Chicago: Chicago University Press, 1979), vol. 1, p. 69.

17 Plowden's addition to his report of *Eyston* v. *Studd* (1574) 2 Plow. 459, 465; 75 E.R. 688, 695, quoted in P. Goodrich, *Reading the Law* (Oxford: Basil Blackwell, 1986).

18 This is not the moment to go into detail about theories of interpretation. The point is that the existence of a distinction between the letter and the spirit assumes a correspondence between the expression of the law and its formal shape.

19 Goodrich, *Languages of Law*, p. 144.

20 F. Cohen, 'Transcendental Nonsense and the Functional Approach' (1935) 35 *Columbia Law Review* 809.

21 Alan Freeman, for instance, writes 'The point of delegitimation is to expose possibilities more truly expressing reality': 'Truth and Mystification in Legal Scholarship' (1981) 90 *Yale Law Journal* 1229, p. 1230.

22 'Whichever device, precedent or legislation, is chosen for the communication of standards of behaviour, these, however smoothly they work over the great mass of ordinary cases, will, at some point where their application is in question, prove indeterminate: they will have what has been termed an open texture. So far we have presented this, in the case of legislation, as a general feature of human language; uncertainty at the borderlines is the price to be paid for the use of general classifying terms in any form of communication concerning matters of fact.' H.L.A. Hart, *The Concept of Law* (Oxford: Clarendon Press, 1961), p. 125.

23 These are 'non-accidental' characteristics of early jurisprudential writings noticed by Gerald Postema in *Bentham and the Common Law Tradition* (Oxford: Oxford University Press, 1986), p. 10.

24 Wittgenstein, *Philosophical Investigations* §85.

25 Kelsen, *The Pure Theory of Law* (Berkeley: University of California Press, 1967), pp. 5–6.

26 Kelsen, *The Pure Theory of Law*, p. 4.

27 Ibid.

28 Ibid, p. 72.
29 M. Heath and N. Naffine, 'Men's Needs and Women's Desires: Feminist Dilemmas about Rape Law Reform' (1994) 3 *Australian Feminist Law Journal* 30.
30 M. Wittig, 'The Category of Sex' in *The Straight Mind and Other Essays* (London: Harvester, 1992).
31 J. Butler, *Bodies That Matter: On the Discursive Limits of Sex* (New York: Routledge, 1993), p. 1.
32 A. Dworkin, *Intercourse* (New York: The Free Press, 1987), p. 150.
33 J. Austin, *The Province of Jurisprudence Determined and the Uses of the Study of Jurisprudence* (London: Weidenfeld and Nicholson, 1954) p. 184; H. Kelsen, 'The Pure Theory of Law: Its method and Fundamental Concepts, Part 1' (1934) *Law Quarterly Review* 475, p. 477; Hume, *A Treatise of Human Nature*, p. 521. See generally Davies, *Asking the Law Question*, pp. 87–90.
34 C. MacKinnon 'Feminism in Legal Education' (1989) 1 *Legal Education Review* 85. See also MacKinnon, *Feminism Unmodified* (Cambridge, Mass.: Harvard University Press, 1987).
35 S. Paulson, 'Kelsen on Legal Interpretation' (1990) 10 *Legal Studies* 136.
36 See generally Kelsen, 'On the Theory of Interpretation'. This article is a relatively recent translation of an early work by Kelsen 'Zur Theorie der Interpretation' (1934).
37 Ibid, pp. 129–30.
38 Ibid, p. 131.
39 Paulson, 'Kelsen on Legal Interpretation' p. 137. Emphasis in original.
40 See the commentary on MacCormick in Chapter 1. 'If understanding in general is to be viewed as the faculty of rules, judgement will be the faculty of subsuming under rules: that is, of distinguishing whether something does or does not stand under a given rule ... General logic contains, and can contain, no rules for judgement.' Kant, *Critique of Pure Reason*, 'Transcendental Analytic' Book II (London: Macmillan, 1929), A132/B171. cf. A138/B177.
41 A. Hutchinson 'Indiana Dworkin and the Temple of Doom' (1987) 96 *Yale Law Journal* 637, pp. 637–8.
42 Michael Detmold is another such theorist.
43 A critique of Dworkin's work on interpretation has been thoroughly undertaken by Stanley Fish, 'Working on the Chain Gang: Interpretation in Law and Literature' (1982) 60 *Texas Law Review* 551; 'Wrong Again' (1983) 62 *Texas Law Review* 229. These articles were written in response to an earlier version of the interpretive theory underlying *Law's Empire*, but – despite the critique offered by Fish – Dworkin continues to make the same mistakes in his later work. See also Sandra Berns, *Concise Jurisprudence* (Sydney: Federation Press, 1993), pp. 53–8.
44 R. Dworkin, *Law's Empire* (London: Fontana, 1986), p. 72.
45 Ibid, pp. 239ff.
46 Ibid, p. 407.
47 Ibid, pp. 407–10. The necessity of 'integrity' in philosophy is a persistent theme which Dworkin sees as connected to judicial integrity.

48   See generally Berns, *Concise Jurisprudence*, pp. 50–1.
49   S. Levinson, 'Law as Literature' (1982) 60 *Texas Law Review* 373, 393.

CHAPTER 3

1   J. Derrida 'Devant la loi' in A. Phillips Griffiths (ed.), *Philosophy and Literature* (Cambridge: Cambridge University Press, 1984), p. 134.
2   I am using the term 'deconstruction' in a more formal sense than is usual. In fact, what I have here called 'demystification' is commonly called 'deconstruction'. This may be the remnants of a Derridean purism on my part. This work in fact began entirely as a deconstruction in which the arguments about power were so deeply embedded as to be nearly useless.
3   P. Goodrich, *Reading the Law* (Oxford: Basil Blackwell, 1986), p. 4.
4   Ibid, p. 5.
5   I. Stewart, 'Closure and the Legal Norm: An Essay in Critique of Law' (1987) 50 *Modern Law Review* 908, p. 908.
6   Ibid, p. 4.
7   cf. M. van de Kerchove and F. Ost, *Le système juridique entre ordre et désordre* (Paris: Presses Universitaires de France, 1988), p. 25.
8   D. Sugarman, 'Legal Theory, the Common Law Mind, and the Making of the Textbook Tradition' in W. Twining (ed.), *Legal Theory and the Common Law* (Oxford: Basil Blackwell, 1986).
9   M. Hale, *The History of the Common Law of England* (Chicago: University of Chicago Press, 1971), p. 3.
10   W. Blackstone, *Commentaries on the Laws of England*. Facsimile of the first edition (1765–69) (Chicago: Chicago University Press, 1979), Vol. I, p. 67. The ambiguity in the term 'goodness' is noted by G. Postema in *Bentham and the Common Law Tradition* (Oxford: Oxford University Press), p. 5.
11   Hale, *History of the Common Law of England*, p. 4.
12   Ibid, p. 40.
13   Blackstone, *Commentaries on the Laws of England*, Vol. I, p. 69; cf. Hale, *History of the Common Law of England*, p. 45; see also Parke B. in *Egerton v. Brownlow* (1853) 4 H.L.C. 1, p. 24; 10 E.R. 359, p. 409; and more recently Garfield Barwick C.J. in *Atlas Tiles* v. *Briers* (1978) 21 A.L.R. 129, p. 134, and *S.G.I.C.* v. *Trigwell* (1978) 26 A.L.R. 67, p. 70.
14   R. Cotterrell, *The Politics of Jurisprudence* (London: Butterworths, 1989), pp. 26–7. See also F. Pocock, *The Ancient Constitution and the Feudal Law* (Cambridge: Cambridge University Press, 1957), pp. 36–7.
15   See generally Pocock, *The Ancient Constitution and the Feudal Law*, p. 36.
16   C. Gray, 'Editor's Introduction' in M. Hale, *The History of the Common Law of England*, p. xxiii.
17   See *Dr Bonham's Case* (1610) 8 Co. Rep. 113b at 118a; 77 E.R. 638 at 652; *Calvin's Case* (1609) 7 Co. Rep. 1a at 14a; 77 E.R. 377 at 393; cf. G. Postema, *Bentham and the Common Law Tradition*, ch. 2.
18   J. Lyotard and J. Thébaud, *Just Gaming* (Manchester: Manchester University Press, 1985), p. 32. cf. Lyotard, *The Differend: Phrases in Dispute* (Manchester:

Manchester University Press, 1988) and *The Postmodern Condition: A Report on Knowledge* (Manchester: Manchester University Press, 1984).

19 Lyotard does not indicate whether the narrators are also sexed, as common law judges were, and still unofficially are.

20 Lyotard and Thébaud, *Just Gaming*, p. 33.

21 Ibid, pp. 33, 34.

22 Lyotard, *The Postmodern Condition*, p. 27.

23 Derrida, 'Devant la loi', p. 132.

24 Kath Hall, 'Starting From Silence – the Future of Feminist Analysis of Corporate Law' (1995) 7(2) *Corporate and Business Law Journal* 149.

25 L. Irigaray, 'Why Define Sexed Rights' in *je, tu, nous* (New York: Routledge, 1993).

26 L. Irigaray, 'The Neglect of Female Genealogies' in *je, tu, nous*, p. 15.

27 L. Irigaray, 'A Personal Note: Equal or Different?' in *je, tu, nous*, p. 12.

28 M. Wittig, *The Straight Mind and Other Essays* (New York: Harvester Wheatsheaf, 1992).

29 The position of the proper name in language is particularly pertinent to the modern 'proper' notion of law. See G. Bennington and J. Derrida, *Jacques Derrida* (Paris: Seuil, 1991), pp. 100–3, 224–5; M. Davies, 'Towards the Common Law: The Limits of Law and the Problem of Translation' (1993) 2 *Asia Pacific Law Review* 65.

30 M. Foucault, *The Archaeology of Knowledge* (London: Tavistock, 1972), p. 25.

31 An empirical critique of the idea of order in law has been undertaken by Charles Sampford in *The Disorder of Law: A Critique of Legal Theory* (Oxford: Basil Blackwell, 1989).

32 J. Salmond, *Jurisprudence* 8th edition by C.A.W. Manning (London: Sweet and Maxwell, 1930), §48, p. 169.

33 L. Wittgenstein, *Philosophical Investigations* (Oxford: Basil Blackwell, 1958), §217.

34 See also A. Ross, 'On Self-Reference and a Puzzle in Constitutional Law' (1969) 78 *Mind* 1. At p. 21 Ross says: 'The chain of reasons and proof must stop somewhere; there must be some foundations (axioms) which are the ultimate basis of all deductions and therefore not themselves demonstrable in the system.'

35 J. Derrida, 'White Mythology' in *Margins of Philosophy* (Brighton: Harvester Press, 1982), p. 219–20.

36 J. Derrida 'Force of Law: The Mystical Foundations of Authority' in D. Cornell *et al.* (eds), *Deconstruction and the Possibility of Justice* (New York: Routledge, 1992), p. 14.

37 Goodrich, *Reading the Law*, pp. 5, 62–3.

38 Derrida, 'Force of Law', p. 14.

39 Ibid.

40 Ibid, p. 31.

41 Parts of this section were originally published in M. Davies, *Asking the Law Question* (Sydney: Law Book Company, 1994), pp. 266–8.

42 J. Raz, 'Legal Principles and the Limits of Law', (1972) 81 *Yale Law Journal*, p. 851.

43 J. Derrida, 'The Law of Genre' (1980) *Glyph 7*, 202.

44 In general, see J. Lyotard, *The Postmodern Condition*.
45 See the opening remarks in a recent article by J. Derrida, 'Onto-Theology of National-Humanism (Prolegomena to a Hypothesis)' (1991) 14 *Oxford Literary Review* 3. Derrida points out here that the existence of different 'philosophical idioms' is both a 'scandal' – because philosophy is supposed to be universal – and the 'chance' which is necessary to philosophical communication.
46 Derrida, 'The Law of Genre', p. 211.
47 Ibid.
48 See also Davies, *Asking the Law Question*, Chapter 1.
49 *Madzimbamuto* v. *Lardner-Burke* [1969] 1 A.C. 645; *The State* v. *Dosso* (1958) P.L.D. 1 S.C. (Pak) 533; *Bhutto* v. *Chief of Army Staff* (1977) P.L.D. 29 S.C. 657.
50 H. Kelsen, *General Theory of Law and State* (Russell and Russell, 1945), p. 116.
51 Ibid, p. 116.
52 G. Hughes, 'Validity and the Basic Norm' (1971) 59 *California Law Review* 695, pp. 699–700; see also J. Stone, 'Mystery and Mystique in the Basic Norm' (1963) 26 *Modern Law Review* 34; T. Honoré, *Making Law Bind* (Oxford: Clarendon Press, 1987), pp. 102–3.
53 Kelsen is relying on the definition of fiction employed by Vaihinger in *The Philosophy of As-If* (London: Routledge and Kegan Paul, 1965); Kelsen quotes Vaihinger who wrote: 'Ideational constructs are in the strict sense of the term real fictions when they are not only in contradiction with reality but self-contradictory'; see H. Kelsen, *General Theory of Norms* (Oxford: Clarendon Press, 1991), p. 256, n. 2.
54 Kelsen's thought has been a controversial method of determining when and how a new regime achieves legitimacy: the cases are particularly interesting for the tension they enact between recognition of legislative supremacy and the power of the courts, and for their appeal to political efficacy or necessity as the final criterion of determining legitimacy: see *The State* v. *Dosso* (1958) P.L.D. 1 S.C. (Pak.) 533; *Madzimbamuto* v. *Lardner-Burke* (1969) 1 A.C. 645; *Mitchell and Others* v. *Director of Public Prosecutions* (1986) L.R.C. (Const) 35.
55 J. Latham, 'Reply to Owen Dixon' (1957) 31 *Australian Law Journal* 253, p. 253.
56 See for instance A.V. Dicey, *Introduction to the Study of the Laws of the Constitution* (London: Macmillan, 1960), p. 39.
57 In fact, according to some theorists, the Queen-in-Parliament is simply identical to the conceptual origin of law: see Winterton 'The British Grundnorm: Parliamentary Supremacy Re-examined' (1976) 92 *Law Quarterly Review* 591.
58 M. Foley, *The Silence of Constitutions: Gaps, 'abeyances', and political temperament in the maintenance of government* (London: Routledge, 1989), pp. 8, 94.
59 Blackstone, *Commentaries on the Laws of England*, vol. I, p. 160.
60 *Madzimbamuto* v. *Lardner-Burke* [1969] 1 A.C. 645 at 723. cf *Edinburgh & Dalkeith Railway Co.* v. *Wauchope* (1842) 8 Cl. & F. 710 at 725; 8 E.R. 279

at 285; and *Pickin* v. *British Railways Board* [1974] A.C. 765 at 786. Lord Reid commented in the latter case (at 782): 'In earlier times many learned lawyers seem to have believed that an Act of Parliament could be disregarded in so far as it was contrary to the law of God or the law of nature or natural justice, but since the supremacy of Parliament was finally demonstrated by the revolution of 1688 any such idea has become obsolete.' The most famous of the pre-revolution opinions was expressed by Coke in *Dr Bonham's Case* (1610) 8 Co. Rep. 113b at 118a; 77 E.R. 638 at 652, and supported by Holt C.J. in *The City of London* v. *Wood* (1702) 12 Mod. 669; 88 E.R. 1592, where it was said that 'an Act of Parliament can do no wrong, though it may do several things that look pretty odd' (at 688; 1602). Though ambiguous, the statement appears to mean that if Parliament does attempt to do wrong it exceeds its powers, whereas if what it does is simply 'pretty odd' the court will uphold it. A much earlier similar view (relating to the powers of the monarch) is expressed by Bracton in *De Legibus et Consuetudinibus Angliae* (London: Her Majesty's Stationery Office, 1879), II, Ch. IX, leaf 107.

61 It must be noted that Lord Reid's comments represent an attempt by the court to limit itself, which it cannot logically do. The doctrine of sovereignty itself is reliant on its articulation in the courts (Foley, *Silence of Constitutions*, p. 94; cf. Winterton, 'The British Grundnorm'. This point will be discussed more fully shortly; see also Chapter 5, n. 14).

62 Moves towards some degree of political union in the European Community will involve a fundamental alteration in the conception of sovereignty applicable to the United Kingdom, suggesting some interesting questions as to how such an alteration can be accommodated by the existing legal doctrines (see S. de Smith and R. Brazier, *Constitutional and Administrative Law* (7th edn) (Middlesex: Penguin, 1994), ch. 4.

63 Raz, *The Concept of a Legal System* (Oxford: Oxford University Press, 1970), p. 10.

64 The contrary view, that Parliament is limited by its treaties of union with Scotland and Ireland, would effectively place it within the category of formally constituted legislatures, theorisation of which is nevertheless subject to the general paradoxes which I outlined in the first section of this chapter, and in the section on Kelsen. Such a view has been expressed in *MacCormick* v. *The Lord Advocate* [1953] S.C. 396, where the Lord President (Cooper) adopted Dicey's later view of sovereignty as absolute yet 'bound by unalterable laws' such as those enshrined in the Treaty of Union (1707). However the question was reduced to one of the court's jurisdiction, in that it was said that the question prior to that concerning the powers of Parliament was whether the court has the capacity to invalidate its legislation: this being answered in the negative, the sense in which Parliament may be said to be bound by unalterable constitutive rules is questionable. See also C.R. Munro, *Studies in Constitutional Law* (London: Butterworths, 1987), ch. 4.

65 For instance to extend its own life, as it did in the Septennial Act (1716), and in the Parliament Act (1911).

66 This is only a brief statement of what is generally known as the paradox
or antinomy of parliamentary sovereignty. P. Fitzgerald generalises it:
'If a rule in a constitution says that all the rules may be amended, does
this apply to the rule itself?' – 'The "Paradox" of Parliamentary Sovereignty'
(1972) 7 *Irish Jurist (new series)* 28, p. 28. For attempts to solve the
paradox see J.L. Mackie, 'Evil and Omnipotence' (1955) 64 *Mind* 200;
Ross, 'On Self-Reference and a Puzzle in Constitutional Law'.

67 Francis Bacon, 'History of King Henry VII' in J. Spedding, Ellis and Heath
(eds), *The Works of Francis Bacon* (1858), p. 160, quoted in A.V. Dicey,
An Introduction to the Study of the Law of Constitution (10th edn) (London:
Macmillan, 1959), pp. 64, 65 n. 2. Fitzgerald comments that one answer
to the problem is that parliament *can* limit itself 'because parliament has'
and cites the Statute of Westminster (1931) as an example of the British
Parliament's self-limitation: 'The "Paradox" of Parliamentary Sovereignty'
p. 28. But this aspect of the Statute has not been tested: the question is
– what would be the constitutional status of an enactment unilaterally
repealing the Statute of Westminster?

68 The situation is more complicated, but still paradoxical, in the case of
a legislature limited by a constitution. See *Attorney General (N.S.W.)* v.
Trethowan [1932] A.C. 526.

69 cf. I. Tammelo, quoted in P. Fitzgerald 'The "Paradox" of Parliamentary
Sovereignty', pp. 32–3 n. 13: 'If Parliament can always pass any law
whatsoever, then Parliament can and cannot pass a law limiting its
lawmaking competence. It can do this because it can pass a law at any
time. It cannot do this because doing this means that Parliament cannot
pass a law at any time.'

70 [1898] A.C. 375.

71 *Practice Statement (Judicial Precedent)* [1966] W.L.R. 1234. Hicks locates a
structurally similar paradox in the doctrine of renvoi in the English conflict
of laws: J.C. Hicks, 'The Liar Paradox in Legal Reasoning' (1971) *Cambridge
Law Journal* 275, pp. 277, and 281–4.

72 Hicks, 'The Liar Paradox in Legal Reasoning', p. 290.

73 cf. R.L. Stone, 'Logic and Law: The Precedence of Precedent' (1967)
Minnesota Law Review 655.

74 If a decision is an 'exclusionary reason' in the sense described by J. Raz
in *Practical Reason and Norms* (Princeton, N.J.: Princeton University Press,
1990), p. 65, then it is effectively a limitation (either absolute or revocable)
on the decision-maker's capacity to reopen the case.

75 R.T.E. Latham, *The Law and The Commonwealth* (Oxford: Oxford University
Press, 1949), p. 523.

76 For a discussion of a similar circularity in Dicey's *Introduction to the Study
of Laws*, see M. Foley, *The Silence of Constitutions*, p. 90.

77 Latham, *The Law and The Commonwealth*, p. 524.

78 As I have indicated, this problem of circularity evident in the analysis
of parliamentary sovereignty is also the basis of Hart's notion of the rule
of recognition: the officials who recognise it must already be officials if
they are to recognise anything.

79 For a recent discussion of constitutional 'abeyances' or silences specifically as a necessary dimension in establishing the legitimacy of a constitutional system, see Foley, *The Silence of Constitutions*.

INTERLUDE

1 S. Kierkegaard, *Repetition: An Essay in Experimental Psychology* (Harper and Row, 1941), p. 134.

2 The term 'arrogant perception' is from Marilyn Frye, *The Politics of Reality: Essays in Feminist Theory* (Trumansburg, N.Y.: Crossing Press, 1983). It has been taken up and used in a compelling way by María Lugones in 'Playfulness, "World"-Travelling, and Loving Perception' (1987) 2 *Hypatia* 3. My reflections about perception are strongly influenced by this article.

3 See D. Cornell 'Violence of the Masquerade: Law Dressed Up as Justice' in Cornell, *The Philosophy of the Limit* (New York: Routledge, 1991), p. 157.

4 J. Derrida 'Force of Law: The Mystical Foundation of Authority' in Cornell *et al.* (eds) *Deconstruction and the Possibility of Justice* (New York: Routledge, 1992); Cornell, 'Violence of the Masquerade: Law Dressed Up as Justice' in Cornell, *The Philosophy of the Limit*.

5 See M. Kramer, *Legal Theory, Political Theory and Deconstruction: Against Rhadamanthus* (Bloomington: Indiana University Press, 1991), pp. 120–1.

6 J. Raz, *Practical Reason and Norms* (Princeton, N.J.: Princeton University Press, 1990), p. 67.

7 The pages on Descartes were excluded from *Histoire de la folie*, where Foucault wrote in summary of the Cartesian exclusion 'moi qui pense, je ne peux pas être fou' (I who am thinking cannot be mad): madness is excluded from the possibility of thinking, from which the cogito emanates. See M. Foucault, *Histoire de la folie à l'âge classique* (Paris: Gallimard, 1972), p. 57.

8 J. Derrida 'Force and Signification' in *Writing and Difference* (London: Routledge and Kegan Paul, 1978), p. 38.

9 Ibid.

10 See the comments made by George Schwab in his Introduction to *Political Theology: Four chapters on the Concept of Sovereignty* (Cambridge: Massachusetts Institute of Technology Press, 1985), p. xiii. See also G. Schwab, *The Challenge of the Exception* (Duncker and Humblot, 1970), pp. 101–7; P. Piccone and G.L. Ulmen, 'Introduction to Carl Schmitt' (1987) 72 *Telos* 3.

11 C. Schmitt, *Political Theology* (Cambridge: Massachusetts Institute of Technology Press, 1985), p. 36; cf. P. Hirst, 'Carl Schmitt's Decisionism' (1987) 72 *Telos* 15.

12 Schmitt, *Political Theology*, p. 5.

13 Ibid, p. 10. In *The Concept of the Political* (New Jersey: Rutgers University Press, 1976), p. 45, Schmitt gives as an instance of such a sovereign decision on the exception the decision of whether another state is a friend or an enemy. cf. Schwab, *The Challenge of the Exception*, pp. 51–5; and G. Hegel,

The Philosophy of Right (Oxford: Clarendon Press, 1942), §324 and addition.

14 Hegel, *The Philosophy of Right*, §275.
15 This phrase is taken by Nancy from the addition to §158 of *The Philosophy of Right*, where Hegel describes love as a 'tremendous contradiction'. See J.L. Nancy, 'The Jurisdiction of the Hegelian Monarch' (1982) 49 *Social Research* 481, esp. pp. 503ff.
16 Ibid, p. 504.
17 Ibid.
18 Ibid, p. 505.
19 Ibid, p. 510.
20 Ibid.

CHAPTER 4

1   S. Kierkegaard, *Repetition: An Essay in Experimental Psychology* (Harper and Row, 1941), pp. 52–3.
2   J. Derrida, *Dissemination* (London: Athlone Press, 1981), p. 123.
3   Ibid.
4   J. Butler, *Gender Trouble: Feminism and the Subversion of Identity* (New York: Routledge, 1990), pp. 142–9.
5   See also G. Spivak, 'Feminism and deconstruction, again: negotiating with unacknowledged masculinism' in T. Brennan (ed.), *Betweeen feminism and psychoanalysis* (London: Routledge, 1989); and J. Butler, *Bodies That Matter: on the discursive limits of 'sex'* (New York: Routledge, 1983), Chapter 1.
6   M. Whitford, *Luce Irigaray: Philosophy in the Feminine* (London: Routledge, 1991), p. 104.
7   Rodolphe Gasché writes: 'To characterise a thinker's work as breaking with the entire tradition is quite a traditional mode of thought. Moreover, such a break with tradition and traditionalism is in the best tradition of philosophical thought.' In *Inventions of Difference: On Jacques Derrida* (Cambridge, Mass.: Harvard University Press, 1994), p. 59.
8   I have qualified 'philosophy' in this case because by definition such a style of thinking would not be within what we currently think of as philosophy, but radically other to it, if such a place can be imagined.
9   L. Irigaray, *This Sex Which Is Not One* (Ithaca, N.Y.: Cornell University Press, 1985), p. 74.
10 Ibid.
11 See M. Lugones, 'Purity, Impurity, and Separation' (1994) 19 *Signs* 458.
12 See Whitford, *Luce Irigaray*, p. 104. Irigaray, *This Sex Which Is Not One* , pp. 192ff.
13 Ibid.
14 J. Derrida, 'Limited Inc abc … ' (1977) *Glyph 2*, 162, p. 190.
15 Ibid.
16 Kierkegaard, *Repetition*, p. 53.
17 In D. Cornell *et al.*, *Deconstruction and the Possibility of Justice* (New York: Routledge, 1992), p. 23.

18 Ibid, p. 27.
19 Whitford, *Luce Irigaray*, p. 104.
20 See M. Davies, 'The Heterosexual Economy' (1995) 5 *Australian Feminist Law Journal*. Irigaray goes so far as to say that heterosexuality is only a mask or alibi for the homosexual economy: it is the social representation of sexuality or the closely confined construction of sexual difference, which takes place only within the realm of the same. See L. Irigaray, 'Commodities Among Themselves' in *This Sex Which Is Not One*.
21 Spivak 'Feminism and deconstruction, again', p. 220.
22 Irigaray 'Commodities Among Themselves', p. 196.
23 H. Kelsen, *General Theory of Law and State* (New York: Russell and Russell, 1945), p. 39. In *The Pure Theory of Law* (Berkeley: University of California Press, 1967), Kelsen offers a different explanation of the distinction, which I am not considering here because it is the dynamic aspect or system which is interesting here, and his explanation of it remains largely the same in each work. See also M. van der Kerchove and F. Ost, *Le système juridique entre ordre et désordre* (Paris: Presses Universitaires de France, 1988), pp. 54–66.
24 Kelsen, *General Theory of Law and State*, p. 133. cf. *The Pure Theory of Law*, p. 234.
25 Kelsen, *General Theory of Law and State*, p. 39.
26 Matthew Kramer argues a similar proposition with respect to Hart, in particular that Hart's emphasis on positive norms ends by 'overwhelming all normativity with factuality': Kramer, 'The Rule of Misrecognition in the Hart of Jurisprudence' (1988) 8 *Oxford Journal of Legal Studies* 401, p. 432.
27 Kelsen, *Pure Theory of Law*, p. 233.
28 Ibid, p. 234.
29 Joseph Raz argues that the basic norm is not created by being presupposed. Certainly the presupposition does not *determine* the basic norm, but it is the precondition, and has an undeniably creative function, in so far as it constitutes the ideational condition under which a norm may be recognised as a legal norm. See Raz, *The Concept of a Legal System* (Oxford: Oxford University Press, 1970), p. 65.
30 Kelsen, *Pure Theory of Law*, p. 234.
31 In this respect also Matthew Kramer makes a complementary argument about the basis of Hart's rule of recognition, that is, that it is founded within an in/ought undecidability. Kramer 'The Rule of Misrecognition in the Hart of Jurisprudence', pp. 429–33.
32 H. Kelsen, *General Theory of Norms* (Oxford: Clarendon Press, 1991), p. 256.
33 To extrapolate (transgressing perhaps the 'proper' character of my philosophical brief?), like other relationships held in place by repeated violence, we often tend to regard as normal our subordination to legal violence.
34 R. Dworkin, *Taking Rights Seriously* (London: Duckworth, 1977), Chs 1–4.

35   N. MacCormick, *Legal Reasoning and Legal Theory* (Oxford: Clarendon Press, 1978) Ch. 9; J. Raz, 'Legal Principles and the Limits of Law' (1972) 81 *Yale Law Review* 823.
36   E. Weinrib, 'Legal Formalism: On the Immanent Rationality of Law' (1988) 97 *Yale Law Journal* 949. See also F. Schauer, 'Formalism' (1988) 97 *Yale Law Journal* 509.
37   MacCormick makes the point that rule cases and hard cases are not absolutely distinguishable because there 'is a spectrum which ranges from the obviously simple to the highly contestable'; *Legal Reasoning and Legal Theory*, p. 198. The difference, if there is one, is certainly one of degree, but to leave the matter there only reinforces the idea of law's essential sameness, whereas its internal difference from itself is a vital element of law's practical (decisive, repetitive) orientation.

CHAPTER 5

1   J. Stone, 'The Ratio of the Ratio Decidendi' (1959) 22 *Modern Law Review* 597.
2   Jean-Luc Nancy writes: 'En disant le droit, le *judex* dit toujours *à la fois* que la réalité du cas est dans le droit *et* que son dire fictionne ou figure cet être du cas': 'In pronouncing the law, the *judge* always says *at the same time* that the reality of the case is within the law, *and* that her/his word fictions or figures that being of the case': *L'Impératif Catégorique* (Paris: Flammarion, 1983), p. 42.
3   My title is from Stone, 'The Ratio of the Ratio Decidendi'.
4   Ibid, p. 599.
5   Taking on board the temporal complexities this is a presupposition which I don't think anyone would want to deny: neither the Realists nor the Critical Legal Scholars have made total arbitrariness part of their theoretical perspectives, but have argued instead that so-called 'legal' reasons are in fact political, economic or sociological. See, for instance, D. Kairys, 'Legal Reasoning' in D. Kairys (ed.) *The Politics of Law* (New York: Pantheon Books, 1982).
6   N. MacCormick, *Legal Reasoning and Legal Theory* (Oxford: Clarendon Press, 1978), p. 215; A. Goodhart, *Essays in Jurisprudence and the Common Law* (Cambridge: Cambridge University Press, 1931), pp. 10–26; R. Cross, *Precedent in English Law* (Oxford: Clarendon Press, 1977), Ch. 2.
7   Goodhart, *Essays in Jurisprudence and the Common Law*, pp. 10–26. cf A. Goodhart, 'The Ratio Decidendi of a Case' (1959) 22 *Modern Law Review* 117.
8   J. Stone, *Precedent and Law: The Dynamics of Common Law Growth* (London: Butterworths, 1985), p. 125.
9   Stone, 'The Ratio of the Ratio Decidendi'.
10   Ibid, p. 616.
11   R. Dworkin, 'Law as Interpretation' (1982) 60 *Texas Law Review* 527; S. Fish, 'Working on the Chain Gang: Interpretation in Law and Literature' (1982) 60 *Texas Law Review* 551; S. Fish, 'Wrong Again' (1983) 62 *Texas Law Review* 229.

12 Stone, *Precedent and Law: The Dynamics of Common Law Growth*, p. 57.
13 N. MacCormick, 'Why Cases Have Rationes and What These Are' in L. Goldstein (ed.) *Precedent in Law* (Oxford: Clarendon Press, 1987); MacCormick, *Legal Reasoning and Legal Theory*, Ch. 4.
14 [1932] A.C. 562. I feel that, like the Bible, this case should need no citation.
15 [1936] A.C. 85.
16 See the quotation from Stone at the head of this chapter.
17 See J. Butler, *Gender Trouble: Feminism and the Subversion of Identity* (New York: Routledge, 1990) and *Bodies That Matter: on the discursive limits of 'sex'* (New York: Routledge, 1993).
18 J. Derrida 'Limited Inc. abc ...' (1977) *Glyph* 2, 162, pp. 231–4.
19 P. Fitzpatrick, *The Mythology of Modern Law* (London: Routledge, 1992).
20 See R. Cross, *Evidence* (7th edition by Colin Tapper, London: Butterworths, 1990), p. 1. J.L. Montrose wrote 'Relevancy is a relative term; evidence is not just relevant "in the air", it is relevant to some fact'; 'Basic Concepts of the Law of Evidence' (1954) 70 *Law Quarterly Review* 527.
21 Hart writes: 'Fact situations do not come to us neatly labelled, creased and folded, nor is their legal classification written on them to be simply read off by the judge. Instead, in applying legal rules, someone must take the responsibility of deciding'; 'Positivism and the Separation of Law and Morals' (1958) 71 *Harvard Law Review* 593, p. 607. Yet in arguing that there are standard cases which anyone will recognise, Hart returns to the uncritical position of there being a natural and pre-interpretive meaning unmediated by any decision. The issue is not whether there are standard cases, but rather by what political exclusions they got to be standard.
22 E. Husserl, *Cartesian Meditations: An Introduction to Phenomenology* (Dordrecht: Martinus Nijhoff, 1960), §6, p. 15.
23 A similar point is made by Howard Caygill in discussing the distinction in early modern philosophy between 'invention' and 'judgement': 'Invention produces the objects of perception which are to be ordered by judgement. However, the difference between the two is nominal, since bringing forth objects in invention presupposes an ordering principle in judgement.' *The Art of Judgement* (Oxford: Basil Blackwell, 1989), p. 16.
24 Phipson writes that 'relevance [is] ... founded upon logic and human experience, and admissibility on law', implying that relevance is determinable as a natural relationship between the evidence and the fact which is to be proved. However, even this most common-sensical understanding of the evidence necessarily involves a reflective, judgmental exclusion, and insofar as it is 'never submitted to discussion', dogmatic. See M. Howard, P. Crane and D. Hotchberg (eds), *Phipson on Evidence* (London: Sweet & Maxwell, 1990) 14th edition, p. 110.
25 Derrida, 'Limited Inc. abc ...', p. 234.
26 J. Derrida, 'The Double Session' in *Dissemination* (London: Athlone Press, 1980), p. 191.
27 Ibid, p. 192.
28 Sir Philip Sidney, *An Apology for Poetry* (London: Nelson, 1965).

29   Derrida, 'The Double Session', p. 193.
30   Ibid.
31   Ibid, p. 194.
32   Ibid, pp. 194 and 206.
33   Ibid, p. 206.
34   Ibid, p. 207.
35   M. Detmold, *The Unity of Law and Morality* (London: Routledge and Kegan Paul, 1984), p. 175.
36   Judge Bridlegoose, Rabelais, *The Histories of Gargantua and Pantagruel* (Middlesex: Penguin, 1955), Ch. 39, p. 398.
37   D. Cornell, *The Philosophy of the Limit* (New York: Routledge, 1992), p. 157.
38   Ibid, p. 169.
39   In 'Plato's Pharmacy' Derrida explains this structure in relation to the game of Platonism: 'It is part of the rules of this game that the game should *seem to stop*. Then the *pharmakon* [a pre-truth undecidable] which is older than either of the opposites is "caught" by philosophy, by "Platonism" which is constituted by this apprehension', in *Dissemination*, p. 128

CONCLUSION

1   C. Potok, *Davita's Harp* (Ringwood, Vic.: Penguin, 1985), p. 326.
2   J. Kristeva, 'The System and the Speaking Subject' in T. Moi (ed.), *The Kristeva Reader* (Oxford: Basil Blackwell, 1986), p. 29.
3   M. Foucault, *Discipline and Punish: The Birth of the Prison* (Harmondsworth: Allen Lane, 1977), pp. 34–5.
4   R. Gasché, 'The Law of Tradition' in *Inventions of Difference: On Jacques Derrida* (Cambridge, Mass.: Harvard University Press, 1994), p. 59.
5   As described by J. Raz in *Practical Reason and Norms* (Princeton, N.J.: Princeton University Press, 1990), p. 166
6   M. Detmold, *The Unity of Law and Morality* (London: Routledge and Kegan Paul, 1984) pp. 217–22.
7   Ibid.
8   J. Derrida, *Limited Inc.* (Michigan: Northwestern University Press, 1988), p. 116.
9   Ibid.
10 I am indebted to Professor Geoffrey Bennington for the formulation of this argument on several occasions and relating to matters which far exceed my present narrow concerns. The argument is reproduced in Bennington, 'Postal Politics and the Institution of the Nation' in H.K. Bhabha (ed.) *Nation and Narration* (London, New York: Routledge, 1990), p. 128.
11 Aristotle, *Ethics* (Middlesex: Penguin, 1955), Book I, x: 1101a, p. 84.
12 St Augustine, 'Concerning the Nature of Good' in W. Oates (ed.) *Basic Writings of St Augustine* (Random House, 1948), Ch. 20.
13 Similarly if the 'end' of 'unalienated relatedness' proposed some time ago by Peter Gabel, or Felix Cohen's dream of a law reflecting reality were attained that would mean the end of law: it would be superfluous and indistinguishable from 'reality'. See D. Kennedy and P. Gabel, 'Roll Over

Beethoven' (1984) 36 *Stanford Law Review* 1, and Felix Cohen, 'Transcendental Nonsense and the Functional Approach' (1935) *Columbia Law Review* 809. As H. Kelsen said, reality 'can be in conformity or conflict with the law only if [it] is not identical with the validity of the law': *Pure Theory of Law* (Berkeley: University of California Press, 1967), p. 213. The same argument applies here: law theorised without some resistance or alienation from reality would not be law, it would just be 'reality'.

14 These paradoxical relations of causality are described by Hegel in the 'shorter' *Logic* and in *The Science of Logic*. For instance in the former he writes 'it is in the effect that the cause first becomes actual and a cause' (§153); 'we then turn the matter round and define the cause also as something dependent or as an effect' (ibid); 'the effect, looked at in its identity with the cause, is itself defined as a cause' (ibid): W. Wallace, (trans.) *Hegel's Logic* (Oxford: Clarendon Press, 1975), pp. 215–17; cf. Hegel, *The Science of Logic* (Humanities Press, 1969), Vol. I, Bk. II, Section 3, Ch. 3, B – 'The Relation of Causality', p. 558.

Bibliography

Aristotle, *Ethics* (Middlesex: Penguin, 1955)

Astor, H. 'The Weight of Silence – Talking About Violence in Family Mediation' in M. Thornton (ed.) *Public and Private: Feminist Legal Debates* (Melbourne: Oxford University Press, 1995)

Austin, J. *The Province of Jurisprudence Determined* (London: Weidenfeld and Nicolson, 1954)

Bennington, G. 'Postal Politics and the Institution of the Nation' in H.K. Bhabha (ed.) *Nation and Narration* (London, New York: Routledge, 1990)

Bennington, G. and J. Derrida, *Jacques Derrida* (Paris: Seuil, 1991)

Bentham, J. *An Introduction to the Principles of Morals and Legislation* (London: Athlone Press, 1970)

Berns, S. *Concise Jurisprudence* (Sydney: Federation Press, 1993)

Blackstone, W. *Commentaries On the Laws of England*. Facsimile of the First Edition (1765–1769) (Chicago: Chicago University Press, 1979)

Bracton, H. *De Legibus et Consuetudinibus Angliae* (London: Her Majesty's Stationery Office, 1879)

Butler, J. *Bodies That Matter: On the Discursive Limits of Sex* (New York: Routledge, 1993)

Butler, J. *Gender Trouble: Feminism and the Subversion of Identity* (New York: Routledge, 1990)

Caygill, H. *The Art of Judgement* (Oxford: Basil Blackwell, 1989)

Cixous, H. 'Sorties' in E. Marks and I. de Courtivron (eds), *New French Feminisms* (Brighton: Harvester Press, 1981)

Cohen, F. 'Transcendental Nonsense and the Functional Approach' (1935) 35 *Columbia Law Review* 809.

Cornell, D. 'The Violence of the Masquerade: Law Dressed Up as Justice' (1990) 11 *Cardozo Law Review* 1047.

Cornell, D. *Beyond Accommodation: Ethical Feminism, Deconstruction, and the Law* (New York: Routledge, 1991)

Cornell, D. *et al.* (eds) *Deconstruction and the Possibility of Justice* (New York: Routledge, 1992)

Cornell, D. *The Philosophy of the Limit* (New York: Routledge, 1992)

Cotterrell, R. *The Politics of Jurisprudence* (London: Butterworths, 1989)

Cross, R. *Evidence*, 7th edition by Colin Tapper (London: Butterworths, 1990)

Cross, R. *Precedent in English Law* (Oxford: Clarendon Press, 1977)

Davies, M. 'Feminist Appropriations: Law, Property, and Personality' (1994) 3 *Social and Legal Studies* 365

Davies, M. 'Pathfinding: The Way of the Law' (1992) 14 *Oxford Literary Review* 107

Davies, M. 'The Heterosexual Economy' (1995) 5 *Australian Feminist Law Journal*. 27

Davies, M. 'Towards the Common Law: The Limits of Law and the Problem of Translation' (1993) 2 *Asia Pacific Law Review* 65

Davies, M. *Asking the Law Question* (Sydney: Law Book Company, 1994)

Derrida, J. 'Devant la loi' in A. Phillips Griffiths (ed.) *Philosophy and Literature* (Cambridge: Cambridge University Press, 1984)

Derrida, J. 'Force de loi: le "fondement mystique de l'autorité"' (1990) 11 *Cardozo Law Review* 919.

Derrida, J. 'Force of Law: The Mystical Foundations of Authority' in Cornell *et al.* (eds) *Deconstruction and the Possibility of Justice* (New York: Routledge, 1992)

Derrida, J. 'Limited Inc. abc ... ' (1977) *Glyph 2*, 162

Derrida, J. 'Onto-Theology of National-Humanism (Prolegomena to a Hypothesis)' (1991) 14 *Oxford Literary Review* 3

Derrida, J. 'The Law of Genre' (1980) *Glyph 7*, 202

Derrida, J. *Dissemination* (London: Athlone Press, 1980)

Derrida, J. *Limited Inc.* (Northwestern University Press, 1988)

Derrida, J. *Margins of Philosophy* (Brighton: Harvester Press, 1982)

Derrida, J. *Positions* (Chicago: University of Chicago Press, 1981)

Derrida, J.*Writing and Difference* (London: Routledge and Kegan Paul, 1978)

De Smith, S. and R. Brazier *Constitutional and Administrative Law*, 7th edition (Middlesex: Penguin, 1994)

Detmold, M. *The Unity of Law and Morality* (London: Routledge and Kegan Paul, 1984)

Dicey, A.V. *Introduction to the Study of the Law of the Constitution*, 10th edition (London: Macmillan, 1959)

Douzinas, C. and R. Warrington, 'The Face of Justice: A Jurisprudence of Alterity' (1994) 3 *Social and Legal Studies* 405

Douzinas, C., R. Warrington and S. McVeigh, *Postmodern Jurisprudence: The Law of Text in the Texts of Law* (London: Routledge, 1991)

Dworkin, A. *Intercourse* (New York: The Free Press, 1987)

Dworkin, R. 'Law as Interpretation' (1982) 60 *Texas Law Review* 527

Dworkin, R. *Law's Empire* (London: Fontana, 1986)

Dworkin, R. *Taking Rights Seriously* (London: Duckworth, 1977)

Finnis, J. *Natural Law and Natural Rights* (Oxford: Clarendon Press, 1980)

Fish, S. 'Working on the Chain Gang: Interpretation in Law and Literature' (1982) 60 *Texas Law Review* 551

Fish, S. 'Wrong Again' (1983) 62 *Texas Law Review* 229

Fitzgerald, P. 'The "Paradox" of Parliamentary Sovereignty' (1972) 7 *Irish Jurist (new series)* 28

Fitzpatrick, P. *The Mythology of Modern Law* (London: Routledge, 1992).

Foley, M. *The Silence of Constitutions: Gaps, 'abeyances', and political temperament in the maintenance of government* (London: Routledge, 1989)

Foucault, M. 'A Preface to Transgression' in D.F. Bouchard (ed.), *Language, Counter-Memory, Practice: Selected Essays and Interviews* (Oxford: Basil Blackwell, 1977)

Foucault, M. *Discipline and Punish: The Birth of the Prison* (Allen Lane, 1977)

Foucault, M. *Histoire de la folie à l'âge classique* (Paris: Gallimard, 1972)
Foucault, M. *The Archaeology of Knowledge* (London: Tavistock, 1972)
Foucault, M. *The Order of Things* (London: Tavistock Publications, 1970)
Freeman, A. 'Truth and Mystification in Legal Scholarship' (1981) 90 *Yale Law Journal* 1229, p. 1230
Frege, G. 'Sense and Reference' in P. Geach and M. Black (eds) *Translations from the Philosophical Writings of Gottlob Frege* (Oxford: Basil Blackwell, 1966)
Frye, M. *The Politics of Reality: Essays in Feminist Theory* (Trumansberg, N.Y.: Crossing Press, 1983)
Gasché, R. *Inventions of Difference: On Jaques Derrida* (Cambridge, Mass.: Harvard University Press, 1994)
Goodhart, A. 'The Ratio Decidendi of a Case' (1959) 22 *Modern Law Review* 117
Goodhart, A. *Essays in Jurisprudence and the Common Law* (Cambridge: Cambridge University Press, 1931)
Goodrich, P. *Languages of Law: From Logics of Memory to Nomadic Masks* (London: Weidenfeld and Nicolson, 1990)
Goodrich, P. *Reading the Law* (Oxford: Basil Blackwell, 1986)
Gray, C. 'Editor's Introduction' in M. Hale, *The History of the Common Law of England*, (Chicago: Chicago University Press, 1971)
Gray, K. 'Property in Thin Air' (1991) 50 *Cambridge Law Journal* 252
Hale, M. *The History of the Common Law of England* (Chicago: Chicago University Press)
Hall, K. 'Starting From Silence – the Future of Feminist Analysis of Corporate Law' (1995) 7(2) *Corporate and Business Law Journal* 149
Hart, H.L.A. 'Positivism and the Separation of Law and Morals' (1958) 71 *Harvard Law Review* 593
Hart, H.L.A. *The Concept of Law* (Oxford: Clarendon Press, 1961)
Heath, M. and N. Naffine 'Men's Needs and Women's Desires: Feminist Dilemmas About Rape Law Reform' (1994) *Australian Feminist Law Journal* 30
Hegel, G.W.F. 'The Shorter Logic' in W. Wallace (trans.) *Hegel's Logic* (Oxford: Clarendon Press, 1975)
Hegel, G.W.F. *The Philosophy of Right* (Oxford: Clarendon Press, 1942)
Hegel, G.W.F. *The Science of Logic* (Humanities Press, 1969)
Hicks, J.C. 'The Liar Paradox in Legal Reasoning' (1971) *Cambridge Law Journal* 275
Hirst, P. 'Carl Schmitt's Decisionism' (1987) 72 *Telos* 15
Honoré, T. *Making Law Bind* (Oxford: Clarendon Press, 1987)
Howard, M., P. Crane and D. Hotchberg (eds) *Phipson on Evidence*, 14th edition (London: Sweet & Maxwell, 1990)
Hughes, G. 'Validity and the Basic Norm' (1971) 59 *California Law Review* 695
Hume, D. *A Treatise of Human Nature* (Middlesex: Penguin, 1969)
Husserl, E. *Cartesian Meditations: An Introduction to Phenomenology* (Dordrecht: Martinus Nijhoff, 1960)
Hutchinson, A. 'Indiana Dworkin and the Temple of Doom' (1987) 96 *Yale Law Journal* 637

Irigaray, L. *je, tu, nous* (New York: Routledge, 1993)
Irigaray, L. *This Sex Which Is Not One* (Ithaca, N.Y.: Cornell University Press, 1985)
Kairys, D. 'Legal Reasoning' in D. Kairys (ed.) *The Politics of Law* (Pantheon Books, 1982)
Kant, I. *Critique of Pure Reason* (London: Macmillan, 1929)
Kelsen, H. 'On the Theory of Interpretation' (1990) 10 *Legal Studies* 127
Kelsen, H. 'The Pure Theory of Law: It's Method and Fundamental Concepts, Part 1' (1934) *Law Quarterly Review* 475
Kelsen, H. *General Theory of Norms* (Oxford: Clarendon Press, 1991)
Kelsen, H. *The General Theory of Law and State* (New York: Russell and Russell, 1945)
Kelsen, H. *The Pure Theory of Law* (Berkeley: University of California Press, 1967)
Kennedy, D. and P. Gabel, 'Roll Over Beethoven' (1984) 36 *Stanford Law Review* 1
Kierkegaard, S. *Repetition: An Essay in Experimental Psychology* (New York: Harper and Rowe, 1941)
Kramer, M. 'The Rule of Misrecognition in the Hart of Jurisprudence' (1988) 8 *Oxford Journal of Legal Studies* 401
Kramer, M. *Legal Theory, Political Theory and Deconstruction: Against Rhadamanthus* (Bloomington: Indiana University Press, 1991)
Kripke, S. *Wittgenstein on Rules and Private Language* (Oxford: Basil Blackwell, 1982)
Kristeva, J. 'The System and the Speaking Subject' in T. Moi (ed.) *The Kristeva Reader* (Oxford: Basil Blackwell, 1986)
Laclau, E. and C. Mouffe 'Post Marxism Without Apologies' in E. Laclau, *New Reflections on the Revolution of Our Time* (London: Verso, 1990)
Latham, J. 'Reply to Owen Dixon' (1957) 31 *Australian Law Journal* 253
Latham, R.T.E. *The Law and The Commonwealth* (Oxford: Oxford University Press, 1949)
Levinson, S. 'Law as Literature' (1982) 60 *Texas Law Review* 373
Lugones, M. 'Purity, Impurity, and Separation' (1994) 19 *Signs* 458
Lugones, M. in 'Playfulness, "World"-Travelling, and Loving Perception' (1987) 2 *Hypatia* 3
Lyotard, J.-F. and J. Thébaud, *Just Gaming* (Manchester: Manchester University Press, 1985)
Lyotard, J.-F. *The Differend: Phrases in Dispute* (Manchester: Manchester University Press, 1988)
Lyotard, J.-F. *The Postmodern Condition: A Report on Knowledge* (Manchester: Manchester University Press, 1984)
MacCormick, N. 'Why Cases Have Rationes and What These Are' in L. Goldstein (ed.) *Precedent in Law* (Oxford: Clarendon Press, 1987)
MacCormick, N. *Legal Reasoning and Legal Theory* (Oxford: Clarendon, 1978)
Mackie, J.L. 'Evil and Omnipotence' (1955) 64 *Mind* 200
MacKinnon, C. 'Feminism in Legal Education' (1989) 1 *Legal Education Review* 85

MacKinnon, C. *Feminism Unmodified* (Cambridge, Mass.: Harvard University Press, 1987)

Montrose, J.L. 'Basic Concepts of the Law of Evidence' (1954) 70 *Law Quarterly Review* 527

Munro, C.R. *Studies in Constitutional Law* (London: Butterworths, 1987)

Naffine, N. 'Possession: Erotic Love and the Law of Rape' (1994) 57 *Modern Law Review* 10

Nancy, J.-L. 'The Jurisdiction of the Hegelian Monarch' (1982) 49 *Social Research* 481

Nancy, J.-L. *L'Impératif Catégorique* (Paris: Flammarion, 1983)

Paulson, S. 'Kelsen on Legal Interpretation' (1990) 10 *Legal Studies* 136

Piccone, P. and G.L. Ulmen, 'Introduction to Carl Schmitt' (1987) 72 *Telos* 3

Pocock, F. *The Ancient Constitution and the Feudal Law* (Cambridge: Cambridge University Press, 1957)

Postema, G. *Bentham and the Common Law Tradition* (Oxford: Oxford University Press, 1986)

Potok, C. *Davita's Harp* (Ringwood, Vic.: Penguin, 1985)

Rabelais, *The Histories of Gargantua and Pantagruel* (Middlesex: Penguin, 1955)

Raz, J. 'Legal Principles and the Limits of Law' (1972) 81 *Yale Law Journal* 823

Raz, J. *The Concept of a Legal System* (Oxford: Oxford University Press, 1970)

Raz, J. *Practical Reason and Norms* (New Jersey: Princeton University Press, 1990)

Ross, A. 'On Self-Reference and a Puzzle in Constitutional Law' (1969) 78 *Mind* 1

Salmond, J. *Jurisprudence*, 8th edition by C.A.W. Manning (London: Sweet and Maxwell, 1930)

Sampford, C. *The Disorder of Law: A Critique of Legal Theory* (Oxford: Basil Blackwell, 1989)

Schauer, F. 'Formalism' (1988) 97 *Yale Law Journal* 509

Schmitt, C. *Political Theology* (Cambridge, Mass.: Massachusetts Institute of Technology Press, 1985)

Schmitt, C. *The Concept of the Political* (New Brunswick, N.J.: Rutgers University Press, 1976)

Schwab, G. 'Introduction' in C. Schmitt, *Political Theology: Four chapters on the Concept of Sovereignty* (Cambridge: MIT Press, 1985)

Schwab, G. *The Challenge of the Exception* (Duncker and Humblot, 1970)

Sidney, P. *An Apology for Poetry* (London: Nelson, 1965)

Spivak, G. 'Feminism and deconstruction, again: negotiating with unacknowledged masculinism' in T. Brennan (ed.) *Between feminism and psychoanalysis* (London: Routledge, 1989)

St Augustine, 'Concerning the Nature of Good' in W. Oates (ed.) *Basic Writings of St Augustine* (Random House, 1948)

Stewart, I. 'Closure and the Legal Norm: An Essay in Critique of Law' (1987) 50 *Modern Law Review* 908

Stone, J. 'Mystery and Mystique in the Basic Norm' (1963) 26 *Modern Law Review* 34

Stone, J. 'The Ratio of the Ratio Decidendi' (1959) 22 *Modern Law Review* 597

Stone, J. *Precedent and Law: The Dynamics of Common Law Growth* (Sydney: Butterworths, 1985)

Stone, R.L. 'Logic and Law: The Precedence of Precedent' (1967) *Minnesota Law Review* 655

Sugarman, D. 'Legal Theory, the Common Law Mind, and the Making of the Textbook Tradition' in W. Twining (ed.) *Legal Theory and the Common Law* (Oxford: Basil Blackwell, 1986)

Turpin, C. *British Government and the Constitution*, 2nd edition (London: Weidenfeld and Nicolson, 1990)

Vaihinger, *The Philosophy of As-If* (London: Routledge and Kegan Paul, 1965)

van de Kerchove, M. and F. Ost, *Le système juridique entre ordre et désordre* (Paris: Presses Universitaires de France, 1988)

Weinrib, E. 'Legal Formalism: On the Immanent Rationality of Law' (1988) 97 *Yale Law Journal* 949

Whitford, M. *Luce Irigaray: Philosophy in the Feminine* (London: Routledge, 1991)

Winterton, G. 'The British Grundnorm: Parliamentary Supremacy Re-examined' (1976) 92 *Law Quarterly Review* 591

Wittgenstein, L. *Philosophical Investigations* (Oxford: Basil Blackwell, 1958)

Wittig, M. *The Straight Mind and Other Essays* (New York: Harvester Wheatsheaf, 1992)

Young, A. and A. Sarat (eds) *Beyond Criticism: Law, Power, Ethics* (1994) 3(3) *Social and Legal Studies*.

Index

absolute justice, 114
acts
  decisions as, 135
  determined by norms, 117–20,
    134
agency, 87, 99
  law separate from, 69
alterity
  jurisprudence of, 2, 3
  in repetition, 128
ambiguity, interpretation of, 32
analogy, use of, 35
application, in normative
    dynamics, 118–19, 134
Aristotle, *telos* of life, 152
Atkin, Lord, 46, 47
Austin, John, 84
  limit of jurisprudence, 18, 20,
    24, 99
  'proper' law, 66
Australia, foundation of law, 93
authority
  of basic norm, 82–3
  of decisions, 127
  as external source of law, 76
  of institutionalised law, 40–1
  in legal theory, 23–4, 26–7
  for natural law, 29
  of Queen-in-Parliament, 83, 85,
    86

Bacon, Francis, 84
basic act, repetition of, 119
basic norm
  chronology of, 82–3, 85–6
  concept of, 28, 64–5, 78, 118
  as essence of law, 81–3
  as fiction, 28, 82, 120
  repetition of, 119

'before' the law (Derrida), 70, 71
  see also pre-legal; sources of law
Bentham, Jeremy, 36, 68, 84
Blackstone, W., 48, 67, 83–4
Butler, Judith, 54, 106, 124, 129
  materiality, 134

case, concept of, 131
categories, 52, 78
  and exclusion, 5, 110
'category of sex' (Wittig), 16, 54, 73
cause and effect, 153
central case(s), 62, 110
  in concept of law, 22–3, 35, 92
  extrapolation from, 33
  as universal, 91
Christian ideals, 47
chronology
  of basic norm, 82–3, 85–6
  of legal subject, 70–1
  of *mimesis*, 136
Church, Catholic, 29
class, 4
coercion, by law, 54–5
cognition, and interpretation, 59
Cohen, Felix, 50
Coke, Edward, 68
common law, 124–5
  as abstract, 67–8
  compared with 'proper' law,
    66–70
  decision-making in, 114–15
  derived from ancient constitu-
    tion, 68
  ratio decidendi in, 124–5
common law theory (classical),
    47–8
  form of writing, 49–50
common sense, 51

community values, 60, 61–2
composite, the law as, 36–7
constitution(s)
    interpretation of, 56, 58
    source of legitimacy, 83
    see also sovereignty
constraints
    on interpretation, 56–7
    on jurisdiction, 97–8
construction
    by language, 52, 53
    by law, 52–3
continuity, and precedent, 128
Cornell, Drucilla, 1, 124, 140
    on the Good, 7–8
    Philosophy of the Limit, 5–6
correspondence theory
    in common law, 47–9
    of language, 45–6
    and law, 46
Cotterrell, R., 68
creation, in legal dynamics,
        118–19, 134
Critical Legal Scholars, 50

decision-making, 39, 114–15
    logic in, 33–4
    rule cases/hard cases, 120–2
    see also ratio decidendi
decision(s)
    as condition of law, 135
    and the decision, 93–5
    ethical space of, 148, 150–1
    on exception, 96, 99–100
    as exclusionary reason, 94
    and illimitability, 85
    just, 113–14
    and momentary system, 139–40
    and precedent, 128–9
    and (re)construction of norms,
        112–13
    as set of norms, 98–9
    sovereign, 95–8, 100
    as transgressive, 144
deconstruction, 4
    of the law, 114
    of law and legal theory, 5–8
    the other of the other, 116

deduction, norm as premise in, 31–2
deductive reasoning, 32–5
definitions
    criteria of, 78
    language and meaning, 48
    as limits, 14
Derrida, J.
    'before' the law, 70, 71
    'Différence', 44
    'Force of Law', 1, 113
    iterability, 111
    'Law of Genre', 78–9
    law of repetition, 104
    'Limited Inc.', 131, 134, 148
    order of appearance, 136
    and origin of authority, 77, 113
    'Plato's Pharmacy', 106
    'violence' (theoretical force), 27,
        75, 120
    'White Mythology', 76
Descartes, R., 94
description, of law, 62–3
description–prescription distinc-
        tion, 51–2, 57, 104
Detmold, M.
    limit of rules, 35
    morality in law, 147–8
    norm and example, 138
difference, 41
    in judgement, 121
    in repetition, 128
differend, 41–2, 62–3, 103
    language and, 43
discrimination, 72
dissent, preceding decision, 95
dominance, culture of, 20
Douzinas, C. and R. Warrington, 1, 2
    limit of jurisprudence, 18–19
dualism, in Western thought, 15
Dworkin, Andrea, 54
Dworkin, R., 99, 120
    principle of integrity, 93
    theory of interpretation, 59–62

eidos, 106, 112, 135
ethics, 92–3, 122, 124, 148–9
    in natural law, 1, 149–50
    and otherness, 8, 150

evidence, relevance of, 132–3
example, and norm, 138–9
exception
    sovereignty as decision on, 96,
        99
    and universal, 91–3
exclusion, 5, 18–20
    of irrelevant, 133–4
    political nature of, 26–7, 110
experience, as otherness, 2–3

facts
    descriptions of, 51
    elements, 126–7
    and language, 45
    and law(s), 45–6, 130–4
    treated as material, 126–7
feminism, 3, 110, 116, 146–7
fiction, 131–2
    of basic norm, 28, 82
    legal, 115, 132
Finnis, J., 47, 50, 99
    rational universality, 21, 22–3
Fitzpatrick, Peter, 132
Foucault, M.
    the Decision, 94–5
    limits and transgression, 13, 16,
        144–5

Gasché, Rodolphe, 146
gender, 4, 5
genre
    of law, 80
    law of, 78–9
    paradox of, 79–80
Good, notion of, 7–8, 47
Goodhart, Arthur, 126
Goodrich, Peter, 108
    common law theory, 47–8, 49
    sources of law, 64, 65, 77, 149
Gray, Kevin, 18
grundnorm see basic norm

Hale, Sir Matthew, 67
'hard' cases, 35, 39, 120–2
Hart, H.L.A., 50, 99
    rule of recognition, 23, 25–7,
        28–9

Hegel, G.W.F., authority of
    sovereign, 95, 96–7
House of Lords, 85
Hughes, Graham, 82
human subject, pre-existing, 70–1
Husserl, E., *Cartesian Meditations*,
    132–3

ideal, law as, 129
identity
    constitution of, 111
    notion of, 109
illimitable limitedness, 83–6
imitation *see mimesis*
indeterminacy, 50–1, 80
    of law, 139
    of norms, 58
individuation, 35–7
integrity, 61
    Dworkin's principle of, 93
interpretation
    of ambiguity, 32–3
    certainty in, 60–1
    constraints on, 56–7
    language and, 50, 103
    norm as scheme of, 52, 57–8
    theory of, 56
Irigaray, Luce, 72, 104, 108–9, 110,
    115
is/ought disjunction, 7, 21, 46, 51,
    55
    and morality, 148
    and repetition of basic act, 119
iterability, 111, 115, 129
    acts and norms, 117–20
    rule cases and hard cases, 120–2

judgement
    logic in, 33–4
    norm as foundation for, 31, 58
    role of will in, 58–9
judges, 40, 45
    and application of law, 121, 147
    ideal, 60–1
    interpretation constrained, 56–7
    'living oracles', 48, 68, 125
judicial responsibility, 92–3, 99
jurisdiction, 97–8

jurisprudence
  laws defining, 17
  limit of, 18–20
  and the universal, 91
jurisprudence of alterity, 2, 3
justice, and law, 1–2

Kant, E., 53
  on logic, 34
Kelsen, H., 52–3
  contradictions in theory, 65
  grundnorm, 64–5, 81
  on interpretation, 57–9
  legal dynamics, 117–18, 119, 134
  limit of jurisprudence, 19–20,
    21, 27–8, 99
  Pure Theory of Law, 75–6
Kierkegaard, S.
  repetition, 111–12
  universal and exception, 91–2
Kripke, Saul, 44
Kristeva, Julia, 144

Laclau, E. and C. Mouffe, discourse,
    42–3
language, 103–4
  as constructive, 52–3
  correspondence, 44–5
  and description, 21
  and interpretation, 50, 103
  and legal discourse, 42–3
  and legal notation, 49–50
  and letter of the law, 48–9
  and meaning, 48–50
  plain, 49
Latham, R.T.E., 86
law
  as abstract, 40–1, 50, 67–8
  as coercive, 54–5, 106
  concept of a law and the law,
    36
  conceptual/practical distinction,
    130–1
  as constructive, 52–3
  critical theories of, 2, 37–8, 63
  end of (*telos*), 151–3
  gaps in, 39–40, 42
  as limit, 15, 123

  and morality, 145–51
  neglect of material side, 92
  as neutral, 4, 40, 55
  political structure of, 3, 38
  as signifying system, 53–4, 130
  spirit and letter of, 48–9
  unity and separation of, 65
Law of Law, 6–8, 30, 67, 78
law and not-law, 103, 114
  paradox of, 78
  in positivism, 75, 149
law of paradoxes, 80–1
laws
  and facts, 130–4
  limits of, 29–37
legal certitude, 140, 143
legal discourse, 53–4
  and language, 42–3, 51
legal dynamics, 117–18
legal memory, 67, 68
legal order, paradox of, 94
legal performance, 134–9
legal person
  chronology of, 70–1
  defined, 70, 71–2, 74
  masculinity of, 70, 71–2, 73
legal philosophy
  centres of, 21–4
  indeterminacy in, 50–1
  limits of, 17–21, 99–100
  of oppression, 4–5
legal system
  criterion of identity, 27
  limits of, 24–9
  primitive/pre-legal, 22, 23, 25
  theory of general, 22
legal theory, 131
  authority in, 23–4
  as constructive, 53
  function of source of law in, 65
  object of, 6, 29–30
  objectivity, 55
  and politics, 63
legality, criterion of, 78, 86
legislation, as creation and applica-
    tion of law, 118
letter of the law, 48–9
limitedness, illimitable, 83–6

limit(s)
    defined, 13–15, 30, 145
    of interpretation, 56–7
    of jurisprudence, 18–20, 99
    of laws, 29–37, 123
    of legal system, 24–9, 123
    legality of, 76
    as political, 24
    repetition and, 107
    of rules, 35–6
    and *telos*, 152
    transgression of, 16–17, 144–5
logic, in judgement, 33–4
Lugones, Maria, 'exercise in purity',
    20
Lyotard, Jean-François, 68–9, 78

MacCormick, Neil, 128
    on deductive reasoning, 32–5
MacKinnon, Catharine, 57
male dominance
    of law, 54–5, 108
    and objectivity, 57
Mallarmé, S., *Mimiqué*, 137
masculinity, of legal subject, 70,
    71–2, 73, 110–11
materiality, 126–7, 149
    determination of, 133
meaning
    and interpretation, 56
    and language, 48–50
mediation, 41
mimesis, 135–9
mimicry, 137
    self-, 131–2
morality, 19
    and law, 145–51

Nancy, Jean-Luc, 97–8
narrative knowledge, 68–9
natural law, 1, 21, 29, 46–7
    and morality, 148, 149–50
    transcendent principle of, 66
Natural Law Party, 29, 46
normative structures, 143–4, 150
norm(s)
    decisions as set of, 98–9
    as descriptive, 51–3

    to determine law, 19
    as determining acts, 117–20
    as frame, 31–5, 52, 57–9
    hierarchy of, 117
    as homogenising limit, 39
    as prescriptive, 54
    and rule of recognition, 25–6
    social, 31, 42
    validity of, 117
    see also basic norm

objectivity
    in interpretation, 56–7
    in legal theory, 55
oppression
    inevitability of, 15
    legal philosophical, 4–5, 103
    and social consensus, 62
other(ness), 2–3, 104
    ethics as, 150
    legal response to, 115
    and the same, 109
    of the same, 111–15
    universality and, 92

paradox
    of genre, 79–80
    of law and not-law, 78
    of origin of law, 80–1, 86, 94
Parliament *see* House of Lords;
        Queen-in-Parliament
Paulson, S., 58
philosophers, role of, 61
philosophy, novelty and tradition
        in, 146
Plowden, E., 48
Pocock, F., 68
politics
    excluded from legal theory, 19,
        37–8, 55
    in interpretation, 56, 57, 62
    in judgement, 33–4
positivism
    aporia of, 81–3
    and common law, 70
    and decisions, 98
    and ethics, 1, 149
    is/ought disjunction, 7, 21, 46

law as abstract, 40–1, 50
and legal certitude, 143
limits of legal system, 24–5, 29,
    74–5
and ultimate sources of law, 75
use of deductive reasoning, 35
see also 'proper' law
postmodernism, 2, 3, 7–8
power *see* authority; oppression
pre-legal
    subject, 70–1
    system, 22, 23, 25
precedent, 127, 138–9
and continuity, 128
prescription, law as, 21, 22, 51–2
problem of relevancy, 32
'proper' law, compared with
    common law, 66–70
property, mechanism of exclusion,
    18
purity of law, exclusion and, 19–21

Queen-in-Parliament
authority of, 83, 85, 86
as source of law, 65

race, 4
ratio decidendi, 124–7, 128
rationality, 33–4
Raz, Joseph
    concept of law, 36
    on decision, 94
    identifying test of legal system,
        27, 78
    momentary system, 139
    theory of general legal system,
        22
Realists, 50, 74, 130
reason
    collective, 68
    and madness, 94
    universal, 127–9
    see also ratio decidendi
reasonable man, and exclusion of
    women, 110
referent, external, 46–7
Reid, Lord, 83–4
relevance, of evidence, 132–3

repetition, 111–12, 121
law is always a law of, 105–8
in *mimesis*, 135
possibility of, 106–7
in precedence, 128
submission to a law, 104–5,
    108–9, 115
see also iterability
rule cases, and application of law,
    120–2
Rule of Law, 144
rule of recognition, 23, 24–7, 28–9
rule(s), 17
    application of, 147–8
    as limit, 107
    limit of, 35–6
    primary, 25
    transparency of, 34

St Augustine, *De Natura Boni*, 152
same(ness), 109–11
    the other of the, 111–15
Schmitt, Carl, authority of
    sovereign, 95, 96
separation, of other, 116
sexual difference, 72
sign
    defined, 44
    function of, 52, 53
social constructions, and legal
    discourse, 53–4
social contract, and founding
    decision, 93–4
social control, in pre-legal society, 25
social limitations, 14, 16, 31
'sound' judgment, 23
sources of law, 143
    heterogenous, 75
    ideational, 64–5, 77, 84, 99, 149
    institutional, 64, 65, 99
    validation of, 75–6, 107
sovereignty
    as creative principle, 84
    and decision, 95–8
    illimitability of, 83–6
    mystery of, 75–7
    and repeatability, 108
    and ultimate decision, 97

spirit of the law, 48, 49
stare decisis, 127, 147
statute, 36
Stewart, Iain, 65
Stone, Julius, 125, 126–7
subjectivity, contextual nature of, 73–4
substantive law, 3
Sugarman, David, 66

telos (end) of law, 151–3
transgression
    invited by limit, 16–17, 151
    of limits, 144–5
truth, 151–2
    process of, 136–7

undecidability, 80, 140
    of sovereignty, 77
United Kingdom, constitution, 65, 83–6
United States, foundation of law, 93
United States of America, constitution, 65
universal reasons, in decisions, 127–9
universality
    central to jurisprudence, 91
    and deductive reasoning, 32, 37
    and the exception, 91–3
    and repetition, 105

usage and custom, as source of common law, 67

values, in law, 33, 51
'violence' (theoretical force), 27, 55, 75, 77, 120

Weinrib, Ernest, 121
Western thought
    dualism of, 15
    foundations of, 3–4
    modern scientific approach, 69
    and mythology, 132
    tradition in, 69
Whitford, Margaret, 108–9, 115
will
    and external constraints, 56
    role in interpretation, 58–9
    and Rule of Law, 144
Wittgenstein, L., 17, 36
    on language, 44–5
    on rules, 76
Wittig, Monique, 'category of sex', 16, 54, 72–3
women
    as legal persons, 72–3
    as the other, 110, 116
    universality and, 92

Index by Auriol Griffith-Jones